COURAGE TO BUILD ANEW

MEDIEVAL HYMN OF UNKNOWN AUTHORSHIP USED AT THE DEDICATION OF A CHURCH

1 *Blessed city, heavenly Salem,*
   Vision dear of peace and love,
Who, of living stones upbuilded,
   Art the joy of heaven above,
And with angel cohorts circled,
   As a bride to earth dost move!

2 *From celestial realms descending,*
   Ready for the nuptial bed,
To his presence decked with jewels,
   By her Lord shall she be led;
All her streets, and all her bulwarks,
   Of pure gold are fashioned.

3 *Bright with pearls her portals glitter,*
   They are open evermore;
And, by virtue of his merits,
   Thither faithful souls may soar,
Who for Christ's dear name in this
      world
   Pain and tribulation bore.

4 *Many a blow and biting sculpture*
   Polished well those stones elect,
In their places now compacted
   By the heavenly Architect,
Who therewith hath willed for ever
   That his palace should be decked.

5 *Christ is made the sure foundation,*
   And the precious corner-stone,
Who, the two walls underlying,
   Bound in each, binds both in one;
Holy Sion's help for ever,
   And her confidence alone.

6 *All that dedicated city,*
   Dearly loved by God on high,
In exultant jubilation
   Pours perpetual melody;
God the one, and God the trinal,
   Singing everlastingly.

7 *To this temple, where we call thee,*
   Come, O Lord of hosts, to-day;
With thy wonted loving-kindness
   Hear thy people as they pray;
And thy fullest benediction
   Shed within its walls for aye.

8 *Here vouchsafe to all thy servants*
   What they supplicate to gain;
Here to have and hold for ever
   Those good things their prayers
      obtain;
And hereafter in thy glory
   With thy blessed ones to reign.

9 *Laud and honour to the Father,*
   Laud and honour to the Son,
Laud and honour to the Spirit,
   Ever three and ever one;
Consubstantial, co-eternal
   While unending ages run.

COURAGE TO
BUILD ANEW

*The Story of the rebuilding of The Friars,
Aylesford, taken from the Newsletters of
Fr Malachy Lynch*

by EDWINA FIELDING

With a Preface by
GABRIEL FIELDING

'*Give us the courage to build anew, quicken our desire to grow and
increase and grant us good success.*'
—CARMELITE EVENING PRAYER

LONDON · BURNS & OATES

BURNS & OATES LIMITED

25 Ashley Place, London, S.W.1

First published 1968

© Edwina Fielding and Malachy Lynch 1968
SBN: 223 31392 0

Made and printed in Great Britain by
Billing & Sons Limited, Guildford and London

Preface

We came to The Friars at Aylesford by way of Allington Castle on the evening of Easter Sunday sixteen years ago. It was a time in our lives when nothing much seemed to be happening, when all the days of the week had only a little colour, when Good Friday itself seemed no more than a diurnal monument to some nearly forgotten oppression or triumph.

If not a good thing then it might be a diverting one to set out on a windy night for the historic castle, to pass an hour or two watching people wending their way along the banks of the river Medway, singing and praying. We knew there was to be a procession, ceremonies of some kind, and torchlight; and though we had no intention of joining in we did want to see what belief might look like from the outside. We were even a little hostile for we had known for some years that the Carmelites had moved back into The Friars on the other side of the river and were resentful of them taking over, so soon, one of Kent's oldest and most beautiful castles.

By the time we actually reached the grounds we were more irritable then before. First we had taken wrong turnings on the roads and later lost ourselves on foot. Wandering with increasing purpose through the wet, unleafed woods we had heard bells tolling in the wind. They fluctuated with every gust, seeming to come each time from a slightly different direction. There was distant singing too which made the three of us think we were going to be too late, that despite the greyness in which we'd started we might miss what we had really hoped to see. When we found that the singing was coming not from any procession but only from the Malta Arms beyond the weir, we began to laugh and tease one another for having been so foolish as to set out at all.

The singing we heard was quite meaningless, very English and jolly; the sound of our time, the celebration of a moment, of a night of some season in a forgotten calendar. It was the same singing we had heard all along the Bank Holiday roads, or in the noise or silence of Christmas. We would hear it again, we knew, at all our Easters.

But at last we found the Castle, its moat full and black, the willows outside the main doors of the Keep just beginning to break, the recorded bells of St Peter's Rome billowing out from the tower. A thin rain was falling on the people standing about on the gravel; in the distance a new kind of singing could be heard, monotonous, repetitive and without fervour, as if the singers were merely chanting something over and over again like children.

We wondered why they were so certain about it, why they seemed in some way to be knocking at the night with it; and why they didn't seem to care whether there were ever an answer or not. Standing there in the half-silence among ourselves and the other people waiting, their faces and bodies not altogether clear, their voices casual and just a little expectant, we all three began to feel that we might have come a long way. Perhaps the fact that we'd managed to get lost on so short a journey had something to do with this, or perhaps the attitude of those strangers suggested it. For, quite unmistakably, they had intention as well as attention.

Cars arrived, there was the flutter of white Carmelite cloaks which we had never seen before but which were nevertheless familiar to us. There were tall men, bald-heads, priests, earnest-looking women, and, most surprising of all, other men who looked like active soldiers or retired ones. The

Castle, the bells, the modern cars, the two kinds of singing, all seemed to be blending to suggest that suddenly we had entered a mixture of the centuries, that we had passed through a barrier of time and place. Our apathy and resentment had dissolved a little at the edges; curiosity and a kind of greed, a hunger, had taken their place.

Some men in the centre of the procession carried a small wooden plinth on which there was a statue decked with jasmine; it was well illumined by tall glass-enclosed lanterns and it rocked a little as does anything which is carried by men who are not quite in step. The rain falling was suddenly visible as the lights inside the main gate were switched on. Fine shafts of it mingled with the yellow tips of the willow buds, with the flowers surrounding the statue.

Soon the bearers and their burden crossed the little bridge over the moat and entered the Keep. The courses of silvery stone, ancient grey arches and oaken doors took them all in amidst restless shadows and the continuing chanted prayer.

In the selections from the Newsletters which follow, this occasion is described not as we saw it but with that inner and outer knowledge which rounds out an event. That one hour which began so much for so many people is given a context and a perspective. Some of the secrets behind it, whether ordinary or mysterious, are revealed; and anyone, curious as we were, ignorant or less ignorant, ardent or even resentful, will find his appetite satisfied merely by reading the actual passage. The full story is told of a procession which, since that day, has become continuous; so that even at this moment it is still going on. And the excitement is that without the Newsletters from which this book has been taken, the procession would never even have started.

The writing of these letters was not an accident; it was rather a forlorn purpose, a hackneyed necessity to raise money by telling just a few people why their help and prayers were needed, why crumbling walls should be restored. But, like all processions when their object is valid, the Newsletters gathered into themselves many happy accidents, great accretions and small, all of them important, each of them ultimately contributing something to the direction and purpose of the writing.

The writing, the style itself, the method of telling changed as the task took clearer shape in the writer's mind. Gradually the financial appeal became subordinate to a greater one which nevertheless, in terms of money alone, accomplished more than had ever been intended. Old walls were not merely restored or rebuilt, new ones were added. A great Shrine was raised on the place of the old one demolished over four hundred years earlier. The new chapels were furnished with new and magnificent works of art which themselves drew in more people, more money and more life.

Father Malachy Lynch, who wrote all these words between 1949 and 1967, was once described to me as 'a man who *is* what he believes'. And it is just such people, most wholly themselves, who are the hardest to describe. Sometimes you think that you may say what makes them different and then suddenly you realize that you cannot define them. I suppose it may be the sense of their reality, the scale of their humanity which may sometimes make you feel uncertain of yourself when you are with them. And this goes against the detachment necessary for a good description. Yet, strangely, when you have left such people you may realize that while you were with them you had found more and more of yourself in their company. Always, with such men, there is surprise and I must admit that with Father Malachy you sometimes have to wait for it. He makes almost a kind of game of this waiting. He seems to tell you that you must be willing to put up with him if you are to reward each other at all.

To look at he is tall and though not fat has plenty of body.

If he is really talking his hands, which are those of a practical man, move slowly; he fiddles with things and sometimes, in a kind of windmilling gesture, he waves his arms about as if he were not only milling his thoughts but were trying to include everything around him into them. When he is excited the windmill turns extra fast; and when he is bored, faster still. I suspect that he is quite often bored, or rather, tired. There are some kinds of piety which tire him even more than his diabetes; but the experience which most irritates him and thus fills him with what may only be described as a desperate intention, is what he calls 'deadness'. When he is confronted by this and is really at his wits' end, he will seize any passing stranger by the arm and substitute him for himself. Then, before you know what has happened, you see him striding away into the distance like a farmer.

His face gives little away, no matter how much you look at it. Its very openness confuses you and you are always tempted to look for some perfectly proper focus or objection. Some people say he has a good nose, Roman or Greek or merely Celtic, and probably ambitious. His eyes can only be described as being worth a second glance. They are very wide apart and conceal their thoughtfulness better than their wit.

As these Newsletters show, to talk to him is often an adventure; people discover in themselves an unsuspected gift for simplicity and truth and are surprised. What Carl Jung calls the 'second personality', that part of ourselves which quite simply 'knows', is suddenly revealed. Although this surprises his friends it doesn't seem to astonish him very much; and in fact he nearly always has materials ready in order to take down notes from the people he's talking to. I have seen him do it anywhere, in his room or summerhouse, in the gardens, on trains or ships and even in coffee houses and hospitals. At any hour of the day he is waiting for some word or sentence that he can use in the context of his own thought or reading.

He is as observant as a child or a countryman, as greedy as a collector and as ardent as a poet.

The Newsletters from which these selections have been made show not only the quality of his mind but suggest a most marvellous energy. Very little escapes the discursiveness and particularity of their direction. Reading them one is more and more aware of a priest who has never stopped thinking and of a man who has never stopped doing. To me, his wide reading seems to be unique not in its facility but in its affection. There is no pride in it to sustain an opinion, no desire to impress. There is only a longing to show and to confirm, to illuminate an already tried conviction. Gradually, as you read on, the apparently unrelated sections of events, thoughts and opinions here set down, take a pattern inside you, confirming lost personal experience until, sooner or later, you find that you've been given a new vision of the time you have known. Yet perhaps the most distinctive quality of all this writing is that of a faultless judgement. Though there is impatience and suddenness as well as a tendency to go the long way round, there is always a kind of exactness and fulfilment in the end, something with which perhaps you were ever in agreement before you realized it.

My wife has been solely responsible for these selections from the writings which cover a period of eighteen years, and it is my impression that in doing so she has managed to take from them just those things which anyone else reading them for the first time would most have liked to remember. In summarizing Father Malachy's achievements she has written:

Now that his great task was completed Father's role was still unique. As writer of the Newsletters, as Priest in charge of Pilgrimages, as the personal friend of innumerable people in all walks of life, he was able to present the fruits of his Catholic judgement to a most catholic array of subjects. Bearing within him his own *clausura* he is able to cut through to truth in a way I have seldom seen in anybody else. The man with a foot in two camps seldom has balance; he veers either to one side or the other; he is brashly worldly or coldly cloistered. In a world where many of the best 'lack all conviction', Father's insights are sure and definite, his balance perfect. With the peasant's wife, one might boldly assert that even when he is wrong he is right!

To anyone who lends himself as much to the reading as the writer did to his thinking, the whole work builds up like a symphony in which the orchestra is ourselves in all our moments of confusion or secret aspiration. It is the kind of writing which is like the best conversation, the sort of talk which Hilaire Belloc once described as 'strong music'. For thousands of people, at any rate, it has proved in a time of Catholic argument to represent most surely the constancy of the Catholic mind, that excitement and serenity which are beyond debate.

GABRIEL FIELDING

Contents

PREFACE, by Gabriel Fielding 5

  I. OF LIVING STONES UPBUILDED 15

 II. MANY A BLOW AND BITING SCULPTURE 68

III. POLISHED WELL THOSE STONES ELECT 116

IV. THE PRECIOUS CORNER-STONE 146

 V. IN THEIR PLACES NOW COMPACTED 210

VI. ALL THAT DEDICATED CITY 244

I

Of Living Stones upbuilded

If you were to come suddenly upon The Friars, at Aylesford, unprepared for what you were to see, you would not, after the first moment, be in the least surprised. This group of large buildings in the Kentish grey-gold ragstone, the oldest of them enclosing a vivid green courtyard, seems to fall into a pattern you have always had inside you. The Pilgrim's Hall has the cold, small-windowed stare which suits the oldest inhabited building in Kent; the great shrine itself, risen from old foundations, gleaming like the inside of a huge shell, is not so much a copy of a mediaeval church as an original recreation, something the early English masons might have built of local wood and stone, using the contours of the river site as an instinctive scale.

All the statues are fresh and dynamic. The ceramics of the central altar, visible through the vast archway to the main chapel, are Byzantine in their black-outlined simplicity, while the inside walls are washed in colours so primitive that they are modern. In the Chapel of the Reliquary the intense stained glass could only be very old or very new, and the tall peerless angels above the high altar remind of the truth of Swedenborg's saying, 'The more angels, the more room'.

All this ought to be amazing and it is. But since there are no discordant notes, nothing that is not somehow in scale with the whole, the total effect transcends mere surprise. The stranger, the pilgrim, is made welcome. He both recognizes and is recognized.

The Carmelites, to whom this great place is Motherhouse, are the oldest Order in the Church. In their liturgy and their spirit they trace their origins back over eight hundred years before the birth of Our Lord, to the time of their founder, the Prophet Elias. From his time onwards there were always hermits living on Mount Carmel, 'the Sons of the Prophet', awaiting the coming of the mysterious and glorious woman who would bring forth the Redeemer. Early in the Christian centuries these men called themselves the 'Brethren of Blessed Mary – Mother of God – of Mount Carmel', in Palestine. By the beginning of the thirteenth century they had received their Latin 'rule' from the Patriarch of Jerusalem; and fifty years after that they were forced, by the Saracen Invasion, to leave their mountain.

One small band of them was brought to England by the Crusader, Sir Richard de Gray, who gave them his manor house by the river at Aylesford while the King gave them leave to settle in the Realm. On Christmas Day 1240 they arrived by boat from the Medway through the water-door into the Hall of their new habitation.

It was here that they held their first General Chapter in Europe and selected Simon Stock to be their leader and it was here that they built the first English church to be dedicated in honour of the Assumption of the Glorious Virgin. In a time when there were no books and few manuscripts this title was a literal expression, a sort of publication of that passage in the Apocalypse which is always taken to describe Our Lady in glory: this woman in heaven crowned with the stars, clothed with the sun and with the moon under her feet.

In those days universal truths had to be expressed more by gesture than by words. Gesture comes from the Latin word *gerere*, which means to do, and the tradition is that Our Lady appeared to St Simon in a vision and cast her cloak about him. Scholars dispute whether this seeing took place at

Cambridge or Aylesford but in any case it was in the direct Carmelite tradition. Their founder, Elias, was told by God to go forth to anoint a king and to appoint his successor. He found his successor ploughing a field with twelve yoke of oxen. He went up behind him in his furrow and flung his garment over him. Not a word was spoken and the young farmer, without more ado, followed his leader at once. Later when Elias was being taken away from the earth, his mantle fell upon Eliseus, a sign that he had left with him a spirit of zeal and service. All this was recognized by the Sons of the Prophet on the other side of the Jordan after Eliseus had divided the river with the same mantle, confessing that the spirit of Elias had gone into Eliseus.

From this story, told in the Fourth Book of Kings, and from the desert custom of symbolizing a contract or a compact by the sharing of a cloak, it was plain that Our Lady was offering her special protection to St Simon and his spiritual children. She is supposed to have said: 'I have spread my garment over you, I have sworn a pact to you', and promised salvation and help to those who called for her protection.

News of St Simon's vision spread quickly throughout the Christian world and when he died at Bordeaux, making a visitation of his European Foundations, he was at once acclaimed as a saint. His relics were venerated at the Carmelite House there for seven hundred years and the 'Scapular Devotion', the wearing of small pieces of cloth from Carmelite habits which were blessed and used as a sign of Our Lady's protection of the wearer, spread quickly throughout Europe. Old Celtic literature celebrated the Cloak of Mary and the devotion it inspired, and the love and use of it persisted throughout penal times in England. To this day a strong feeling about the mantle is part not only of the tradition of Ireland but of France, Spain and Portugal as well. French history records that a Scapular was one of the last possessions relinquished to her gaolers by Marie Antoinette, when she was being prepared for the guillotine; and when the body of Pope Pius X was exhumed, his scapular was found to be intact and fresh as when he first put it on.

This phenomenon has been repeated often in the history of the Cloak. When the bodies of the parents of St Thérèse were exhumed, everything in the coffins had decayed including the shrouds, but the scapulars on both were as fresh as if they had been recently imposed.

But such detail is only incidental to the great stream of official history. The doings of tyrants and power-seekers are more fully recorded than the hard and monotonous lives of such people as the Carmelites and other religious whose numbers were so drastically reduced owing to their fearless nursing of the sick during the times of the Plagues. At the time of the vision St Simon was in great trouble. Then as now the wind of change was blowing very violently in the Church. The ranks of mendicant friars were just coming into history at this time. They differed from the settled orders of monks in that they had no great possessions, were vowed to poverty and were prepared to subsist on alms and to live a more or less wandering life, preaching and teaching.

Although they aroused some resentment among parish clergy who saw their flocks crowding to hear them preach, to bring them their overdue confessions and to give them money, these Friars were there to stay. The centuries before the Reformation were full of their tumult and their influence was greatly strengthened by their teaching in the newly founded universities of England and Europe.

St Simon, although a contemplative, was supremely practical and saw that in the different climate and circumstances of Kent there was no future for his body of desert hermits. Therefore under the patronage of Sir Richard de Gray he petitioned the Pope for a mitigation of their Rule so that they too could become friars. The Carmelites have remained as such ever since and every movement in the Order seems to be a harking back to the spirit and temper of those early centuries when the Friars were a 'shake out' from the entrenched ranks of the Church.

We get glimpses only of life at The Friars in the years before the Reformation; there were enclosed hermitages, which are still standing, used by some of the Community; but for the most part the Carmelites must have gone around the countryside, with the pilgrimages and in the villages, preaching and begging. They must have offered some hospitality to travellers on the Pilgrim's Way to Canterbury; near-by Boxley Abbey was drawing crowds of the pilgrims to see a mechanically animated crucifix, made by some clever monk to foster devotion; but there was not anything so exciting at Aylesford, just the church and the bridge which the Friars had built across the Medway and a coming and going between them and the other houses of the Order.

St John Fisher of Rochester was only a few miles from The Friars. He must have come often to look for prayer and consolation in the constant devotion being offered through Our Lady, and to offer it in his lonely stand against tyranny and heresy.

But a St John Fisher, a St Thomas More, were not enough to halt the dreadful tides which were sweeping through the Realm of England. In 1538 Henry VIII's strong-arm man, Sir Thomas Cromwell, ordered the destruction of the church at Aylesford: 'Proceede to the dissolution and the defacing'. That was the decree and as Father Malachy wrote in 1958 when they were excavating the old foundations, 'The despoilers did their work well. They left the bones of the dead who were buried in the church but they took away the stones which covered them so that they will now remain forever the nameless dead. We came upon them as if "sown in the rich

earth" in the old sanctuary. . . . There were many broken
floor tiles and bits of glass. . . . There were also some beautiful
Gothic window heads of the fourteenth century. . . . That is
all they left: no broken image, no broken altar stone, nothing
marked with the Sign of the Cross.'

The Manor House was given to Sir Thomas Wyatt of Allington Castle down the river. 'I have reserved for you The
Friars at Aylesford', wrote Cromwell to Wyatt. Allington
Castle now belongs to the Carmelites; but that is another story
which is told later in this book.

In the four hundred years between 1538 and the Vigil of
All Saints in 1949, the story of The Friars was much like that
of the many great 'seats' in England. The almost accidental
grandeur and beauty of such places attract the families whose
prosperity has gone beyond the amassing of a sheer weight of
property and who seek the intangible qualities to add to their
glory. But when prosperity fades the almost monolithic quality of such places invites despair. They can absorb repairs into
their very fabric, slough off tiles, flake off paint and even sink
a few feet into the ground. At one time The Friars was the
seat of several generations of the Earls of Aylesford. The first
Earl was a Prosecutor General and was notorious for the prose-
cution of Blessed Oliver Plunket, the last Catholic martyr.

By 1668 it was in the hands of a Sir John Banks, a rich merchant of Maidstone. He was one of a dozen or so of these
people whose wealth came mainly from provisioning His
Majesty's ships.

On 24 March 1668–9 Pepys Diary was given the entry:

To the Mill House (Chatham) and there did give order for
a coach to be made ready; and got Mr Gibson whom I carried with me to go with me and Mr Coney, the surgeon, towards Maydstone, which I had a mighty mind to see. A
mighty cold and windy, but clear day and had the pleasure

of seeing the Medway running winding up and down mightily and a very fine country and I went a little out of the way to have visited SIR JOHN BANKS, but he at London; but here I had a sight of his seat and house, the outside of which is an old abbey just like Hinchingbroke, and as good at least, and mightily finely placed by the river: and he keeps the grounds about it and wall and house very handsome. I was mightily pleased with the sight of it. Thence to Maydstone which I had a mighty mind to see, never having been there. . . . In the street I did buy and send to our Inn, the Bell, a dish of fresh fish . . . and so staying till four o'clock we set out, . . . I light out of the way to see a Saxon monument, as they say, of a king which is of three stones standing upright and a great round one lying on them of great bigness though not so big as those on Salisbury Plain. It is near to Alesford where Sir John Banks lives so homeward to Chatham, Captain Allen's and there light.

In 1923 Lord Conway, the owner and restorer of Allington Castle, wrote an article for *Country Life* about The Friars as it then appeared. He said:

Few houses in England offer examples, and such good examples of the work of so many generations, or so picturesque and harmonious a grouping of various styles. . . . The Courtyard is for the most part sixteenth-century remodelling of older buildings and there are many inserted windows and doorways of the same date. . . . To disentangle the work of these various generations and reconstruct the building as it existed in successive centuries is no easy task. . . . The Gate House, with its finely panelled upper rooms, is a separate dwelling house, apparently intended for occupation by people of a certain quality.

In 1930 the fourteenth- and fifteenth-century cloisters and

claustral buildings were badly damaged by fire but the owner,
Mr Copley Hewitt, who was at that time High Sheriff of Kent,
was, with his wife, very much devoted to the place and took
immense pains to see them restored perfectly. However, the
years of the Second World War, which took away all labour
from 'non-essential purposes', meant that many of the buildings became very badly run down again. Someone even went
so far as to describe the place as a 'rickle of ruins' and indeed
many of the roofs around the Courtyard had fallen in, horses
had been stabled there during the War and the great hall in the
restored wing had been used as a dance hall. This hall, an upper room, was ready for the Carmelites to turn into a simple
and beautiful chapel with its oak-beamed roof from the old
ship Arethusa, as soon as they took possession; but one in-
habitant of Aylesford was heard deploring the change: 'When
I think of the lovely dances we had there with the soldiers and
all, I could have wept when I saw the way it is now.'

For years the Carmelites had 'had an eye' on the place.
Almost unnoticed by the Kentish people the Carmelites had
returned to Faversham, only twenty miles away. There they
had restored a shrine to St Jude and built up a Catholic parish.
Father Elias Lynch had taken over a German colour printing
process and accumulated a good deal of money from it. For
years he had hankered for the ancient Motherhouse and kept
the name alive with a kind of magic appeal. This so affected
his brother, Father Killian Lynch, that when he was made
General of the whole Carmelite Order, he called all the
Provincials together and asked them to decide to buy back
The Friars.

From his printing monies Father Elias was able to provide
most of the £25,000 needed; and since many of the Provinces
of the Order had been very hard hit during the War, this was
just as well.

Before he was appointed General, Father Killian Lynch had

been a Provincial in America and had lived there for many years. He was able to see things in a big way and did not hesitate about the purchase; but once it again belonged to the Order the task of restoring it had to be placed in very capable hands for though it was so historically glamorous it was very much in decay. The Order did not know what was to be done with it when it was restored, either, but since it was so obviously, as the Edwardians used to say, *meant* that they should have it back, they were content to proceed with the task in hand, which was, immediately, to preserve the place for the generations to come. A good builder and organizer must be provided, and fast. Father Malachy Lynch had to be sent for.

He had just completed a great task of rebuilding, at Llandeilo in Wales, where he had been sent thirteen years before, without even the resource of a Catholic population to support him. He regarded it, he says, 'as a great good fortune' to have thus had the 'opportunity of learning mendicancy the hard way' and while he was there he had managed to bring together a parish, to build a small but beautiful church and to start a new college. This had proved to him the truth that, 'going back to the original and living on alms and expecting them was practical wisdom'. And he goes on to say, 'The experience of building this church has proved to me in practice what I always believed and taught my students: that one can build with very simple materials, with untried craftsmen, and that the result will always be fine, uncomplicated and clean. Everything in that church was made by hand, the vestments, the altar vessels and the furniture; it seems to have been a rehearsal for Aylesford.'

But he was not at all anxious to take up this new task, 'I was not taken in by accounts of the place and had always avoided even the mention of it', he says, so when Father Killian came on a visitation to Llandeilo he must have been rather holding his breath and trying to appear invisible. But sure enough, the request came and he had to accept the commission and pull up his roots in Wales. His lack of enthusiasm came from experience because, as he says, 'I knew all about the trials of getting building permits and scarce materials. So you see it wasn't my own private adventure and didn't even involve an act of faith but rather of sufferance.'

There were only a few Catholics in rural Kent at the time and even amongst these the Order was very little known and had no prestige. In this Conservative countryside anything or anybody unusual is suspected at once of 'madness' and soon there was to be talk of 'the mad Prior of Aylesford'. At the beginning there were only five of the robed friars to cause a stir, but they seem to have done so nevertheless. There were two priests, Father Malachy and a Maltese priest, Brother John, an ex-soldier who came almost directly from Mount Carmel, and two energetic Spanish lay brothers with no English. These men must have looked on the huge ruin with bewilderment. But in the face of emptiness, ritual asserts the dignity of man at his humblest, as can be seen from the Newsletter of the time: the simple actions of their long tradition became a declaration of trust and intention:

In the Summer of 1538 the brethren of these returning friars had most probably gone out over the old bridge of Aylesford. They must have looked back over the meadows to take a last look at the Priory they were leaving, they must have seen the Church of the Assumption and the Pilgrim's Hall and the Water-gate on the Medway, for the last time. The rest is silence.

More than four centuries afterwards, on an Autumn afternoon, there was a stir on the bridge again, the white-robed friars had returned. Unexpected publicity had brought many clergy and people for another event. Spontaneously a procession formed, it moved slowly over the bridge singing the Litany of the Saints, and through the narrow street which is Aylesford, hushing it to silence. It came quickly in sight of the ancient walls on the outskirts of the village and to the great door of the Gatehouse, where the *Magnificat* was sung, then in the chapel with its open waiting tabernacle, the *Te Deum*. A prior was installed at once and was given a copy of the pre-Reformation seal of the Prior of Aylesford. That part was soon over and the people departed, but some remained to keep vigil with the friars during the night. It was cold and great wood fires had been laid in all the open fireplaces. The chimney smoked and filled the house with the smell of burning wood. People were huddled uncomfortably in the chapel and in the bare halls. At midnight the office of All Saints was said once more, and at dawn, the Mass was offered and Life returned.

After the War the Pope had given permission to the Carmelites to found a secular order of women. People in the world have for centuries been able to attach themselves to an Order as 'Tertiaries', so that they can pray with them and benefit from their sacrifices and spiritual teaching. This Institute of Our Lady of Mount Carmel was to be an order of tertiaries with three-year vows of poverty, chastity and obedience. They were to help the fathers and learn to pray, and later it was hoped that they would be able to go back into the world taking the spirit of Carmel with them, in an informal way. In the usual empirical way of the Church they were given ten years in which to flourish or else to go out of existence.

Father Elias preached a splendid sermon when the Institute was first installed at Allington Castle: he said that during the War the Pope had seen a group of British W.R.N.S. being conducted round the Vatican. He had asked about the organization to which they belonged and was told that they were there to 'back up the British Navy'. Here Father Elias became carried away in his sermon and added that His Holiness had cried, 'Whatever they can do, we can do better!' How this would have sounded in the precise Italian of Pope Pius XII is hard to guess, but however it was, he gave permission for these auxiliary orders, thus lending weight to Father Elias' further lapidary statement that 'behind every great man you'll find a great woman'. He spoke of St Brigid of Kildare, St Clare, St Jeanne de Chantal, and the help and encouragement *they* had been able to give to their saints.

But now, in 1949, the Institute in its strength over at Allington Castle, was two years away in the future and at Aylesford there were only three women auxiliaries to install in the Gatehouse a fortnight after the return. This Gatehouse had been built for 'persons of quality' and indeed these women had quality, for otherwise they would not have been there; but the quiet life of the original tenants was not for them. A life of hard work, facing almost impossible situations every day, was to be theirs from the beginning.

In the expectation that this group of women would soon grow out of the Gatehouse, Father Malachy was instructed by the General to look out for a large place nearby, out of which they would not grow in a hurry. So when the Carmelites were given the opportunity to buy Allington Castle for a very small price, this seemed to be the perfect solution. They used the Castle for a number of years for retreats, etc., and at the same time helped to look after the pilgrims at Aylesford. But to return to the first months of the Carmelite tenure of The Friars:

Soon there were sixty workers and staff to be fed every day and then the pilgrims started to come unbidden; the Prior General and the Curia of the Order had planned to use The Friars as an International House for the students of history. They had not discerned that Our Lady was *making* history and writing a new and vivid chapter herself.

Some day we will be given credit quite wrongfully for making Aylesford a place of Pilgrimage. The first pilgrimage came very soon after we had taken possession. A Legionary from Ealing wrote saying: 'We are bringing our legionaries to Aylesford. Will you meet us at the Bridge at 3 o'clock?' We did, and one hundred legionaries led by Dom Ambrose Agius, O.S.B., of Ealing Priory descended from coaches and moved across the bridge as if it had happened often before. And of course it had, many thousands of pilgrims in the same spirit had come across the bridge in the days when England was Catholic. That was how the first organized pilgrimage began: it was not our doing. Everything that has happened at The Friars has that quality. We can regard it quite impersonally; but it is not difficult to know who is behind it all.

Father Malachy's Newsletters, from which I have taken these extracts, seemed to become an 'institution' in much the same way as the 'happenings' so far described. In October 1951 he wrote:

Soon after our return, the Prior General asked us to organize a pilgrimage to Rome from Aylesford for the Seventh Centenary of the Scapular Vision. It was obviously most fitting that a pilgrimage should come from the land of 'Simon of England'. An International Congress had been arranged for August 1950 to which the Holy Father gave his special blessing. In great innocence and without experience we started to organize a pilgrimage. It was all done by an amateur staff, most of them voluntary helpers. It was during this time that the Devil discovered his presence to us in sinister and unexpected ways, which were very frightening. Everything possible went wrong on a grand scale; only to go right in the end. That pilgrimage was said to be the largest single pilgrimage of the Holy Year and possibly the largest pilgrimage ever to leave England for Rome. There were three special trains, a special boat and several planes to transport over one thousand five hundred pilgrims.

What had gone wrong in the first place was this: the Agency in charge had promised everything; but six months later, by seeming accident, we found that they had made no arrangements at all. For this and for other very serious reasons we had to bring in another agency. At such short notice that was a great anxiety. The new agency could not cope with such large numbers and so instead we had to provide twenty-five guides ourselves. When we tried to extricate ourselves from the first agreement we were threatened with a High Court case and a writ was actually served on us: I don't know if you have ever read one of these frightening documents. I can only say that the first reading is the worst until you get accustomed to the sinister jargon of it. Well, we made a desperate novena to St Joseph in preparation for his Feast and actually on his feast day the directors of the new agency were in conference with us at The Friars. As a result of this they took over the original pilgrimage.

But of course a great deal had to be done and Father had to fly to Rome and Paris with the directors of the firm to make new bookings: 'I remember, when looking for accommodation in Paris calling on Mr McClusky, the head of an American charity organization. When I told him our numbers he exclaimed, "Holy Smoke! Only God can help you."'

The pilgrimage got off but –

I felt it necessary to warn them beforehand about the difficulties that might arise and to indicate the proper spirit. They all said they were rather unfairly 'muzzled' when anything did go wrong, but I can only say now that we have seen and experienced human nature at its very best. The pilgrims obviously were given great grace. We have a great bulging file of letters which are most touching and most consoling and which make us feel very humble when we realize how comparatively little we were able to do in the long run. In Rome, for instance, when the telephone system broke down and we could not get in touch with the different hotels and all our plans went amiss, when the 'B' pilgrims were put into 'A' accommodation so that a monumental man found himself delivered at a convent with a coach-load of ladies – well, there was nothing to be done but to call upon St Joseph to whom we had commended the temporal affairs of the pilgrims. Yet out of all the subsequent letters there were less than half a dozen which were complaining and only one which was abusive in a bitter way.

The wry bond which this traditional pilgrimage forged between the Aylesford community and the travellers was to be continued right up to this day in the Newsletters. As Father Malachy said:

In the old days the people of every land went on pilgrimage and often the pilgrim's way was hard and dangerous. They were glad to keep vigils because they felt they were visiting Our Blessed Lady or the Saints. One can see this spirit surviving in many of the great shrines of Our Lady, in Chartres and Fourvières. You will always find Our Lady giving audience, surrounded by a blaze of candles which are the continuing prayers of the faithful. Some places, like Rome, have been indelibly marked and made sacred by martyrdom, for the blood of the martyrs nourishes the good ground of the Church. Persecution and time have not been able to blot out the memory of these. Similarly, where saints have lived, something of their spirit seems to remain; and when we visit these places we are more nearly in communion. Many of our pilgrims, on the coach pilgrimage particularly, told me how profoundly they felt this at Ars. It is so different from many other places which the pilgrimage took in. And there is Lisieux of course where there is only that humble convent church standing amongst the ruins. When we toiled up the steep climb to the Basilica and we first caught sight of that welcoming statue of the Little Flower facing down the hill in a gesture to all pilgrims, we forgot whether the sculpture was good, bad or indifferent; but we knew that St Thérèse was on that mount holding out her arms of welcome and bringing pilgrims in endless procession to Our Lady.

However, I must not linger on these experiences, because every pilgrim will have his own secret, about which comment is useless. With the monks of old each one must say, 'My secret to myself'. He must affirm only that, 'Our Lady is alive and all the saints of God are alive and active; and that we join up with them mysteriously in our pilgrimage upon this earth; and that in their company we are reconnoitring the image of purgatory and the city of God'.

In this same letter there is more news of the building:

The old Pilgrim's Hall is practically finished. It is not a restoration at all in the 'wooden' sense, but a re-creation with a great number of craftsmen of every description working with zeal, skill and real dedication. Even now, with the work half finished in the Courtyard, visitors say how beautiful it is. The Courtyard itself, with its remains of the old hermitages and the Elizabethan and Tudor buildings, is regarded as one of the finest in England. During the year we have spent over twenty-five thousand pounds. That is not a great sum when one considers the modern costs of building: acres of floor and roof to be renewed. In addition to the contractors who are doing this work – several of them craftsmen and a good deal of voluntary labour—we have our own brothers which relieves us of considerable expense in labour costs. We have spent over five thousand pounds upon oak timber alone and that will give you some idea of how fast the money goes; but it would be sacrilege to do this work in any other way except the best way. In inspired language the Church has spoken of Our Lady as a 'Merchant's Ship', 'She is like a Merchant's ship bringing her treasure from afar', and what treasure she has brought us from every direction for The Friars! workers and materials.

When you realize that little over a year ago we had to dig our way in along the main drive and the big door was closed and we entered to find the whole of that hallowed place half way to dissolution, you may imagine the change now. The work is being done by a London firm. Many of their special craftsmen have to be accommodated. All these workers, with the addition of a dozen of our own community and ten members of the Institute at the Gatehouse, voluntary workers and visitors, who are always pouring in, have made of The Friars a little township in itself. When we first arrived all this would have seemed wild and impossible had we tried to envisage it. Yet with a 'footling' kitchen, but with a cook of genius and a devoted staff, all this transformation has come about in so short a time. I always think how literally true it is when we say that lesson in Our Lady's Mass: 'The land which was desolate and impassable shall be glad, and the wilderness shall rejoice and shall flourish like the lily.'

But for all this, of course, the money had to be found. And there is far more money in the world than there are ob-

jects of value. Since all that the owner of money has to show
for hours of his life, for his effort, his pain and good luck is
capital, this always collects an aura of magic. So it is not surprising that many people would rather give some of it away to
God rather than see it all turned into dull goods. Consequently
there was a steady trickle of alms coming into Aylesford for
the rebuilding and the upkeep; but there were no rich patrons
and much more money was needed. So Father Malachy decided to send what he called 'stones' cards out to pilgrims:

> The Stones Card is not an original idea at all but it came
> to me in a curious way. In Wicklow, high up on a hill which,
> they say, dates from pre-Celtic times. The most primitive
> way of marking a grave here was by putting a stone or
> stones upon it—and the bigger the chief the bigger the stone!
> In this old cemetery there are many graves and many heaps
> of stones to mark them; for it was the custom for each
> mourner in a funeral to carry a stone up that narrow path
> and there place it on the grave. That was the explanation
> of a noble and austere simplicity, so good to see and to
> wonder at. Yet, though seemingly so casual it was so
> eloquent that it has endured for many generations.
> By a strange freak of memory that burial place gave me
> the idea of stones for Aylesford. If all pilgrims, or even
> pilgrims of desire, were to send or bring a stone or its
> equivalent, how very quickly we would restore this dese-
> crated shrine. We are not heaping stones on a grave, but
> building again on a shattered place – *vivis ex lapidibus* –
> out of living stones. I am asking you in Our Lady's name
> to do a simple and noble deed of charity and reparation.

He was quite firm and sure about pledging Our Lady's
gratitude, spiritual and material, to those who gave to her
causes. In February 1952 the Newsletter was written from
hospital and Father recalled how, although it was his first time

to be an in-patient, he had not known good health during the twenty years which had succeeded his student days in Rome:

A specialist told me that I had to be resigned to ill-health and the taking of various medicines every day. In fact he was rather doubtful about my future at that time; and then, five years ago, another specialist told me that I had some two years to live. A little while after this pronouncement a priest friend of mine was staying at Llandeilo in Wales. It happened to be Easter time when the first great tax on tobacco had been announced. Not without some scruples, I was smoking my pipe, and answering my concern he suddenly remarked that I should edify him by giving up smoking altogether. He told me that he himself had been a chain smoker and had 'given' it to Our Lady. That sounded just too simple but he quoted a French saying: *'Donnez-lui l'oeuf, elle vous donnera le boeuf.'* 'If you give her an egg she will give you an ox.' Though it doesn't rhyme in English the meaning is, of course, that if you give her a small thing then she will give you a big thing.

So I edified him by hanging up my pipe there and then and asked Our Lady for decent health and to be rid of the chemistry of all my pills. I had often tried to give up smoking and had suffered horrors of desire. That last time it was no trouble at all and to my great astonishment the ox came in the shape of normal health after twenty years of futile doctoring. All that long-standing trouble cleared up and I was able to dispense with medicines altogether.

In the Spring of 1951 Allington Castle, a great historical building, already superbly restored by Lord Conway, was offered to the Carmelites for just fifteen thousand pounds – about a quarter of its real market value. There was an old connection between The Friars and the Castle which had been the birthplace of Sir Thomas Wyatt and of generations of his family, and now for the second time the two buildings were to come under the same ownership. As forecast, the Institute had outgrown the Gatehouse and needed new quarters. Although the Order could not 'afford' another great place, they could not now afford to turn it down either. This meant months of worry, conferences with bank managers and special novenas. But by July 1952 enough money had come in from unlooked-for sources:

> This all proves how practical it is for us mendicants of Our Lady to go on practising our profession. Only in this way can we receive the reward of faith in the good providence of God. After all, we are trying to honour the Mother of God and restore her dowry. As Our Lord himself is bound to honour her, we cannot but be blessed.

Father Malachy presses home his point:

> At the end of the last century a pious Dutchman started a business in one of the big cities of England. To begin with he was unsuccessful. Then he formed a company, making Our Lord one of the directors. At the meetings they even left an empty chair for him, and his share of the profits was devoted to the education of priests. Almost at once the business grew and flourished exceedingly, so that very soon a great seminary was founded and endowed and is still being helped from the profits of this business. What a blessed way of preventing the piling up of profits from becoming an end in itself!

> I am forming a Company and issuing shares in Aylesford and Allington. The company will be made up of shareholders. These two great concerns, with such immense spiritual possibilities, are directly to do with Our Lady's work and nothing else. Allington Castle still has a debt of

eight thousand pounds and we must make a start on re-building the Church of the Assumption this year.

The shares will not be repayable and the question of interest will be left to Our Lady. The interest will go on accumulating in time and eternity. She has been beyond all measure practical in the restoration so far; she will be practical in a surprising way with her shareholders. It will be her company. It cannot fail in any respect; she will repay a thousandfold even in temporal ways.

Cradle Catholics who are not English will probably not be able to understand how this simple idea could have upset so many people. But, during the eighteenth and nineteenth centuries not only had England built up a most sophisticated and delicate monetary system, she had simultaneously consigned all forms of religious enthusiasm – including belief in the intervention of God and the saints in worldly matters – to the 'lower orders' of Christianity. These lower orders were of course the Low Church denominations and Roman Catholicism; but even amongst these people national attitudes are inclined to be pervasive, and the running together of business and religion could not fail to give us a shock.

The Bishop of Southwark, however, continued to confine his criticism of Aylesford to the Community's choice of processional hymns; while the rest of us thought about Our Lady's Company and came to the conclusion there was no reason why she should not have it. Some of us even joined it.

Bishop Cyril Cowderoy had been a supporter of the Carmelite invasion of his diocese from the moment the restoration was planned. As part of a hierarchy whose return to England after the Reformation coincided with the Gothic revival in architecture, it must have been a great joy to him to be able to foresee a day when Catholics would no longer have to go to Europe to see true architectural expression of the Faith. Like

St Simon Stock, the first English Prior of an order imported from the Holy Land, this English bishop no doubt saw that, with a modified Rule to fit the climate and local circumstances, nothing but good could come from the re-settling of this exotic international order, steeped in the spirit of early Christianity, among his work-worn parishes.

He made frequent visits to Aylesford, officiating at all the great ceremonies. From the very beginning he was moved by the early Christian spirit of prophecy to make such utterances as : 'This will be a great shrine of Our Lady – perhaps one of the greatest shrines of the Church.'

Father Malachy writes:

Father Bruno, the great French Carmelite, explaining how the order of Carmel is a prophetic one, says that prophecy is in a sense 'The clarification of the present' – seeing in the present with clear vision what others will only see when it has been fulfilled. 'The veil is lifted for a moment and then you have the pain of waiting; but what is fulfilled is more beautiful than your seeing.' That is why everything that has been done here appears as if it could not have been done in *any other way*. But if you ask me how that is, I cannot tell you, but Father Bruno's explanation helps. People, events, may be seen in this way. Where Our Lady is concerned it is shining logic. You see the beginning which lights the end, not fully, because the end is more beautiful than your seeing. It explains why everything which has been done here appears as if it had been there for a long time and as if it could not have been done in any other way.

It is this feeling of the presence of all time happening simultaneously at The Friars – perhaps in a point of light sparkling on a leaf above the altar, perhaps in the slow movement of a procession – which has affected all of us at one time or another. There is even a sense that time might be disturbed, that things might work out differently, so little do hours matter in the presence of an immutable eternity. There is a strange little story Father Malachy tells in his Newsletter of July 1954. He is describing a day when more than twelve thousand children came to The Friars to hear the bishop:

A minute before going to ask the Bishop's blessing to help to preach to the children, it was reported to me that one of them had been drowned in the river. The boy who saw it all happening said that the other child had fallen in at a certain place, that he had come up once and then disappeared again. This boy was able to point out the marks on the mud-bank of the clutching fingers when the child surfaced. The suspense was painful indeed. Next day it was confirmed that there was no boy missing. Nor had anyone seen any boy looking as if he had been in the river. It was most mysterious. In the village somebody said, 'A miracle has happened at The Friars – a boy has been drowned!' That was Satan's sneer. It was easy to see and feel who was behind the whole incident: the one who is always 'lying in wait for her heel'.

Of course it could have been a trick or a lie; but sometimes one wonders if God might not simply have wound the whole reel back in answer to prayer. Writing about prayer in the same Newsletter Father Malachy gives the idea that nothing is impossible:

There is a mysterious language of prayer which is yet so simple that a child can understand. People who have achieved simplicity and children pray best and of such is the kingdom of God. They do not misunderstand homely ways of talking to Our Lord and to his Mother and to the Saints. It is better to talk *to* them than about them. For lots of people prayer is putting on a solemn act. To have to suffer this is terrible and so heavy an affliction that you want to run away and blow bubbles.

I turned on the radio the other day and heard the B.B.C.'s 'Lift Up Your Hearts' – a programme to which scores of people send in letters asking for consolation in their troubles. In this particular edition a district nurse was answering. She told of a letter from a woman who had lost God. She had prayed and prayed and never had an answer. The district nurse said: 'God had answered. He had said No.'

That stupid slander of God horrified me. It set up a kind of defiant shouting within me. 'Knock and it shall be opened.' 'If you ask the Father *anything* in my name. . . .' Sometimes we ask for a stone and he gives us bread and we do not know it. We would make of him a serving man. He has answered even before we prayed. We could never have thought of asking him for our eyes to see with, our hands to work and pray with. As a matter of fact, God cannot say No. Impossible. There is nothing negative in God. He is positive act, as the philosophers would say. His Yes is creation and he is always saying Yes, Yes, endlessly Yes. Lucifer said an irrevocable No and he fell like lightning from heaven. Judas said No and went out into the darkness. We are always saying No to God and he is always saying Yes to us by keeping us alive. We must not slander God. In all creation only man is free to say No to him.

In a country where there is little theological teaching and even less knowledge of the saints, it is not surprising that there's a strain of astonishment at the ignorance which surrounds Aylesford. The Newsletters often reflect this:

Not even by accident can those who attack the Church be right about her (Our Lady). They could be silent but always they proclaim their difference. When her Glorious Assumption was proclaimed they protested. It was widening the gulf. And yet seven hundred years ago the hermits from Mount Carmel dedicated their first Church at Aylesford under that shining title. Nor was it a new discovery then but an ancient truth. The Blessed Mother does not widen the gulf between God and man, she bridges it.

When I was at our college in Llandeilo in Wales, a devout little man came to measure the Lady Chapel for a carpet. He was very religious, as are most of his race, very wistful and very shy. He was scared of offending and burning to know. Very simply he told me he believed Our Lord rose from the dead. But was he God? Was he alive now in any way that mattered to *him*? Of course he was. He was surprised Catholics believed so much.

'What about his Mother?' he asked.

I said, 'Has he left her dead in the dust?'

He was most bewildered as at something very strange and new and asked again, 'But is she alive now? If so, where is she?'

'If she is alive and in heaven, is it like her – is it as we read of her in the Bible – to be doing nothing for you and me if we ask her? If *she* is not alive it won't much matter to you and me or to anybody; because if he has not raised up his own Mother, what hope have we? But if she is alive and you go up to heaven, you will see her flaming in the breath of the Holy Spirit and you will know yourself for a clod and a boor not to have blessed her when she said that all generations would call her blessed.'

He understood – just as had his countrymen, 'smitten by sickness', hundreds of years before Wales was robbed of the Faith. And he was not a clod at all; but began paying lovely, heavenly-sounding compliments in Welsh to the Blessed Mother of Jesus.

To a generation whose philosophers are tempted to doubt even their own reality, it must be a weary task to be persuading them of the reality of any heavenly order. In 1952 Father Malachy wrote:

Perhaps we are now seeing the final working out of the Reformation. It is not finishing in any splendour of evil but is shabby, boring and empty. I read in our local paper some time ago how twenty thousand people went to see an actress setting a bonfire alight. The bonfire was in the middle of a field. It was a wet evening and the field was churned to mud by the crowds. Many of the women left their shoes after them in the mud. This is what has taken the place of the lovely festivals of the Church. The poor bored people will worship sticks or stones or an actress rather than nothing at all.

The life of Père Lamy seemed to him more real and interesting than such items from the newspapers:

I have had many and happy lessons from reading, for the third time, the Life of Père Lamy. I would prescribe the reading of it to all inclined to self-pity and solemnity. It was very good for me. On one occasion the French priest was asked when in difficulties, 'And how are you going to get out this time?' His reply was, 'You don't get out. You sink into it.' [And Father adds:] You think you are going into the abyss when in reality you are sinking into the bottomless abyss of God's Providence. That is how it is with us here. We must go on sinking. . . .

A year earlier this had nearly been literally true. In 1953 Aylesford had been badly flooded:

The writing of this Newsletter has been interrupted by the great flood which has brought sudden horror to so many people and places. Indeed we had enough of the horror here to understand and pity their plight. We have no wireless so on Saturday night we went to sleep without knowing what a storm was brewing. At two o'clock I was awakened by a great shouting which reached me above the howling of the storm. At first I thought it came from the animals in the zoo not far away or that it might be Brother John overhead having a nightmare. It was Major Hewitt giving the alarm.

Sister Joanna had left her fire burning and was awakened by its crackling. She jumped out of bed into a foot of water. The Courtyard was a swirling flood of waters coming in a mighty rush through the Watergate. Some people had come for a quiet religious weekend! Soon they were all working with the utmost speed clearing the ground floors before the flood. One of the masons, sleeping in St Jude's, was awakened to find all his belongings afloat around him and the water rising. Two brothers went waist deep to rescue the pigs and poultry. They were only just in time to save all the pigs and don't know to this day how they lifted the large pigs on to the bank behind. Brother Nuño, trying to save the poultry, climbed on a roof which collapsed. He only saved himself with the greatest difficulty. It was quite weird to see our timber for the building which had been stacked carefully inside sheds floating off on the rushing waters, to see another flood of tree-trunks and every kind of flotsam moving in from another direction.

It is incredible that so little damage was done. Only the river wall and the flood banks will have to be rebuilt. That will be a costly business.

Six months later the flood of bills was still with them:

The last letter was written in the midst of floods and their aftermath. Though we have had no help yet to repair the ravages we have good hopes. I am sure the floods will have proved to have been a blessing very much in disguise, and now I am hoping that all who receive this letter will help us to deal with these other floods of bills. They are much more dampening to one's spirit than the flood waters of the Medway. Work that costs enormously more than it should, the maddening vexations, the alarms and shocks; they are a part of the suffering of everybody nowadays. It is a continual mortification.

But it is a great and speedy means of detachment, better than the hair shirt and the picturesque penances of the desert. The more suffering and anxiety, the more detachment. One can be numb with fear and anxiety and not from want of faith. It is this very fear that flings one on the Providence of God. If our faith were the easy operation of a heavenly slot machine how superficial and vulgar it would be.

How pleasant then to return to Père Lamy and the excellent news a visionary always brings:

Père Lamy often saw Our Lady and the angels and the saints—and Satan. What sparkling conversations he was able to have with them and sometimes overhear: 'I am always in the gap', Our Lady said to him more than once. And he says of her so candidly, 'She is endlessly good. . . . The Blessed Virgin offers our prayers to God. She touches them up. She makes them into something pleasant. She is a ragpicker, divinely clever. She knows how to get rags out of places where you see nothing. She constantly finds a few little things and she gilds them.'

The Devil appeared to this ragpickers' priest: 'If she is good and kind, he is tricky. We are like a grain of sand in his presence. If his power were not limited, a puff, or not even a puff . . . one ought to put things more clearly and warn people: you fight Satan with prayer but prayer is the strength of God.'

He confesses he did not realize enough the disproportion between man and the angels,

'You keep on learning every day. *He* was in the sacristy and he was annoying me. I said to him, "Ah, you dirty beast!" St Gabriel said to me, "Don't forget he is an archangel. Don't argue. Respect Lucifer; he is an archangel that failed. He is like the son of a noble family brought down by his vices. You respect the Creator's masterpiece even in his destruction. . . . If you set about giving him deed for deed it is a real tinker's fight." '

'When a soul gives up praying I count it as my own.' It is Satan speaking in Père Lamy's hearing. 'Give up praying and I will give up bothering you.'

'He may say what he likes; I will take good care to go on praying. I would pray if it were only to make him angry, even if I had not the love of God', replies the priest.

A few years ago Father Bruno, the great French Carmelite writer, brought out a book on Satan which was a best-seller. It has been translated into most languages but I may tell you it is heavy going. It had a flaming cover with Satan in the centre looking much like Blake's version of him. This cover was repeated in a large way in a bookshop window in Paris. It attracted crowds of fashionable men and women, with more women than men, and held up the traffic; but if the crowds had known him as the Abbé knew him, there would have been no traffic hold-up.

But what a marvellous eyewitness the Abbé was of his good angels – 'What is very beautiful about them are the gold plates of irregular shape set like mosaic all over the upper part of their bodies.' And he describes the human likenesses in which they appeared to him, 'They are like athletes'. 'Wrapped in light so different! When you see

fifty together you forget to pray to God. They get light
from God.' 'They are there around us; we so nearly see
them: we do not pray enough to them, "Good evening,
my good angel", and so on.'

The seer is a homely priest and yet all that he writes is
in scale. Adam Kossowski in his paintings at Allington
depicts his angels like that, great towering beings over-
shadowing the earth and men. Suarez wrote three-quarters
of a million words on the angels; they must have been
around him in force when he was dying. He confessed he
never thought it could be so sweet a thing to die.

Adam Kossowski's work glows almost wherever one looks
in the completed shrine at Aylesford, the great angels round
the central altar, the ceramics on the altar, the scraffiti drawings
in St Anne's Chapel with inset ceramic groups, the glowing
colours of the Mysteries round the Rosary Way:

I am sure [Father Malachy says] that Our Lady chose
Kossowski for her work here. I am not saying this to
disarm criticism; for a Polish artist as great as Adam could
not go far wrong in his treatment of Our Lady and the
Saints. And his personal history must have prepared him
for the great work he is doing here.

He suffered an austere novitiate. Before the War he had
already achieved fame in his own land when he, with so
many more of the nobility of his race, was taken by the
Russians to a Siberian lumber camp, thousands of miles
from anywhere; so far indeed that there were no guards to
prevent escape, which could only be to death in the wilds.
Buried alive in the horrors of an Arctic winter, many died
every day.

One day he sketched an outline of the Annunciation on a
piece of paper and made a promise that if he survived to be
free again, he would devote his life to honour the good

God and Our Lady by his art. He attributes his survival to Our Lady's help. After the War he painted his first picture in London. It was the Annunciation he had sketched in bondage. He sent it to an exhibition and it won a prize, enough money to keep him until he was brought into touch with us. And since that time he has been constantly painting and making ceramics for Our Lady of Aylesford.

Among the first works executed for The Friars were a series of the fifteen Mysteries of the Rosary cast in ceramic ware and mounted in wooden shrines around the Rosary Way in the garden. In technique they are an exciting revival of a fifteenth-century medium associated with the Della Robbias and each group is a work of art in itself. The colours shine through the soft glaze and there is a primitive dignity in the composition of each scene. The Renaissance, coming late through Poland, has given a Byzantine cast to their faces. Yet, at the same time, there is a freshness and originality which liberates them from any traditional mould.

From the beginning the life at The Friars has been threaded by processions; processions by torchlight, in sunlight or beneath the diffused light of rain clouds. We take to them naturally because they can signify so much for us. Solitary yet companioned we wander into them, we circle the mystery and in this circle our life seems enclosed in the progression from birth to death, the slow march of our seasons, the Church itself. Step by step we pace out these concepts as they do in the East.

All visitors to Aylesford have, at one time or another, moved slowly round and past that great progression of mysteries defined by Adam Kossowski. His vision is peerless, the ceramics forever significant reminding one of Boethius' definition of eternity: 'That immortal life from which nothing of the future is absent and from which nothing of the past has drained away.'

Since the Return the first great procession actually to be planned was for the Feast of Our Lady of Mount Carmel in July 1951. In May of that year Father Malachy was asked to Bordeaux to attend the seventh centenary of the Feast of St Simon Stock.

Bordeaux was en fête for the Feast of St Simon of England [he writes]. I rejoiced greatly but the magnificence of it all gave me uncomfortable thoughts. When the relics of St Simon are brought back to Aylesford a few weeks from now, the ceremonies will have to be under the open sky in the Sanctuary of the desecrated church he built. This will not, however, take from the welcome we are preparing. There will be a Cardinal of the Curia to represent the Pope, the Archbishop of Bordeaux, other great prelates and dignitaries of the Church and State and pilgrimages from many countries. Many thousands will escort St Simon's relics over the ancient bridge and give them welcome home.

Preparations had to be hurried forward. The site of the old church was nothing like fully excavated, there was no roof over the outdoor altar. In the event all went well:

A few months before the rededication ceremonies we were quite certain that 'all would be well and all manner of things would be well'; although at the time it looked quite impossible that any considerable part of the restoration would be finished. But it was. The Great Court in particular was more beautiful than we had planned, not only in essentials but even in its gracious detail. The work of uncovering the foundations of the Sanctuary of the original church was begun only a month before the ceremonies.

One day I was standing with a naval chaplain and some officers from Chatham Dockyard looking at the great heaps of earth and thinking in terms of wheelbarrows and voluntary workers. One of the naval officers with great sense said, 'Get a bulldozer!' And then with greater sense he sent me a cheque to defray the cost. When the 'Son of Thunder' had been working for a week the lawn was a sorry sight, but the foundations at last were showing. Mr Jarmin, a landscape specialist, who has been giving his labour of love to The Friars for nearly two years, was reassuring. He was truly part of the special providence of Our Lady, he and his small band of voluntary workers. It was no time at all before great heaps of earth became contours and the ragstone base of the altar had been built high above the foundations, and the thirty hundredweight of altar stone placed upon it.

The Directors of the Aylesford Paper Mills, who have shown a most practical interest in the restoration, made a noble gesture. They offered to be responsible for the canvas to cover the altar and Sanctuary during the ceremonies. The estimate they received from the firm was six hundred pounds for three days. We said 'No' several times and then we saw that we had not trusted Our Lady enough. We changed our plan and decided to erect a permanent canopy. The old oak beams were found and the work started just a week before the ceremonies. One day a Scottish Presbyterian engineer came on to the site to consult me about something quite different. He said, 'I am the only man in Great Britain who can give you copper for your roof; it would look lovely against that copper beech'.

And so the copper came, with the coppersmiths to put it on; and it was finished just one hour before the ceremonies on that Saturday morning. All the ceremonies were in the open. If it had rained! It rained all day on Thursday; it came down in torrents, but it didn't shake our faith. We knew again that 'all would be well and all manner of thing would be well'. Friday was clear; on Saturday morning the sun was shining into the cloisters. The Prior General's Mass was to begin the Triduum. The choir of Carmelites and many other pilgrims had come the evening before . . . the director of the choir had come from Rome. My lasting impression of that ceremony was of a long procession of white Friars, coming with unexpected suddenness to the altar through the sunlit cloisters, singing the *Magnificat*. It was like good news heard suddenly – and then there was the incomparable Introit:

'How beautiful are thy steps, O Daughter of the Prince: thy lips are like a dripping honeycomb and the fragrance of thy garments like frankincense. Let us sing to the Lord a new song.'

On the Sunday Bishop Cowderoy offered Mass in the presence of the Cardinal, after which the whole company set off in procession to the outskirts of the village where the relics of St Simon were to be met:

There were more than twenty-five thousand pilgrims for that welcome home. There are very few Catholics in the village, yet the people truly sensed the greatness of the event. There were flowers on the window sills; all along the way stood little girls in long white dresses with lilies in their hands. It might have been in France or Spain – and it was spontaneous. The Vicar was as helpful as he could be and loaned the school on the other side of the bridge; but the chimes in the church could not be rung. That was not his fault, it is the old law of England; but at The Friars three old bells had been slung in the branches of the great beech tree behind the altar and their sound, sharp and very clear, came to us over the stir and singing of the waiting multitude as the relics were carried in to the altar. They gave a curious sense of remoteness, as if they came from the far past.

Contrary to previous arrangements Bishop Cowderoy insisted that the relics should be handed over half way across the bridge. This was a sudden inspiration and must have meaning. Seven hundred years ago St Simon of England had gone over that bridge to make his last visitation of his many foundations abroad. He died at Bordeaux and there his relics were venerated during the succeeding centuries. Now, with his relics on the bridge, St Simon had truly returned and this strange return has no meaning unless it makes a bridge across the years, joining again the England of Our Lady's Dowry with the England of the present – so starved of the joy and hope Our Lady can give.

On the evening of the Feast more than a thousand came for the torchlight procession. The relics of St Simon were carried round the grounds, and there was solemn Benediction from the open-air altar. This was an afterthought to the general arrangements, but it made of The Friars for that one evening a little Lourdes. Our Lady appeared there for the last time on the Feast of Carmel and St Bernadette declared she was more beautiful than ever. Significantly the Most Reverend Father Silvirius, Order of Discalced Carmelites, and many of the Carmelite family from all over France were holding a great congress at Lourdes to celebrate the Seventh Centenary of the Scapular Vision. They too were closing their ceremonies with a torchlight procession.

The best news of all about the Triduum is the knowledge of great graces which have been given to many. Several taking part had the gift of faith, and the scapular has been the means of healing to others. . . .

On the tomb of Cardinal Merry del Val in Rome is his epitaph written by himself: *Da mihi animas, cetera tolle.* 'Give me souls, take away all else.' It is souls that matter. Although they are noble enough, all the works and crafts at Aylesford are no more than a means. Sure signs are the many who come and have the gift of faith, and there have been many cures. One sudden and complete cure is now being considered by the Ecclesiastical Authority. But from this and other cures I can now see that what happens spiritually is the real miracle. Quite clearly one sees that Our Lady does not bring about cures in order that the cured may live in a mediocre fashion ever afterwards. It is the immense awakening of the spirit to life and activity, and all the spiritual consequences that are the surest sign . . . I am sure the Blessed Mother cannot be present in great love without bringing healing to the souls and bodies of her children.

We are often asked to send scapulars to be worn by the sick and we have had reports of many cures. Here is the letter of a small but startling little girl writing to thank somebody to whom I sent scapulars blessed at Aylesford for her father who was very ill. It is a model of good reporting:

Dear Miss O'C,

I hope you will have a Happy Christmas. I am sending you one pound for Father Malaky. It is my first Holy Communion money. I was sorry to hear the floods had got into his house and hope he got them swep out. My grass children are all dead for this year but they will come again. Daddy thanks you for the scaplars. Mammy put them on him when he was sick and he was sick no more.

Love from Jeannah.

In 1953, continuing on the same subject, Father Malachy wrote:

> We are always under siege here, always there is evident the sinister counter-sign. I am sure Our Lady is here surrounded by a great multitude as St Simon saw her. She has answered the prayer we make to her most often, St Simon's, 'Show us a sign, thou dost protect us'. Here is one of the many which she has shown us recently. It is so clear that she must wish it to be known.
>
> On Easter Sunday Eve this year I found a man and his wife and little girl of six looking rather lost in the cloisters. I brought them into Benediction and afterwards they walked with me around the Rosary Way. The mother explained that the little girl had brought them to get holy water for her stoup. Only holy water from Aylesford would do and she brought them fifty miles to get it. She was going to a convent school and had a wisdom which embarrassed her parents. Through the most painful circumstances imaginable, the mother was a lapsed Catholic and had no faith at all. The father is a scientist and at that time had no definite belief.
>
> His wife had been extremely ill for six years and looked so awful that she attracted my sympathy at once. She asked if she might come and stay for a few days. She did, and felt a little better from her continual pain and extreme discomfort. She had a kidney infection combined with high blood pressure and other complications which resulted in headaches, pains and sickness of all kinds. She could not sleep without drugs and these no longer killed the pain.
>
> She went home and came back after a few days with a friend and they both began to work in the garden. On the second day she was exhausted almost from the start. She climbed a bank above the Rosary Way and sat down to rest

under a hawthorn bush. Quite suddenly all pain left her
and health came surging back and more energy than she
had ever known. She has had no need since for drugs or
medicine and for three months now has done the work of a
strong man. She has kept all the gardens here with only
occasional help, and now she has turned her hand to the
large vegetable garden and the orchards. When she was
examined by her doctor he was greatly surprised. Though
he would not believe it was supernatural he could not
disprove the fact. He is ill himself and asked her to pray for
him, so he must suspect that this is something beyond his
reach and skill. She has recovered a fervent faith and her
husband too is on his way back to the Church. In fact, this
little girl of six and a half made him say three rosaries with
her before she would go to sleep one night. He came back
perspiring.

There is authority in the New Testament for belief in the
particular power of the prayers of children: in the Autumn
of 1953 Father Malachy was describing a new kind of
pilgrimage:

> Last Sunday the first pilgrimage came by water. Quickly
> the people came off the boat through the old doorway from
> the river into the Pilgrim's Hall. The river was again
> bearing pilgrims along the way travelled by the first
> hermits when they came from Mount Carmel. There was a
> triumphant air about it, something indescribable I had not
> felt before. I know I shall have it always.

The sight must have given a particular confidence to Father,
fresh as he was from looking at a pattern which was becoming
familiar at Aylesford: that of a child leading its parents into
truth by the sheer force of its will: 'a little child shall lead
them'. That day he had been talking to a woman who had

been coming to The Friars to give thanks for the transformation of her life. Although not a Catholic she was married to one and had a little Catholic daughter with whom, from a sense of duty, she had been praying the Rosary. Her husband was the victim of a severe neurosis which was ruining their family life; but somehow the little girl had prevailed upon him to go and stay at Aylesford. He had returned from there changed, and the mother now knew what had happened. Now she herself was coming into the Church too.

On Ascension day, 1954, there were nearly a thousand children at Aylesford, with their Sisters and teachers:

> It was a heavenly day and the children seemed to flow in around the outdoor altar. It was not walking nor marching and each one appeared to be separate, as if Our Lady were giving them welcome one by one. There they were in their great numbers, like the 'heaven's embroidered cloths' spread at Our Lady's feet.

On the same day came Mr Adrian Gilbert Scott to survey the site for plans for the rebuilding of the church. Although he had told us that it would be months, perhaps even years before he could start in earnest on the work, it was his second visit within weeks.

He came at the end of Mass so I asked the children to say the Memorare with me that he might be inspired to build a noble shrine for Our Lady. After lunch he was seized by a frenzy of inspiration and shut himself away and worked furiously all the afternoon. I began to see the children's prayers being answered at once, so before the procession I asked for another Memorare for four intentions:

> More people for the Saturday evening talks, 'For a Better World'.
> That the debt on Allington might be paid off at once so that we could get on with the church.

An intention for the building of our workshops about which we were almost in despair.

Lastly, for little Sheila McIntosh who was having a heart operation that afternoon.

Sometimes she is sudden with the answer and clear. When the architect and the children had gone I was called to the telephone: a lady who had been to the previous Saturday's talk wanted to arrange transport for three or four others. Very soon after that there was a long-distance call to the Gatehouse. I went rather listlessly and wonderingly to take this personal call.

'Who is speaking?' I asked.

'I am a reader of your Newsletter. Is the debt on Allington paid off yet?'

'No, as a matter of fact we have been busy accumulating more. There is upkeep and overheads and repairs. . . .'

The unknown voice said, 'I understand. Would you like a cheque for a thousand pounds now or would you like me to make you a covenant to pay a thousand a year for seven years?'

I chose the covenant offer! The man who made it had not been to Aylesford and was calling from the North of England. He wished to remain anonymous, 'Just the grateful father of a family'. He said he would confirm his offer by letter on the following Saturday. It was as brief as that. I was walking on air and am still levitated in spirit.

Then there were the workshops: a week previously I had received a donation for shares from the head of a building firm. I telephoned him about the workshops and he came to see me. We spoke the same language with the same brogue too and I knew that the answer was here. He took the plans away saying he would write the next day. He didn't so I thought he would be slow.

We were celebrating the Feast of the Mediatrix with great splendour and for great reasons. The Sisters from Allington sang the solemn Mass and their singing, as always, was full of light. It was late in the morning on the last day of May, the last of the Crusade of Prayer. At nine came an excited message that a foreman and a party were erecting offices on the site of the workshops and had already begun digging.

This took my breath away and then came two letters which I was expecting: one from the person who had telephoned, very simply confirming his offer: and the other from Sheila's father. It said:

I thank you for your letter. As you say, God answers our prayers in His own and the best way, for Sheila died on Thursday evening . . . she was greatly loved. . . . On us the loss on earth of this gay and gallant little girl leaves such a void. . . . The expression on her face as she lay in death was peace itself and it took away from us the soreness and bitterness of her loss which was very great. I have no objection to your using my name or using my letter in your Newsletter. She loved Aylesford.

Sheila had come here several times with her parents. She was most lovely, unforgettable. Not only the prayers of a thousand children went up to Our Lady but a heavenly child to take them. Is it any wonder that the day was so full of blessing. I do not ask you to pray for her. She will pray for us.

The whole of this conjunction of events, the triumph, the pain, seemed to be contained in the great prayer of the Mass on that last day of May. Father Malachy went on:

A great Mother-General had come with sixty of her

Sisters. I never see Sisters in a body like that without a feeling that they are the far forward companies of the army of God, and that only an act of God could push them back. That act could never be. Many look as if the final battle were already won. The Church *is*. She is not an argument nor a debating society but the army of God on the march, fighting and always winning against impossible odds. Is not Our Lady 'terrible as an army set in battle array'? There were many children and the large chapel was full. The Mass was long and I must have spoken for a long time. They were so rapt I could not stop. Nobody seemed to mind. Aylesford was timeless that day as never before.

There were many more outdoor ceremonies that summer, always with an eye on the weather. In September Father Malachy wrote:

> Despite the cold wet summer we have had many pilgrims. The weather did not seem to matter on most days, but it would have mattered a lot on the feast of Carmel when seven thousand pilgrims came and the Ordinations were in the open.
>
> Half-an-hour before the ceremony my heart sank. People arriving from all directions reported rain on the way. Already there was a drizzle and they were putting up their umbrellas. The Bishop's secretary telephoned the Air Ministry: the forecast was rain.
>
> Then the sun came out and the Mass went on under the sky over the old foundations. It was fine all day.
>
> Aristotle defines a slave as a 'living tool'. To see an ordination is to see a man being made into a living tool of God. He is a consecrated thing. You see the Bishop anointing his hands in a terribly meaningful way, as if they were an altar stone: and then his hands are bound by a linen cloth and he is prostrate on the ground during the

most solemn invocation – separate and apart – as if he were dead.

From this comes the priest – with sacrifice and forgiveness and blessing and healing in his hands. There is no emotion. It is a stark creation which cannot be undone. Emotion could not support it for a moment. By the Grace of God a priest! From ordination derives what Cardinal Manning calls the 'mystic pedigree of one whom the Church ordains; without father, without mother, without genealogy, having neither beginning of days nor end of life, but likened to the Son of God, a priest for ever'.

The building of a church is little in comparison with the making of a priest. Father Brocard Sewell, one of those ordained, now belongs to the Aylesford Community and is already heavily engaged. He was associated with Eric Gill in the early days and came to the altar by indirections.

Since then Father Brocard has become a very well-known member of the Aylesford Community, publishing the *Aylesford Review*, a literary magazine which is highly thought of among writers although perhaps a little puzzling to the pilgrims. The local doctor, a friend of his, is accustomed to Father Brocard's 'happenings' at his Georgian riverside house. Suddenly at teatime Father will sweep in with an assortment of literary and musical people from London and abroad: a Canadian string consortium, Colin Wilson, a Dominican-priest poet from America, Henry Williamson . . . Father Brocard keeps them all on their toes and back numbers of his magazine are collector's items.

In the wet Autumn of 1954, as the fifth anniversary of the Return was approaching, it seemed good to Father Malachy further to strengthen the links of prayer and friendship between Aylesford, Lourdes and the great Carmelite shrines of Europe, by making pilgrimage to them.

But before he could set out there was much to be done: in the last five years the community at The Friars had grown, much restoration had been accomplished and it had become a spiritual centre for many thousands of people; but it was still an island in a sea of unbelief, still it was 'line-fishing' in the apostolate, still the graves of the founders were open to the sky.

The Mass on the Solemnity of the Assumption had been an important event. Father Paulus, a Dutch Carmelite, had composed a special Mass and for the first time the 'stations', lovely antiphons celebrating the Assumption, were sung at intervals in the procession to the altar. It 'began under a darkening sky with a roll of thunder and the Mass proceeded to the accompaniment of heavenly fireworks. The choir was heard but above it the majestic and startling rattle of artillery.' Nobody got very wet although people were baling out their houses in a nearby village; but the need for a proper church was heavily underlined.

But it was still the workshops which were presenting the problems, as Father wrote: 'The workshops have jumped up. They are now ready for roofing. There is a mighty lot of building in them, laundry, pottery, carpentry, shops, weaving, loom-making, garages and stores.'

The trouble was that they had been more or less obliged to build them exactly twice the intended size because building regulations forbade the use of proper roofing materials on a one-storey building. Aesthetically – almost religiously – speaking, they could not have an aluminium roof at The Friars, so two storeys high it had to be. In time the extra space would no doubt be useful; but in the meanwhile the extra money had to be found while they were still without even *materials* for the new church. Old ragstone had to be found; all that had been on the site had been used already. Even the small bits had been disposed along the Rosary Way:

I went to the quarries. I was all eyes for months looking at old walls and houses but always there was complete disappointment. Then we thought it time to pray in real earnest.

One busy day a message came to me that somebody with a van wanted to see me; he had been waiting more than an hour. He was a little man and black as a sweep. His profession was demolition and he was pulling down an old mansion a few miles away.

'I see you are doing some building here', he said. 'I can sell you five hundred tons of faced ragstone and thirty thousand old peg tiles. I must have them out in a few weeks.'

The price was half the one quoted from other sources and in a few days notice came from the Bank that the greater part of a legacy for The Friars had been paid into their account. This was enough to pay for the materials and then came an ultimatum from the architect that 'The wall opposite the west door must come down, to give us room and a vista'. That wall was built of stones from the old church and now they were to go back:

I have do doubt at all about who is creating these situations in which one must act, and at once. It has happened so often before. That is why I say this Restoration is impersonal. The pace is set from the other side and one has a sense of great urgency.

So, with the peg tiles stacked under the great beech tree near the foundations and the ragstone being brought in at a rate of fifty tons a day, Father Malachy was able to set out for the Three Day Congress in Saragossa for the Feast of Our Lady of the Pillar to speak of Aylesford. He was to be in Lisieux for the Feast of St Thérèse and in Avila for the Saint's

Feast Day on 15 October. At these places and at Lourdes he promised to offer Mass and to pray for the Friends of Aylesford:

> We set out as pilgrims. There were four of us, two recent converts of Aylesford, one who had been cured at Aylesford, and myself. We made a pact with Our Lady and the two Teresas which kept us out of restaurants and expensive hotels and bound us to three rosaries every day. Before long we knew that Our Lady and the Saints were helping us and in many and curious ways they disclosed their identity. Again that mysterious sign language of the other world!
>
> We had no bookings beforehand but I had an introduction to a Sister at Lisieux. Very simply she told me how she came to be there: she had entered Carmel as a girl and was heart-broken when she had to leave as both her lungs had become affected. She was cured through the intervention of St Thérèse and now, though she was no longer a Carmelite and belonged to a different Order, she had come by amazing 'indirections' to be engaged in an apostolate directly concerned with her saint.
>
> We talked for a long time and I shall always remember her comment: 'If only we realized fully the Communion of Saints, we should die of happiness.' She led me to the Carmel next door and in a few moments I was talking to the Mother Prioress who renewed the pact which Mother Agnes made with me a few years ago, always to remember in their prayers the old Motherhouse of Aylesford and its apostolate.

In the Carmel at Lourdes Father Malachy made a similar pact with the Mother Prioress. It was there that he came to know, on the authority of an aunt of Bernadette, that Our

Lady had last appeared there on the Feast of Our Lady of Mount Carmel. He wrote:

> You will be tired of hearing from me how the Feast of Carmel replaced the old Feast of the Assumption as the patronal feast of the Order after the vision of St Simon. By appearing to Bernadette on the last time on this scapular feast, Our Lady was linking her vision at Lourdes to Carmel and to Simon in England. All this is delicate and gracious but it is very clear; as clear in its implications as her last appearance to the Children of Fatima as Our Lady of Mount Carmel. It is a sign that she has not forgotten Simon or Aylesford nor turned away for ever from her Dowry.

At Lourdes Father Malachy gave thanks for two years' relief from the diabetes which had been making his life difficult. He had been taking insulin but when he returned from Lourdes he found that it was the *cure* which was affecting him; he was getting severe headaches from the insulin and it was not until he had cut the dose down to nothing that he felt the benefit of the 'pool of healing'.

From Lourdes the party motored on into Spain:

> It was St Teresa of Avila who opened our eyes to Spain, and Teresa herself becomes in her own land most vividly alive. Across the Pyrenees, that land which is neither east nor west, the Spain of Castile and of Aragon, sombre as El Greco's landscapes, unfold to the distant Sierras. They seem to be full of silence and penance.
>
> Everywhere mules and donkeys, high-spirited beasts, and the strong patient oxen ploughing the scorched plains and the tinkle of bells and the labour of animals and men that has gone on unchanged from dawn to dark for more than a thousand years.

Father was much taken by the air of purpose which even the animals have in that land. After his journey he was telling some of the Aylesford pilgrims about a pig he saw surging determinedly down a village street. Without a flicker of its ears, with no shadow of hesitation, this animal had turned into a doorway and disappeared.

At evening time in the dusk the working beasts, the cattle and the goats and the shepherds and the sheep with their sheepdogs fill all the roads home and they are not really at all heavy, but animated, having *fulfilled* a day; men and creatures which God has from the beginning joined together in toil and dependence. They are fulfilling time and not using it up as we are. It is intimacy with the earth and with living things and the terrible familiarity of life with Our Lord and Our Lady and the Saints which has made the Spanish soul what it is: noble and with great spirit and dignity. With the Knight Don Quixote they know that 'A man must not make a jest of his soul'.

When the party arrived in Saragossa for the Congress of All Spain:

It was Our Lady's name which was flashing in the night above the tallest building. She was carried in procession in a thousand images from all Spain. There was the Lady of Monserrat, her face black as night; faces dark and secret, 'Most holy dark, cover our uncouth love'. Faces enigmatic, old, venerable, majestic; Our Lady sorrowing.

At that Congress General Franco laid Spain at Our Lady's feet. One evening I heard more than a hundred thousand young men and women making an act of consecration for all the youth of Spain in the great square of Our Lady of the Pillar. When the Cardinal had finished speaking there was a hush; and it began quite suddenly as one voice or act. It was mighty and startling but it did not lift you up, it cut through you, though the night to the sky. It was clean and final, a fearful thing: then they turned away without emotion as if it were something which need never be done again. The cry of the martyrs was in that final word to Our Lady, of more than four thousand priests cut down without a single defection; and countless other martyrs, religious and lay, spoke in it too.

It has been the fashion to slander Spain's deliverer. Truly he was a man sent by God and of Our Lady's commissioning. From a great prelate in Valladolid I heard how Franco and his wife heard Mass together and received Holy Communion on the Feast of Carmel. On the next day he began the war which delivered Spain from Communism. For him Our Lady of Carmel is Our Lady of Victories and his home is under her protection. He always carries with him a relic of St Teresa of Avila which he recovered from the Reds. He lives and has fought his battles in the Communion of Saints and has known the wonder of God's providence and his people know it too. That is why their gratitude is almost impersonal, why it has such dignity and reserve.

It is said that every Irishman is half a monk and it is true. But every Spaniard is more than half a Carthusian. The men of the grey plains under a pitiless sun! These terrible landscapes withered from drought and the cold winds from the Sierras which sweep the dust. For the greater part of the year there is no rain. The land is irrigated by most primitive means but still the waters of the Ebro never reach the sea. No government can yet change this condition and what follows looks like poverty; but it isn't. Upon my soul I have never seen such noble people. The poorest woman is womanly and to see them washing clothes by the wayside is a dignified sight. They are without envy because they have great possessions; every dusty village is full of children, beautifully dressed and radiant; the baptized! That character is as plain as plain can be. 'Their eyes are shy with secrets.'

One sunny morning on our way home we passed – too quickly – a cavalcade which made our shining car and a million other things seem irrelevant. Mounted on donkeys with pack saddles young women with such good faces and riding some hundred yards apart were travelling to the town we had just left. Their little mounts with their sensitive ears were strong and lively. They sat superbly, those riders, and one was reading, another knitting and two others were equally engaged. The animals had shining harness and needed no guiding. Their riders were completely indifferent to the irrelevances passing by, and there flashed across one's mind the vision of another Rider riding into another city. That is Spain, where time is fulfilled.

I was wondering aloud about it to Brother Nuño, the Spaniard, when I came back. He said to me, 'Conscience is terrible in Spain'. His father runs the village bakery where he is still baking as they baked hundreds of years ago. He is up in the morning at three and has eight bakings a day; but after a long life he is poor. During the Civil War he scorned to make money out of the needs of the poor and often he gave his bread away because bread was life.

Another Spaniard, Brother Simon, told me of a father and his little boy who were being tortured to death in the most terrible way because they would not betray their comrades to the Reds. The father cried out every minute while he could, 'Courage, my son; a few more minutes and we shall be in heaven'. Conscience is terrible in Spain.

But from the large austerities of Spain the travellers were due to return to the cold November of Aylesford, shrinking in on itself for the Month of the Dead. As usual the shocks were in scale:

> The ragstone had piled up around the old foundations while I was away. The roofs of the workshops were almost completed and I was dismayed when I saw the size of them. The ground floors will be ample for our pottery and weaving and woodworking and on the empty first floor there is a vast space. Then I was told of the need for a bigger sewage disposal works costing thousands of pounds (forty thousand booked pilgrims came this year, that's why). A whole lot of troubles came at once: the Winter coming, with no income to keep this vast place going – and there was an east wind! For a fortnight I was as empty as that first floor, not unhappy but terribly afraid. I felt the burden too heavy and regretted having gone away. And then the cloud was lifted and light came: let us use this space for accommodation for pilgrims, I thought. There will be room for seventy-five cubicles.

Since it is the beggar who is nearly always in the right he needs great conviction and even greater humility to overcome the irritating effect of his rectitude. In one of his later News-letters Father Malachy describes a marvellous Belgian mendicant who was given permission by his Abbot to go and preach about the refugees from behind the Iron Curtain and to appeal for help: 'At the end of his sermons people gave him nearly everything they had. I even heard of a chemist who went to hear him and found himself thanking God he'd forgotten his cheque book.'

Father Malachy is no mean beggar himself. In England it is apathy and spiritual dullness which makes a famine in the soul. Cubicles for pilgrims, well-fed pilgrims, may not have the same interdenominational immediacy as food for refugees; but Father has always been able to make people feel that Our

C

Lady's plans for the English were an important part of world Christianity. And of course, since the beliefs of advanced countries are such a powerful force for good or ill in the rest of the world, he could only be right.

When the late Bishop Ullathorne was asked what is the best book on humility he is said to have replied: 'The best book on humility? *I* wrote it.' But when Father Malachy confesses to doubts and misery as to whether the Newsletters are in the best possible form, it is not 'humility with a hook in it'. He considers himself only as the 'basket of the sower', and is grateful for every crop that grows. Here is his appeal for money for those cubicles:

> Didn't St Benedict say a monastery was for sick souls, not for healthy ones? Your alms will be giving Our Lady rooms for her pilgrims. You may never be able to give her a house, but you might give her a room for the one she didn't get in Bethlehem. This is the only Shrine being restored in England this year, so far as I know. Bishop Cowderoy has said we should let it be a reparation for all Our Lady's desecrated shrines. She is calling us to it and she is urgent as we know. This unrelenting pressure! I am sure it is right.

> We have twelve thousand in her Company now. Could you canvass or cajole? Make it twenty thousand before the Feast of the Immaculate Conception. We will be Our Lady's church builders and what a church it will be! The church of the Assumption of the Glorious Virgin, restored out of 'living stones'. Send her a gift in thanksgiving for a year which has been full of her love:

> Our Lady went into a strange country and they crowned
> her for a queen,
> For she needed never to be stayed or questioned but
> only seen;

And they were broken down under unbearable beauty:
as we have been.
Our Lady wears a crown in a strange country, the crown
He gave,
But she has not forgotten to call to her old companions:
to call and crave.
And to hear her calling a man might arise and thunder
on the doors of the grave.

Chesterton's Queen of the Angels – wearing her crown again. If the very simple unsophisticated people of this land could only see her! But how can they unless we show her to them as her great knight saw her? This Newsletter is Our Lady calling to you. Perhaps in answer to it twenty thousand of 'her old companions' may arise before the end of her year, to 'thunder on the doors of the grave'.

As I have said before, 'Give her an egg and she will give you an ox'. Gifts of jewellery have proved a very substantial help, and a covenant with the Friends of Aylesford means that a contribution is almost doubled. Bequests? It was a bequest from the late Miss Dixon which enabled us to pay for the ragstone and peg tiles already on the spot. Notes and valuables should be sent by registered post. For the Rosary Way and the gardens we would be grateful for bulbs and shrubs; any quantity, any kind.

I am sending you a Spanish Madonna to bring you greetings for Christmas and the New Year. I leave it to Our Lady to thank you in her own way.

Very gratefully in Carmel,

W. MALACHY LYNCH, O. Carm.

II

Many a Blow and Biting Sculpture . . .

For those who cannot resist the temptation to make heavenly
equations, the next part of the story may seem perfectly
logical. The Carmelites had been able to outwit the Devil in
putting The Friars on its feet again. Already it was a stumbling
giant, 'a giant that had not yet begun to walk'. The Devil,
fallible because hindered by hatred, though a powerful
archangel just the same, was due for his turn. Father Malachy
suddenly became gravely ill and this is how he wrote of it
later, when sufficiently recovered to do so in January 1955.

It is nearly always the unexpected that happens. I did
not expect to find myself in a hospital on Christmas Day;
neither had I expected all that led up to it.

I went down with an undiagnosed illness a week before
Christmas. There was a high temperature with a migraine
headache which, in the space of a few days, reduced me to a
state of utter misery. Half-way through the week the doctor
got the pain under control but the temperature persisted.
Then there was an unexpected crisis. Although I had taken
a sleeping tablet I was quite unable to sleep for several
hours so they brought me some tea. I then fell asleep only
to awake and find myself in the toils of what they call a
rigor. I shook and shivered and gibbered as if I were
freezing to death. The people who were with me immediately heaped everything they could find on top of me. Within
a few minutes my temperature was normal again but by

68

this time everyone was so frightened that a specialist was called in. Although I didn't acknowledge it I had reached a state of indifference and needed no food – the senses had all gone. I had a feeling that my body was not there, but just a vast empty expanse. If light were to break over that grey universe which is oneself I think it would be what we call dying; and it would be very easy.

Years later Father was again at the point of death. He could describe it only as a kind of 'light-hearted surrender, familiar in a way, and gay too'. But illness is so much worse and in both cases it was for the miserable aftermath of mental and physical suffering that he was snatched back.

I was bundled into the hospital to a high, badly proportioned room and I was alone in it – at least for a few moments. Now the specialist appeared with two other doctors, the ward sister, two nurses and others. He had a four-square Napoleonic stance. He looked grim and was treating his 'case' with all seriousness and solemnity. I suppose it was ceremonial and was expected of him; but it had a peculiar effect on me because I felt quite irresponsible. He delivered a little homily which I had probably brought upon myself, saying he would have nothing more to do with the case if I did not obey.

While my arm was lashed to a board and liquid was dripping into me from bottles slung over my head I must have had a kind of flight from reality, as I was projected back twenty years to a beautifully proportioned high room in Merrion Square, Dublin, where I was examined by a brilliant young woman specialist to whom I had been sent by my Provincial. She tackled her cleric very delicately. She was saying, 'There is nothing wrong with your heart, thank God. There's nothing wrong with your chest, thank God. There is nothing wrong there." And so the examination went on. Then she sat down at my feet and began to talk – not as a specialist, she said, but as an ignorant woman. She said to me, 'You know *you* have all the secrets'. I got her off that line at once; but as she parted with me and asked for my prayers, I said to myself, 'You vital woman. There's nothing wrong with your soul, thank God.' Actually she was dying of cancer and in two months she was dead. The news of her death was heart-breaking.

But if I were a doctor that is the language I would be using. You cannot fake it; it comes from the supernatural and is like oil or balm poured into a wound. Contact with the world of grace gives a touch faculty for which nothing else can make up.

That day there were injections of penicillin, a portable X-ray was wheeled in for photographs of Father's chest and by the evening he was able to see his brother, Father Elias Lynch.

That evening, Father Elias came. I am sure he was fairly certain I was finished. Somehow I was very certain I was not. He seemed more cheerful when he came on the Friday evening.

Since Father Malachy had had very little sleep on the previous night the specialist prescribed a different brand of sleeping tablets for Christmas Eve:

I had had two hours sleep when Father Christmas appeared at three a.m. After that there was a lull. I put out the lights and closed my eyes wearily to induce sleep. The room seemed to expand and to be filled with a mighty throng. On my right I could see a procession of funny fussy little women all creeping quietly along and taking up their positions around my right shoulder or in that direction. One rather elderly lady, dressed in the style of twenty years ago, came slowly. She took a good look at me before she took up her watch. I turned to my left and a procession of most odd people in scarlet were all disappearing behind the bed. They didn't seem to have any faces so I said to myself that I must peer more closely. I picked out one and I saw when he passed that he had a face like a horse. I thought what a boring lot they were. Then I looked up at the ceiling and that was fantastic. Formless, faceless sprites were intent on holding a kind of awning over me. Down they swooped and just when I felt they were going to wrap me up in some comfort, the whole thing finished. I couldn't stand the procession going round me on both sides so I kept my closed eyes on the goings-on over my head, which I couldn't begin to understand. They dangled things first at a high level and then swooped almost to the level of my face. It was so real that I thought they wanted to give me something. I put out my hand and opened my eyes and there was nothing. I explored all the corners of the ceiling where there was something different going on in each. One corner was full of half-born faces, in another there was a ridiculous dance of some sort going on to which I could not give a name. So I was subjected to this entertainment for a couple of hours and had no sleep.

I put on all the lights at six o'clock when the nurses came in, all gay and Christmassy. The priest came with Holy Communion. It was, I think, the first Christmas in my life that I had not been to Mass and possibly the first Christmas as a priest that I had not sung Mass. Here I was trapped; but I tried to say my rosary afterwards. It seemed incongruous. Then I began to make my dispositions for the day because I knew what was coming. I said to myself that I must keep my eyes open at all costs but that I wouldn't be able to close my ears.

Father Elias had brought me a novel called *The Key above*

the Door by Maurice Walsh. He had said, 'That's a topping
good yarn'. Since, at this stage, I was beginning to feel
strangely well on account, I am sure, of all the prayer at
Aylesford, I said to myself, 'Christmas or not, I am going to
read this book and I will read it all day'. So I started off in
the company of Long Tom King of Loch Ruighi. At once
I was in the wild air of the mountains, shooting grouse in
the Wicklow hills, or not bothering but sitting watching the
evening and silence descend upon the brown mountains.
And Long Tom brought back to me some great men of that
place, men who descended from the mountains to the
sheep fairs in the Autumn – whitening all the roads with
their flocks – whose stature was immense and whose voices
rang as clear as a bell; men who were sudden in their
rolling speech and whose words were half-battles, full of
theology. That book was strangely evocative to me and it
was the mountainy men who came to me when I read:

'. . . or else what, Sir?' He smiled contemptuously.
'Or else you can sit on the hot hob of hell for a thousand
years,' said Long Tom. 'And God forgive me for using
such language before a lady.'

As I had expected, Christmas soon got into full swing.
The hospital had provided the most lavish fare for the
patients and indeed a lavish programme. The nurses were
most kind and worked hard and I think that the patients
enjoyed their Christmas very much. There was carol
singing and children dancing, singing to the right of me
and to the left of me, from below and above my head, all
the noise and bustle of a travelling zoo. Then the Salvation
Army appeared outside and made a mighty onslaught
against our windows, with all the clanging blaring instru-
ments full blast. It was apocalyptic and kept on for nearly
an hour.

During this time there was a deputation of shy nurses and one made a pretty speech. Then the door opened and I had a real breath-taking surprise. There stood Queen Elizabeth the First with a train of nurses in attendance. From my very lowly angle she looked tall and her face cold as alabaster. She addressed me as 'sir', in a very few words, and pointed coldly to the lamp-shade which was slightly awry. A little nurse swiftly put it right and as she turned regally with her train and left me I saw that it was the assistant matron under the disguise. A moment later in came the Mayor of Chatham, in all his chains, and the Mayoress. He was beaming benevolence, having shaken all the hands in the hospital, and called me 'holy father'. Then I returned to Long Tom King.

The Bishop came in the evening. He quite expected me to be very ill indeed. He said to me, in a hesitating, musing way: 'Our Lady has very funny ways – very comical ways. I wonder what reason she had for frightening everybody and shutting you in here for Christmas?' Strangely enough, I could have given him five reasons there and then. He gave me his blessing, saying, 'Get well quickly and build Our Lady's church.'

The next day I left the hospital. My clothes hung upon me and my hat came down over my ears. Father Bede, an impressive giant, had come to fetch me to an unknown destination. He had a borrowed Jaguar so I was very comfortable and it was an afternoon beyond description. He told me about the Aylesford Christmas and I was soon tired laughing. I closed my eyes for a minute and the ghastly circus of that monstrous boring regiment began all over again. I had had enough of that so I kept my eyes open and the sheer loveliness of that evening quickly filled me with wonder. There was one shadow. I thought of spending a month among chocolate walls and chocolate Sisters.

Then we came to this beautiful house, the Esperance Nursing Home at Eastbourne. Father Bede helped me up the steps and in a moment I had staggered into Paradise. Two white Sisters carry me ambrosia all day long.

Now don't pity me. Pray for me and it will have very exciting results; but that is enough of *me*. I am sorry for the irrelevance which has taken up so much of this letter.

Father spent six weeks in the Esperance Nursing Home where the Sisters of the Holy Family nursed him back to health again. In his next Newsletter he said:

The Curé d'Ars describes illness as an 'austere interview with God'. But I must say that from the first I felt like singing in that happy place. The lives of the Sisters are dedicated so completely to prayer and work. Manifestly they are full of joy in the midst of sickness; and joy like this is a sure sign of grace.

The aftermath of an illness is worse than an illness itself. There are times when black blots out black, so dark and depressing seems the outlook. All this has to do with the body and its ills and not with faith. The Good Lord uses suffering to hold us back from what is not his Will and when the light comes again one can see the pattern on looking back.

Two months before he became ill, Father Malachy had been fortified in his concern for the Church Suffering by an article on Soviet Power in the *Daily Telegraph*. In after years the great long all-night vigils at Aylesford were to grow out of this concern; but in the meantime he was feeling his way. It now occurred to him that they might found a praying army, based on Aylesford, to counter the war of attrition which was being waged against the Church in Communist-dominated countries. One day he deliberately waited after breakfast to talk to Father Brocard Sewell about it.

> I outlined my dream; and after I had told him the facts he looked up in a very sudden way and said to me: 'Father Prior, I don't like mass movements. Begin small and you'll end big. I don't like these anti-movements either. They are too negative.'

> He trod, and not softly, on my dream. In fact he stamped it out of existence and I laughed because I understood. I knew he had spoken with more than natural wisdom.

But Aylesford, great rocky reef that it had become in the world's tide, could not fail to attract flotsam and jetsam from the storm-tossed places.

In 1955 they were visited by Father Aidan McGrath. He had been for many years a missionary in China and had seen a flourishing Catholic community grow up around him. Then persecution came, directed against the Legion of Mary of which he was head. Always when in danger he would go to the Carmel to ask for the Sisters' prayers.

The Communists had a great disembodied rage against Our Lady who was inspiring great bravery amongst Chinese men, women and children whom they threw into prison, and martyred. Torturers would ask the children: 'Where is this lady?' And when they replied very simply that she was in heaven, they would say, 'She is not! She is in Shanghai and we will catch her.'

Father Aidan was arrested. In spite of the supernatural fortitude he had witnessed in the Christians, he confesses that he was craven with fear and fright and was miserable beyond words. They stripped him and beat him; they took his breviary and rosary and trampled on them. A raw impudently aggressive youth was his interrogator: he promised him that the Chinese Communists were coming to liberate Ireland. They had no hesitations at all and were going to conquer the whole world. English or Americans, they literally kicked their prisoners round. Father McGrath was wearing a scapular and for three months they could not see it although it was not hidden by clothing and was plainly to be seen. He was thrown into a bare cell. From every side came screams and the sound of beatings and of persons gone mad. Suddenly a great peace took possession of him. He lay down on the floor and fell asleep and woke up refreshed in the morning. For over two years in the prison that peace never left him. Father Brandsma, the Dutch Carmelite who died in Dachau, described very much the same thing: he suddenly realized that his tiny cell, in which they first imprisoned him, was a haven of peace and comfort; a sort of retreat house.

Father Aidan said: 'I was brought up in the Faith and yet I felt I never knew Our Lady until that night in prison. Nor did I know what prayer really *is* until then.'

This Communism is a smudge over the earth and on men's eyes. It is really the religion of Satan and he can never produce anything but a stale resemblance of good because he is 'the ape of God'. His image, gross, cunning, evil, is stamped on the faces of the inhuman creatures who seem to be the masters of this world and whose works are cruel and abominable on a colossal scale. Communism, because it is a corruption of Christianity, can never be anything but corrupt – and corruption of the best thing there is, is truly the worst form of corruption. Nor is Communism anything new or hopeful, it is not even paganism; for that can never hold sway again, not even in the East where Buddha, with eyes closed, still broods, still dead asleep!

For heaven's sake don't be impressed when half-educated people talk about the great religions of the world, about Christianity as if it were a competitor, usually fighting a losing battle.

Always the ape of God is trying to simulate the works of grace by natural means. Natural religions are of the earth earthy and only end by muddling us up in the gross aspects of nature. Our religion, which is unique, is the religion of *grace*. This is the mighty inner life of God given to us in Baptism and increased in us all the time. Grace perfects our nature and produces those splendid spiritual effects which would in the ordinary way be beyond our reach. This is *super*-natural.

The prevailing philosophy of this country has been, and is still, 'Liberalism', which affirms that nature is perfectible by its own means; educate it, feed it, clothe it well and give it security and you will have a paradise on earth. It is wrong, manifestly wrong; but solemn humbugs still love to be called liberal and to talk about 'Liberal' ideas. Maritain has described the *liberation* they have achieved as the 'letting loose of wild beasts to lay waste the earth'. St Paul said, long ago: 'By the grace of God I am what I am and his grace in me has not been void.' This is true not only for men but for nations as well. If St Paul's teaching about the need for grace were not sufficiently convincing, surely there is enough, even in the history of this century, to put an end to the illusion of the naturally good man.

Still preoccupied with the manifestations of grace among the faithful in the suffering half of the Church, Father Malachy wrote: 'Just after the War I took down and edited a story of two and a half years in the life of a Polish lady departed to Kirghistan by the Russians in 1940. The story is contained in only a few pages, but in its searching of the depths and its resolution of the terrible conflict of a soul, it is greatly moving.'

It should be added that when Father Malachy was writing this Newsletter in May 1956, Serov, the Russian who had been responsible for the deportations of millions of Poles and the murder of many thousands of the finest Polish men, women and children, had come, 'roaring out of the skies in a shining jet plane' and been accorded a most courteous reception in England. Father naturally had his own reservations:

From Friday to Sunday they were filling up the trucks with human freight. Then, on that Sunday morning, the train moved out on a fourteen days' journey to Kirghistan. On the second day they crossed the Polish frontier, 'The most unhappy day of my life'. They sang the national anthem and a hymn to Our Lady. The Jews in the truck joined in both, they were the most unhappy people of all. It was heart-breaking to hear and see them all crying: men, women and children. On 1 May 1940 they reached a large town called Pawlodar where a meeting of Kirghist communists was celebrating May Day. There were a hundred trucks on their train and they were loaded seventy to each truck. During the fourteen days' journey they had been given only five buckets of soup. The Communists went through the performance of welcoming them and then they were counted, selected, distributed.

Now it was hard to think of God in all that degradation. He was lost to many in bitterness and gnawing hatred. And yet, among the Kirgies, there was goodness and kindness to remind them of him. Madame X, the Polish lady, knew and loved the Russian language for its beauty. In retrospect she could appreciate the Russian landscapes – the very emptiness of them, the 'beyond' in them; they gave her the curious liberation of great distances and there were all the colours and sounds of that strange land and the poignant loveliness of the Russian music and singing. But to the hungry and miserable, to those cast away and to the lost, there is no beauty in the senses. All that comes to them through the bitter soul is fear and dread and the creeping cold of the forever displaced. They enter another world, subhuman; and in every waking moment there is the touch of the brutal and the irrational; an absence of reason, cruel and impersonal. On the plane of the senses it is not poverty nor emptiness, but worse than destitution. On the plane of the soul it is darkness.

This would be just a horror story and depressing did we not see beyond the darkness. Even when God's children are sent into the valley of the shadow they still find him. On the face of it it seems to be mere brutishness; but we of the Faith can see it as a permissive act of God, sending millions into a strict religious order, into the desert. It is the good God swiftly multiplying his saints and martyrs. The Celtic monks regarded a *terra aliena* – a foreign land – almost as a necessary discipline for sanctity. It was their white martyrdom. But the horror story is entirely relieved by God's mysterious visitations.

Madame X had a brother with her. One day he came 'home' with frost-bitten hands. He was in despair, frozen and hungry. He was only a boy but when his mother spoke to him of God and of suffering as expiation, he understood and never complained again although he was dying of hunger. One evening they found him a few yards away from the door of their hut. He was dead. Madame X never forgot that date, 11 February 1942. She and her mother nearly died of grief and she thinks that something did die within them.

A Ukrainian carpenter whom they knew, an Orthodox Christian who used to pray secretly before an eikon concealed in his hut, made a coffin for the dead boy. Most of those who died were wrapped in sacking and buried anyhow. All their group attended the funeral. Since there was no priest they prayed and sang a hymn and left him among the Kirghies. Polycarp, a martyr of the early Church, has said, 'Call a person a martyr and you need no further praise'.

Many other young people died for they were not able to stand the privations as well as the older people. For these there was suffering and endurance and for some a secret strength which seemed to wrap them around. There was one man whom they used to see in the evenings kneeling in the open and praying for hours at a time. He was a source of strength to everybody and had a sure peace about him.

To Madame X also there was given the grace of prayer. One day she was offered the position of clerk which would have meant escape from the worst aspects of her servitude; but it would have meant separation from her mother and she refused. That night when the family was asleep she was praying when suddenly God spoke to her. It was sure but mysterious, a voice in her inner self. It brought relief and a deep peace: 'and in that moment I forgot all my suffering'.

The end of the story leaves you thinking not of tyrants but of the good God. After her return to freedom she still had the haunting fear that the tyrants might yet rob her of her soul's salvation. It was not the hatred of tyranny but of tyrants that wrecked her peace. In her soul's fierce struggle she had said: 'It is not for me, Father, to forgive; therefore it must be the gift of God.' And God have it to her. Time and God's overwhelming goodness helped her to fulfil the hard law of forgiveness of enemies. She was happily married to a Polish officer who had had a similar experience to her own and they had a little boy, George, whom I baptized. He came to claim her love and to redeem her soul from bitterness.

She bought a missal with her first savings and she said that it is only in the Mass and particularly in the Preface that she can adequately give thanks to God, joined with the mighty sacrificial will of Christ. In him is our peace; in him all sorrow is changed to joy. 'It is truly right and just that we should always and in all places give thanks to thee, Holy Lord, Almighty Father, Eternal God.'

After Our Lord himself it is only the saint who is also a great poet who is able to illuminate the dark mystery of suffering.

When Blessed Henry Suso writes in the fourteenth century about temporal suffering, his language is all light:

There is nothing more painful than suffering and nothing more joyful than to have suffered.

Suffering is a short pain and a long joy.

There is probably no man living but who derives good from suffering. A man who has not suffered, what does he know?

Never was a skilful knight in a tournament so gazed at as is a man who suffers well. He is gazed at by all the heavenly court.

Patience in suffering is superior to raising the dead.

All the saints are on the side of the suffering man.

This is true not only of men but of nations. When we think of the suffering nations we think with Belloc of 'Europe and the centuries'. I think of Ireland with her calm and light. After a long darkness she has come to her 'inevitable day'. A nation that has not suffered, what does it know? Suffering marks a people, it gives to people a mysterious distinction.

In the context of their suffering Father Malachy writes of the Poles:

The Poles have proclaimed this year a Marian Year.

Three hundred years ago King Casimir proclaimed Our Lady Queen of Poland. The devotion of Poles to Our Lady is a truly astonishing thing. It is a most noble work of grace that marks them, every one. To them she is never the subject of argument or doubt. She *is*. She is Poland in a more than legal or even mystical way. One of them said to me about praying with her, 'We pray, we thank, we accept'. A Queen suffers with her people. She knows the way in which it is a 'short pain and a long joy,' and 'they accept'. Our Lady of Czestokowa with her scarred face is marked with the wounds of her country's history. That face is said to be the truest likeness of her. A copy is venerated here at Aylesford and this year, 1956, we are expecting many thousands of Poles to come and find her. She has been called 'the hope of the half-defeated'.

We of the faith who live in the Catholic Church, in its long perspectives in time and eternity, can know and live these divine reconciliations. As Belloc writes with such power in *The Path to Rome*:

'I begin to think this intimate religion as tragic as a great love. Yes, certainly religion is as tragic as first love, and drags us out into the void away from our homes. It is a good thing to have loved one woman from a child, and it is a good thing not to have to return to the Faith.'

Father Malachy writes:

It is the first intention of Aylesford to pray for the lapsed.

Take away my faith or yours and what is left? I have met many lapsed and can imagine what that final emptiness may be – at best just good manners and an accepted code of behaviour. Now the word 'lapsed' comes from 'labi' the verb to slip. The lapsed are those who have slipped away; they have not turned their backs and walked away. But therein is the beginning of death or rather an absence of real joy and life. They are of all men the most miserable, or should be. If they felt it, their misery would be a sign of life returning.

To the three first intentions of The Friars and Allington Castle, namely: to pray for the lapsed, for the awakening of the spirit of prayer and an inner life of faith throughout the Church, and for conversions to the Faith, was now added a fourth, the cause of the Suffering Church. Aylesford gives to the pilgrim, 'A place where prayer has been valid'. In the words of T. S. Eliot:

> If you came this way,
> Taking any route, starting from anywhere,
> At any time or season,
> It would always be the same: you would have to put
> off sense and notion.
> You are not here to verify, instruct yourself or
> inform curiosity.
> Or carry report. You are here to kneel
> Where prayer has been valid. And prayer is more
> Than an order of words, the conscious occupation
> Of the praying mind, or the sound of the voice
> praying.
> And what the dead had no speech for when living,
> They can tell you, being dead: the communication
> Of the Dead is tongued with fire beyond the
> language of the living.
> Here, the intersection of the timeless moment
> Is England and Nowhere, never and always.

In return Aylesford requires from its pilgrims prayer and alms, alms to build the place and keep it going, prayer to bring the strength of God. A shrine is a microcosm of the Communion of Saints. You see the pilgrims bringing their suffering and their petitions and their prayer to Our Lady and the Saints, so that the prayer which comes from God can go back to him in a way which sweeps the world into heaven and heaven into the world. If St Thomas Aquinas was 'a great mill' then so too is The Friars.

Father Malachy says:

Prayer is the gift of God, it is a joy, without it we dry up and wither. Let us pray together, we have great reason and great need. As Blessed Henry Suso says, 'Prayer is a gift worthy of God, not in a hundred years of asking could you earn it'.

If you are baptized and living in the grace of God, the Holy Spirit of God is working in you and through you but not without you. As a result of this working together all your prayer, all you do, is supernatural. You might as well think of launching a planet with your little finger as of doing one supernatural act worthy of eternal life without the Holy Spirit. Through the Word made Flesh, through baptism into him, all the baptized live in him a life ordered to eternal life. Without him it is natural life with a natural end. With him it is supernatural and its end is eternal life.

When we live in the Communion of Saints there is a timeless 'now'. Let me put it as simply as I can. We are all bound up with the past and live in it as if it were now. If the hermits had not come to Aylesford, if St Simon had not seen Our Lady, well, we would not be here today rebuilding this ancient shrine. Thousands who have come here and who have prayed and found grace, would not have come. We are all of us bound up with the pattern of the past and it is really in the Communion that we have our roots and our life.

This way of seeing life whole and not in unrelated bits has to do with the Carmelite spirit which is prophetic. We are all prophets, not in the sense of crudely guessing future events but in seeing always the unfolding pattern of God's wonderful providence and its shining logic. This *seeing* is of course a gift of God. Without grace we cannot see it in this sense and for all who do see it it must be the beginning of real prayer. It is a gift not to the 'prophets' only but to all men. But there are degrees of seeing; you may see it fitfully or dimly or steadily all the time, and to see it steadily all the time is to share in prophecy and to see the future in the present. To many it is a discovery which comes late in life. In a flash, they may see the shining hand of God in everything that has happened to them. Then it is an astonishing revelation. I have often heard it from souls near to the gate of heaven and wistfully looking back, 'God has been very good to me, Father'.

Once you are awake to the Providence of God you can see its logic and you can prophesy. You see he cannot but be economical of time and opportunity and circumstance because nothing escapes his fearful care or his most terrible love. When people come to Aylesford, whether they know it or not, he has led them. It cannot be otherwise. They come seeking and when they come they begin to ponder and reflect and go away troubled with the mystery of their souls. To pray for the lapsed, for a real awakening of Faith in all those who believe, to pray for conversions: if Aylesford is not for these, what on earth *is* it for? Why these elaborate preparations? Why our prayer and labour? Why your sacrifice to restore it, why all these surprising happenings? Is all this waste and leading up to nothing? Of course not, it shows more than a hint of great things to come. God is all powerful to realize all his purposes beyond our wildest dreams. It is only Satan who leaves us with emptiness and frustration. You see lives meant to be full of the mystery and glory of God – and at their ending, a tired yawn!

St Augustine says that God would in no wise permit evil out of which he cannot bring good. This is absolutely sure and explains everything. Do remember it and apply it because it is the answer to the great evils which seem to be a denial of his goodness. A headache or an earthquake or a world war; he must bring good out of them. Paul Claudel has used as a sub-title to *The Satin Slipper*, the great statement, 'The worst is not the surest'. This has intrigued me for years and actually what is meant is that the best is the surest and the more you are awake to God's providence the more clearly you can see this. Constant under whatever guise of evil, whatever God wills is the best for us and for the world. He *permits* evil but he *wills* good. Blessed are they who suffer and know why, and nobody will ever be able to make just reproach to God because the wonderful fact of God's good and loving providence is predictable and sure.

When God's grace is working in people it is amazing what you see; you see a shining face and know a soul has been given the gift of faith. Souls, whether in grace or out of it, can be an open book.

Many non-Catholics, versed in the ways of God and devout, are still puzzled by the great place the Mother of God holds in the life of prayer of the Carmelites, in fact in the whole Catholic Church.

The answer is easy, perhaps too easy [Father Malachy has written]. She is alive now in heaven in a state of life beyond imagining, flaming in the breath of the Holy Spirit. She did not become an angel in another life, she is still, and ever will be in eternal relationship, the Mother of God. We shall see her in that life we call heaven and be glorified by the sight of her. If she is not alive, neither shall we be after the few short years of precarious life here. But Our Lord is

risen from the dead and surely he who made the commandment, 'Honour thy father and mother', has not left his own
mother dead in the dust. All this is simple and obvious;
otherwise there is no Communion of Saints and we would
have no communion with anybody and would be praying
into a void. It would all be a game of make-believe because
there can be no communion of living men with the dust.
Even though it be 'a sweet-memoried dust', it is dead.

With the next step in our answer, imagination does not
help us. How can this heavenly woman give audience to
millions of people on this earth at once and all the time?
That clamour of the multitude: 'we have no wine', never
ceases. But there is that mysterious partnership, 'whom
God hath joined together', between Our Lady and her Son.
This power of Our Lady in heaven has puzzled even the
saints. When Our Lord was told that his Mother was
standing outside, he said: 'What is that to you and to me?'
It was a rhetorical question and *we* know how extremely
much it was 'to you and to me'. We say: 'If you ask, if I
ask; but if *she* asks!' And I suspect that she does not have to
ask, that she is not there just to hand on our petitions –
that is too human a way of regarding her. She is herself
the supplication of all humanity and it is as if all the needs
of humanity, bitter and sweet, were crying out in her.
Dante, who is the Christian thought of the Middle Ages,
sees her coming to the help of one who did not ask her.
She was not *asked* at Cana. Hers was the quick-eyed
charity, the intuition of a woman, the daring initiative;
don't we know it well?

The Order of Carmel is the oldest Order in the Church
and it exists to honour her. Since the Church is Christ to
all men and Carmel's Rule and way of life have long been
recognized by the Church, you will see that Our Lord has
an order which directly fulfils his own commandment and

honours his Mother. The vocation of Carmel is the vocation of the Mother of God to give Our Lord to men as graciously as ever she did. It is as simple as that and is why there is so much about her in these letters.

Devotion has been defined as 'love in flames'. Many people, coming to Aylesford, become so caught up in the spirit of Carmel that they ask for a way in which to fulfil the mysterious love they've been given. The Holy Spirit of God often 'gives' us a special saint – it may be St Francis or St Dominic or St Thérèse – in an intimate kinship of grace. If Our Lady is 'terrible as an army set in battle array', then there must be an especial fire about devotion to her, an urgency. The *caritas dei urget nos,* and we 'burn with giving'.

The Scapular is the only universal piety of the Faith that has its origin in England and the apostolate of Aylesford is of course most closely bound up with this devotion to the cloak of Our Lady. In Spain they greet a Carmelite by kissing his scapular and to those who belong to the Scapular, Father recommends a simple devotion:

> If every morning you were to kiss her scapular saying: 'Mother of God, use me today', she would use you. You have only to put the intention in the very centre of your will and you will become 'a living tool of God'. It is very simple. Even children will understand and practise it. They are the world's greatest realists and make wonderful apostles.

There was also the more formal Third Order Secular to which, in 1956, six hundred people already belonged. Besides the Aylesford Chapter there were centres in London, Birmingham, Manchester and Leicester. The Rule is simple and is 'meant for people of every profession and walk of life in the world. It has to be simple enough to be useful to busy people, but it is not so easy that it doesn't mean at least one step beyond mediocrity.' The main obligations are to say the Little Office every day, or one Rosary, and to set aside at least fifteen minutes every day for meditation or 'a bit of quiet'.

No one needs to belong so much as those who have great desires for goodness and need help. It is not the *doing* of a thing which is hard as the *beginning* to do it.

The spiritual advantages of belonging to the Third Order, or Tertiaries as they are called, are many and may be reckoned in a formal way. But the easiest way of understanding is to see Our Lady 'adding' to everything you do, your prayer, your good works. With her you will always be giving and be richer for what you have given.

Since the time of Oliver Cromwell's Protectorate there has been a slight residual distrust in English minds of church statues, a reverberation from the Puritan past about 'graven images'.

Aylesford is full of statues of Our Lord, Our Lady, St Anne, St Joseph: all the Carmelite saints, and even one of the Franciscan, St Anthony of Padua. They are beautiful statues which lessens their offence in the muddled theology of our time; but it is not until we are given the full context of the Communion of Saints that we in our narrow island can fully enjoy them. Father Malachy writes:

Words trying to express the supernatural become hackneyed and in the end say nothing. The statues of the saints say even less. Yet we cannot get on without words and the statues seem to localize a presence or, in some dim neutral fashion, to take us beyond ourselves.

What Our Lord looked like or Our Lady and St Joseph we shall not know this side of eternity. It is more real to think of them as *presences*. Presence has to do with the soul

and the rational nature. You can say a person was present
but you could not say that a cat was present. Have you ever
noticed that some people seem to carry life with them and
some death? I have known one great priest who seemed to
fill a room with his presence, and everyone in it with him
seemed to become more alive. I have known the other
sort, whose presence seemed to empty a room of air and you
became tongue-tied and could hardly breathe. Our Lord's
presence must have filled the whole world just as now it
fills every church where the Holy Sacrament is reserved.
You sense Our Lady's presence in this way at Lourdes and
Fatima, you feel it very strongly at Aylesford. What is it?
It is a mysterious contact with life. We who are bleak and
wanting, receive life. It is an enlarging and unexpected
freedom given of another world, a secret discovery and
everyone's secret to himself. Even if we were to see Our
Lady and St Joseph we could not communicate our vision
except in stammering speech. It would remain almost
completely our own – *meum secretum mihi*.

But a simple way of knowing something about the saints is
to pray with them. Novenas of prayer to St Joseph, the two
Teresas and to St Jude are called for in the Newsletters, to
end on the feast day of the saint concerned. About the two
Teresas Father Malachy wrote:

These two great saints are still bound by their vow to
honour God and the Blessed Mother of Carmel. Their
images are over adjoining doors in the great court and facing
one another over altars in the large chapel. We have not
put them there just for ornament. The saints are given to
us by the Holy Spirit to be ministers of grace in the living
communion of life which we share with them. They are
there in heaven to construe what we on earth say in pain
and exile. We pray *with* the saints, especially during novenas.

St Thérèse said she would spend her heaven doing good upon the earth. Let us all ask her to keep her promise: 'Little Flower, in this hour, show thy power.' The saints are all different and we get to know their ways. The ways of St Thérèse are delicate as a rose and as mysteriously beautiful; sometimes there is a thorn in the rose she gives. They all teach us patience except perhaps St Jude.

About St Teresa, that 'undaunted woman of desires', there will be no end of writing till the end of the world. I was in her strong-walled and turreted city last year for her feast. There was a mighty clamour of sermons and bells and fireworks and lights and a million noises – an echo of the fire and spirit of their saint. They carried her more than life-sized statue out into the great square. It was a seated figure, heavy and solemn like Queen Victoria, may she forgive them for that! Past it filed all Avila, high and low, Church and State, in all the considerable splendour they could muster; last of all came the Army, a body of smart cadets with drawn swords led by high officers. That quick march past and their sharp salute of swords to their saint-commander was worthy of her as indeed her statue was not.

She was all fire and so human withal. Once when she was crossing a ford she narrowly escaped drowning. With some impatience she cried out, 'Lord! If this is the way you treat your friends, no wonder you have so few.' She had great courage and daring with God. She was rapt to high heaven but she never had a rest from the twisted and crooked business of the world. Always there were contracts to be drawn up, house-hunting, loans to be raised, prioresses with no heads for business to be dealt with and debts to be paid off. There are many in Our Lady's Company who must pray with Teresa during her novena about houses and debts and law suits etc. and she will understand very well.

Practically all she wrote in its rich variety has come down

to us. She who never meant to do anything but unburden her soul and tell all God's most wonderful works, created a great language and a literature.

Years ago when I was in Nijmegen, Father Titus Brandsma, then a University professor, afterwards the Carmelite martyr of Dachau, showed me the original manuscript of one of her works. It was written with a 'running pen' with scarcely a correction, a strong and generous hand revealing her character, making a page beautiful to look at. I remember to this day how Father handled that precious manuscript most lovingly and how his face lit up as he showed it to me; but even in the cold impersonal print of modern books you feel you are meeting someone. She exercises a strange power. You don't *argue* with her. You begin to adapt your behaviour to her noble company.

In the first volume of her life she describes her terrible illness which lasted for three months. She was wracked by pain from head to foot and in fierce torment until she was almost completely paralysed. In her vivid way she describes her sufferings which could only be likened to the pains of the suffering Job. She was unconscious for four days. In her convent they were sure that she was dead and a grave was dug and in one of the monasteries of the Order they had sung her Requiem. Her father, in great grief, would not allow the body to be buried and when she had returned from this seeming death she found wax on her eyelids. 'Then, instead of the dead body they expected at the convent, they received a living soul for the body was worse than dead and distressing to behold.' Like Julian of Norwich and many another great contemplative, God allowed her to die almost-the-death of the body. One thinks of the epitaph on the tomb of Duns Scotus at Cologne: *Bis mortuus, semel sepultus* – 'Twice dead, once buried'. It was not the last of the dying of St Teresa. During that terrible experience she explored the frontiers of pain to the last movement: 'I could move, I think, only one finger of my right hand.' She could never again have any fear of death, only the fear of being dead.

'And when I found', St Teresa continues, 'while still so young I was still so seriously paralysed and that earthly doctors had not been able to cure me, I resolved to seek a cure from heavenly doctors. I took for my advocate and lord the glorious St Joseph and commended myself earnestly to him; and I found that this my father and lord delivered me both from this trouble and also from other and greater troubles concerning my honour and the loss of my soul; and that he gave me greater blessing than I could *ask* of him. I do not remember even now that I have ever asked anything of him which he has failed to grant. I am astonished at the great favours which God has bestowed on me through this blessed saint, and at the perils from which he has freed me both in body and soul. To other saints the Lord seems to have given grace to succour us in some of our necessities; but of this glorious saint my experience is that he succours us in them all and that the Lord wishes to teach us that as He was Himself subject to him on earth, just so, in heaven, He still does all that he asks.'

Most of the nuns Father Malachy knows put St Joseph in charge of their material worries. 'He is slow but sure', they say. There is a funny little story told about a poor Carmel to which a Catholic man once brought a Jewish friend. Downstairs in the chapel there was a statue of St Joseph upon which was pinned the message: 'Holy St Joseph, send us a cow.' The Jewish man was really upset: 'Tell those silly women to take that paper down. *I* will send them a cow.'

In Singapore the Little Sisters of the Poor have a home

where some hundreds of old ladies and gentlemen, mostly Chinese, are being very well looked after. The Chinese themselves have a great respect for old age and therefore the Sisters have from the very start of their good work had a great deal of local and governmental support. A visitor to the home noticed that the statue of St Joseph had a cigarette tucked under its arm and on enquiring the reason was told that, though the Sisters lacked for little for their old people, they were not able to afford the cigarettes they would have liked for those who craved a smoke. They had therefore asked St Joseph to see to it, and fearing he might be busy had put a cigarette on his statue just to remind him.

Only a few days later the most efficient customs authorities caught a boat smuggling in tobacco from Indonesia and confiscated over three thousand cigarettes which they presented to the Sisters for their old people. . . .

But it's St Anne if you want a husband. Father Malachy was reminded of this when a Mr L offered to Aylesford, in thanksgiving, a beautiful thirteenth-century statue:

> Mr L, who is Jewish, had said that it was a statue of Our Lady but that she had two children with her, one on each arm. When it was brought it was found to be St Anne with Our Lady on one arm and the Holy Child on the other. This was given as a museum piece but suddenly it dawned on us that this was Our Lady symbolically bringing her mother to us; and so St Anne will be on a pedestal in time for the beginning of the novena for her Feast. I am ashamed to say I had never thought of St Anne at all, but you see how that did not make any difference. She is here and need give no thanks to me or to anybody here, but to one of her own race. I discovered that there has been a great cultus of St Anne going back a long way and extending even to England. I discovered too that everybody seemed to

know a homely rhyming verse, 'Pray St Anne, get me a man, and any old thing won't do'.

This surely belongs to a time when people knew the saints and what they expected of them.

And of course, in a Carmelite house, St Elias must not be forgotten. It was in Northern Ireland that Father Malachy had had his most vivid reminder of the presence of that saint:

Recently I was in Northern Ireland and came upon a Carmel I had never heard of before. It is in a lovely country-side, a few miles from a large town. It was after seven o'clock in the evening when a young relative and I arrived at the Lodge gates. We were very hesitant but a most friendly woman unlocked the gates and brought us to the Carmel. There was such undoing of bars and bolts that I felt ashamed; but someone had been sending them the News-letters from Aylesford, and they knew about the Prior, who somehow does not seem to be me. In a few minutes the Mother Prioress and the Community had come and drawn back the curtains from the grille and were so welcoming and kind that I did not know what to do with myself. They recalled all the fathers who had visited them for the past fifty years. I had been all unsuspecting of this affec-tionate regard, a proof that Carmel is one family of Our Lady, with its free and happy courtesies still unaffected by the world. The longest memoried Sister, and the most lively, was eighty.

Certainly the Prophet Elias is alive to them. The day I was there was the eve of his Feast and the Sisters were con-vinced that he had something to do with my unexpected visit. They told me of a tradition that Elias sometimes visits the poorest Carmel and in their early days this honour had been theirs. He did visit them and it was this clear-headed, long-memoried Sister who told me so. He came in the guise of a poor man and they gave him a cup of tea. If I had been inventing this story I would have given him a griddle cake and a drink of cold water, as befitted the founder of monasticism. But tea for the Prophet – no! A Sister drank from his cup afterwards and was cured of a malignant disease. On another occasion he was seen in the Choir and they knew him by his mantle. You will notice that he *visits*. I would certainly have made him *appear* and I would have been wrong. Our Holy Father Elias is the *homo passibilis* of St James, a man like unto us, knowing the depths and the heights. He visited the woman of Sarepta, and was very kind to her in her distress. 'There was no lack of flour in the jar, nor was the cruet of oil diminished.' Why should he not have a care for poor Carmels?

I was staying in the hotel of a young relative of mine in the town. At lunch on that day the dining-room was very full of dour people. At a single table at the head of the room I noticed a little man who did not seem to belong; he seemed to be isolated and out of it. On the Feast of St Elias I was due back for an evening Mass at Aylesford. I came down for an early breakfast to catch the morning plane from Belfast. There was my little man sitting all alone in the dining-room at his table for one. I bade him 'good morning' and he was friendly but somehow detached. He told me he had been all round the world and had had a long audience with the Pope. Then he gave me a real fright – that quiet little man – he said: 'My name is Elias.' When I had recovered I said, as quietly as I could, 'Are you the Prophet Elias, by any chance?' He did not seem to understand, nor did he know that it was his feast day. Then he gave me his address in Newfoundland. I quite expected it might have been Mount Carmel!

The Arabs say we are not dead because Elias lives. Elias is not dead and Carmel is not dead because the

Prophet lives. He was an ever-present figure to the hermits of old and in the foundations at Aylesford are the foundations of an altar, dedicated under the title of John the Baptist, who came in the power and spirit of Elias; and the great altar there, under the sky, is a swift recall to Elias standing by his altar, built up again in the midst of the people: 'The shadow of a great rock in a weary land.' That was nearly three thousand years ago. At that moment in time it was the only altar in the world to the one true God: there, at the world's centre, between East and West, on the holy Mount of Carmel.

The Prophet Elias was God's angry man: 'Elias rose up like a flame and his words burned as a torch: How long do you halt between two sides: if the Lord be God follow him, and if Baal, follow him.' It is a challenge sudden and sharp, timeless because the Prophet lives. It is in the spirit of Carmel not to argue with God but to know God's will, simple and stark like that.

Aylesford was originally intended as a House of Carmelite Studies and in a way this is what is has become. Here they study the will of God through Revelation and from the pattern of events as they happen. For them each day has its special message and they teach that the daily Collect is most important since it is the voice of the whole Church praying together. To follow the Calendar of the Saints and to study the appropriate lessons they see as most important and relevant. In November 1955 on the Feast of St Raphael, Father Malachy wrote:

I have been trying for days to begin this last Newsletter of the year; but now at last I am off to a flying start with St Raphael the archangel leading me. This is his Feast and I read in the lesson of the Mass this morning, 'At this time the angel Raphael said to Tobias: "Kings have their

D

secrets which are best kept, but it is not so with God's doings. To reveal and publish them is man's privilege. A life of prayer and fasting and almsgiving is more profitable than storing up treasures of gold. Does not almsgiving preserve us from death?"

Nowhere is a great Archangel, one of the seven who stands before the face of God, he who is called 'medicine of God', prescribing medicine against death. So it is by the archangel's leave that one can speak safely and without hurt of the works of God.

Over the years it is apparent that there have been many proofs of the abundant works of God. Although publication of them has never been sought, Father has been bound at intervals to touch on them in his Newsletters. He does it with a kind of nonchalance and it is only when you see the phrase 'by indirections', that you begin to realize there may be some strange and delicate story hidden in what follows. For him, the word 'happening' has content, it has not the accidental quality that it has for the Existentialists.

All the time there are cures. Of many kinds: there are the secret cures of dead and crippling attitudes of mind. When these are suddenly lost or changed, when a kind of mental somersault liberates someone from self-pity, a sense of injustice or some cruel obsession, then this might be called a 'miracle of disposition'. It is quite private but wholly effective and the results are subtle and lasting: the end result which so many psychiatrists seek in months or years of the deep analysis of their patients. Other more public kinds of cure, the physical liberations which we call miracles, can and do happen. Aylesford, it is clear from many hundreds of letters, is rich in both. About the latter kind of cure Father writes: 'They happen often and we now take them for granted. There is always as much fuss about miracles as if they could not happen. Here, we are in the fortunate position that we have no need nor inclination to prove them. They just happen and a number go unrecorded.'

A great many people write to the Carmelites about answers to prayer which, in one way or another, they connect with Aylesford. Such letters are replied to and then stowed away in a file. One morning in 1957 Father went through some of them, and he records:

I can quote from only a few of so many letters and then only briefly. So many of them begin like this: 'I am over-joyed to tell you. . . .' And I have an idea of what is coming. Another one says, 'Something I had thought almost impossible has come about in quite a simple way'. There are many stories of conversions after long prayer, and others of lapsed Catholics returning to practice and fervour after many years; often suddenly and for no apparent reason. For example there is this letter: 'I feel I must write to you and tell you what a wonderful day this has been for me. It was wonderful not because of what I did, for I did not do anything except visit the chapel and the shrine and say the rosary. But it was wonderful because of what happened to me.'

But from time to time there is a physical cure recorded; this is from Father's letter of January 1955:

A man and his wife had come to Aylesford to become Tertiaries. For twenty years she had suffered from a slipped disc which seemed to disjoint her hip on one side. It was quite an objective deformity and it made her hobble. She and her husband went round the Rosary Way and prayed hard as she had urgent reasons for asking for release from her pain. Afterwards they both returned to the little chapel in the cloisters. There the pain grew worse and twice she felt as if something or somebody were twisting her back. When she left the chapel she was no longer crooked but straight. Her doctor afterwards said to her: 'All the curvature has gone, your spine is now perfectly normal.'

Yesterday, for the third time, she came to see me and confirmed all this. She is a very quiet person and no lover of sensation. She herself is the best proof of what she says.

Then, in addition to these kinds of cure, there are the prodigies of charity. They too are sometimes recorded in the Newsletters:

Last Autumn I was very busy dictating letters in the office when I was told that a poor woman wanted to see me. I went at once. Katherine B was seventy-five and had lived in a small room until she could no longer look after herself. She had arthritis very badly and could hardly move without pain. Her clothes seemed to be a living part of her or as if they had lived with her and shared her life for a long time. She had been born in Kilkenny and had been in England practically all her life; yet you would never have guessed she had been away from Ireland for so long as she had retained the most beautiful untainted speech, something all her own. She spoke in short sentences in the language of the 'Pale' – from the Plantations of Queen Elizabeth the First. She said she was 'perishing cold' for instance, and I could not drag myself away from her, from this hard-working woman who had kept to herself all her life long. This was the wonder that was awaiting me on that busy morning, this woman so fiercely alive and independent.

Years before her father had left Katherine two hundred pounds as her 'portion'. She had saved it all and now, in the most off-hand way, she said, 'There it is, Father; take it for Our Lady's church,' but I could not because she was going to a home of the Sisters of Nazareth and I knew that they needed the money for their own work. Yet, in the end, they themselves gave Katherine her way. Some weeks later, in a short letter – one or two sentences and no trimmings – she sent us the money she had kept for Our Lady for fifty years.

Then there were the leukaemia cases. The bare facts of Pauline Scott's cure were briefly mentioned in Father's letter of Summer 1956, though they were not fully published until some years later when the cure was finally established. Then, in *Family Doctor*, a magazine published by the British Medical Association, the whole story was related and set off sensational reports in the popular press.

The simple facts are as follows: at the age of eight the little girl was dying of acute lymphatic leukaemia. Nothing more could be done for her either by the local specialists or in London. Her own doctor brought her to Aylesford for the Blessing of the Sick. Although she was not a Catholic she was willingly enrolled in the Scapular and blessed with the Relic of the Cross. Two days later she became terminally ill and was given only hours to live; but on the Feast of the Precious Blood she suddenly began to recover. A fortnight later the specialist who had earlier written: 'The prognosis is, of course, hopeless', now wrote: 'This child appears to be spontaneously recovering without further treatment.' Her doctor sent both these letters to Aylesford.

Since then Pauline has grown up in a perfectly normal way, not differing much from her contemporaries on the housing estate where she still lives. She has not become a Catholic nor is she unusually religious.

Another small child, Peter Corless, was only two and a half years old when his parents brought him to Aylesford in the last stages of the same disease. After receiving the Blessing of the Sick he had what may well have been a natural remission lasting a year, during which time he and his parents stayed often at Aylesford and his father became a Catholic. But ultimately he died and Father wrote:

Little Peter Corless died. The good Lord gave him to live a long life in a short time. He was officially dead a year ago and his father says he was allowed to live to bring him here to Our Lady and the Faith. He is buried in the cemetery at Aylesford. The little white coffin was in the small chapel overnight in front of the Shrine of Our Lady and St Simon. I offered the Mass of the Angels the next day. Most of our community and the lay community went to the graveside. The greatest consolation, after the Mass, is to hear our Holy Mother the Church, which is Christ, celebrating a child's entry into eternal life. Whether children live or die there is suffering. When they are baptized they become God's children and the parents give them to his will. Often it is not so; but you can trust God with his treasures: 'for such is his Kingdom'.

His father asked me, 'Will Peter become an angel?' The answer to that is, No. The angels are the *heavenly* creation of God. We cannot imagine what they are like. Paul Claudel had the scale of an angel when he wrote: 'I saw a great white angel rising from the sea, filling the whole space between earth and sky.'

'Is he in heaven?' Peter's father asked me.

'Yes, most certainly.'

'Will he grow up or will we see him as a child?'

Peter's soul was as large when he began to live as it will ever be. It was breathed into the body by God. That is the homely way in which Scripture speaks of the creation of the soul. It doesn't grow, it doesn't develop, nor does it evolve. It is bigger than the Universe and has two faculties which it can never lose: the mind and the will. Supernatural life is created or breathed into it by baptism. That life of the spirit is beyond imagining. When Peter died his mind would have had all knowledge of God's creation in a flash by sudden illumination. In his state of grace he will have had knowledge of the angels and the entire heavenly creation. Finally, he has eternal life in the Beatific Vision of God. There we must leave him alive and ageless in eternal life.

Here Father quotes from St John Chrysostom who lived in the fourth century and once wrote to a bereaved friend:

Thou hast not lost thy son but bestowed him henceforth in Eternity. That is not thy child that is lying there. He has flown away and sprung aloft in the boundless height. When thou seest the eyes closed, the lips locked together, the body motionless, O! be not these thy thoughts: 'These lips no longer speak, these eyes no longer see, these feet no longer walk, but are all on their way to corruption.' But say the reverse: 'These lips shall speak better, these eyes shall see greater things, these feet shall mount upon the clouds, and this body shall put on immortality and I shall receive my son back more glorious.'

From another letter I add Father's affirmation:

Chesterton said: 'Here dies another day during which I have had eyes, ears, hands and the great world about me. And with tomorrow begins another. Why am I allowed two?' He said this about a single day and yet still there is the fear of death. But dying is easy. Even the Pagans could die nobly. Socrates said to his judges: 'You go to life and I to death. Which of us to the better part, God knoweth.' I am sure it is not the fear of dying which pains us but the fear of being dead. But there are no dead. I believe in the

Holy Catholic Church, the Communion of Saints, the forgiveness of sins, the resurrection of the body, life everlasting.

This is a tremendous affirmation of what *is*. We believe in life everlasting. This is the creed which built the cathedrals, flinging great walls of masonry against the sky. This is what inspired the music of the *Credo* of Palastrina's Mass, *Papae Marcelli*, the end of which almost hurls you into eternity, so great is it. With the loss of the old faith comes a slow dying, worse than dying, for it is the corruption of a good thing and that is the worst form of corruption. Only by the grace of God can the majestic creed be believed and only by that grace can Christian Europe be reborn and England become part of Christendom again.

To die, 'fortified by the rites of the Faith', that is one thing, to die in ignorance and without hope as thousands are daily dying in England, that is another. In 1957 Father had many opportunities to go about in the desolating materialism of contemporary society and what he saw shocked him.

The other day we were asked by someone at The Friars to offer an urgent Mass for a friend of his who was undergoing a serious operation. I was told that he was a writer, very intellectual and belonging to a very anti-clerical family. He was half-French which inclined him to very severe logic in his outlook. The nurse in the hospital when I visited him declared that he had been dead for fifteen minutes after the operation, that his heart had ceased to beat during that time but that it had unaccountably started again.

He told me that he was very glad to see me but that he did not want to talk about religion at all. None the less he talked non-stop for three-quarters of an hour and needless to say I had heard it all before and found it very tiring. He spoke of the moral anguish of so many and the elemental fears that all men know in their souls and said that the doctors who will treat only the bodies of their patients should be able to help more with their mental states. He had a good innings with me and after he'd spoken for three-quarters of an hour, I said, very quietly to him: 'I have not come to argue at all, but God in his great courtesy and kindness has sent a priest to you.' I was using the language of Dame Juliana of Norwich whose *Revelations* I had been reading in the train on the way to see this man. I said I would give him my blessing and after that, quite illogically, he said: 'I will come to Aylesford as soon as I am able. That may do me more good than all the doctors.'

Trouble and death reveal many secrets hidden beneath everyday faces. There was the woman dying of cancer in the Council house who had never gone to any church and who had slaved all her life for her invalid mother. She was as good as gold. As a Friar, I was new to her; but somehow, not strange – and this I cannot explain at all. Coming down the stairs I saw in a lower room the old mother of over eighty years, a good woman from next door, and others. I have been haunted ever since by that strange peering look they gave me, as if they were seeing a ghost. Again a priest had brought to them the courtesy of God. In a few weeks that woman had suddenly gone. Is it a race memory they have or is it, perhaps, 'the shades of the shaven men . . . come back in shining shapes at last'? It may be the brown habit of the Friar that calls back what was so familiar in England in the days of the Faith.

I could fill this letter many times with examples of this kind. Truly these are the 'secret people' of England of Chesterton's poem, dying, millions of them, without the last courtesy of God. With holy anger he takes us back in his poem to the 'unspeakable Henry', and to the King's servant, Sir Thomas Wyatt of Allington Castle, who had The Friars for loot in the Reformation: but he was even more merciless towards the Lords of the Industrial Revolution, 'The new people who took the land', than he is to the 'last sad squires who ride slowly towards the sea'. 'They have bright dead alien eyes, they look at our labour and laughter as a tired man looks at flies and the load of their loveless pity is worse than the ancient wrongs.'

On Christmas Day I went to visit a mental hospital. There were three thousand patients in it. It was a desolating experience and the memory of it haunted me. It is a strange world. I walked through wards seemingly endless. The lady I went to see was in Ward no. 11, and I was told there were ninety-six in each ward. The wards were clean and well lit and the patients were clean and there were many wireless sets and televisions; but they all looked the same, abandoned and hopeless. I am certain that the vast majority of them should not be there at all. They are just harmless old people needing love and care. They looked like the castaways they had become and represented for me a terrible indictment of our faithless age. Is this what St Paul means when he says that, 'In the later days', there will be a generation of 'lovers of themselves more than God, without affection'. The poor people are handed over to the Welfare State, on them is the burden of a loveless pity.

I was telling our Spanish brother, Nuño, of this experience and he was surprised at the numbers involved. He told me that he had lived for some time in a town of twenty thousand inhabitants. He was always around and about and knew everybody in the town. He does not remember that there were more than three or four who were so afflicted. They were cared for at home and everybody knew them and had charity for them. All this dreary segregation must have to do with the loss of the Faith.

I am sure that it is this experience that has discovered to me the English mystic, Dame Julian of Norwich. She was born in thirteen forty-two and became an Anchoress. She lived at the time of the Great Plague from which a fourth of all the people in Europe died. In her own city there were fifty thousand dead and yet her *Revelations* take us into a spiritual world which is full of the courtesy and kindness and great homeliness of the good God. Her very language is balm to all the ills of body and soul and there is not a hint in her writings of reproach to God. She gives a picture of fourteenth-century England, an England which I cannot believe to be entirely lost. Her revelations are of the high things of the soul and of God, and reading her is not only to have the savour of high heaven but of the apple orchards round her cell in the springtime. But a blighting wind came from the fiend, as she calls Satan, a withering wind that has blighted the land for more than four hundred years.

So many of the people who have come here since the Restoration began to find the world increasingly big and strange and cruel, and they themselves lost in it, and afraid. It is that terrible desolation which follows when a country loses its conviction and its faith. Listen to Dame Juliana in one of her Shewings:

'He showed me a little thing, the size of a hazel nut, lying in the palm of his hand and it was as round as a ball. I looked thereupon with the eye of understanding and thought: "What may this be?" And it was answered generally thus: "It is all that is made."

'I murmured how could it last? for it seemed so little it might suddenly have fallen to nought; and I was answered in my understanding: "It lasteth and ever shall because God loveth it." And so the world has its existence by the love of God.' And then she explains: 'For to a soul that seeth the Maker of all, all that is made seemeth very small.'

And yet how often we are tempted to think that the world is out of the control of God and that he does not care for his creation. The whole of it to him the size of a hazel-nut! And who would be afraid of death when in her Shewing she sees her good and courteous Lord receiving us at the end into his Father's House: 'I saw him royally arrayed in his own house, filling it with joy and mirth, himself endlessly to gladden and to solace his dear worthy friends, most homely and most courteously, with marvellous melody and endless love, in his own fair blessed Countenance.'

It is a real temptation to quote from the *Shewings* at great length. Could anything be lovelier than this? 'Our Lord, full of lovely pity, deep-seated and penetrating, far and wide – as a watchman surveying endless kingdoms.'

But if Father were merely contrasting England as she is today with some dream of the Middle Ages, it would not be very helpful to us; nor indeed would it be if Aylesford were only a manifestation of mediaeval romanticism. But he knows what a Catholic society can be, having had the good fortune to be brought up in Ireland, in an homogeneous country society where the Faith touches everything from a man's disposition to the set of his hat or the shape of his house. And it is the living tradition of Christianity with all its ramifications in the material world that he is trying to convey to us in the Newsletters. Here he is writing again about his countrymen:

Messrs M. J. Gleeson had offered to do up the back drive for us. On big occasions when there were many coaches and cars we were just smothered in dust and pilgrims were complaining of the stony paths and saying it was worse than Lough Derg.

One fine morning a steam roller and a tar sprayer were unloaded from a carrier. There were four fine Irishmen with it. They were marvellous workers and so much more that one could not easily forget them. Three of them were young, very reverent and shy. The engine man was portly like St Thomas Aquinas, with a slow rich brogue which seemed to come out of the depths of the big man. St Thomas himself could not have been more wholesome or well-balanced. All these men were strong and vigorous and yet they had about them a strange and quiet reserve. I have noticed it often among men of the old Faith and the old Catholic culture. This 'quiet', or whatever you would call it, reminds me always of the repose you find in great painting. It is a supreme achievement of the great artist. The subject does not leap out to assault you nor do these men. You could, if you were very ignorant, take it for backwardness, but when the engine-man said, as he said, often: 'it is strange!' you knew that it meant reflection in the real sense, that he was a man, pondering and wondering.

It might not be exact to describe such men as 'educated', but their material education from simple surroundings and good substances, the wood, stone and iron they have always handled, together with the dimensions of the Faith, means that they are capable of sound and considered judgement in most things. William Douglas Home considers that many people from our industrialized society are almost ineducable because of their inchoate early lives. Father writes about Sister Catherine, a great educationalist and friend of his:

On a weekday Sister Catherine came from Burnt Oak in Middlesex with four hundred of the thousand children in her schools. Sister Catherine knows that you cannot have education without religion, even though this is the last thing to bother the dry minds of the Ministry of Education. They want a nation of contented technicians and workers. They do not understand that men are not just machines for sifting information and moving things about, not knowing why they are alive at all. Thinking back I do not recall ever having heard of education when I was being brought up, nor did Sister Catherine, I suspect. Pity the children with their exams at Eleven Plus, to decide whether they are going to Grammar Schools or to the Secondary Modern Schools which are described as being, 'for the less intelligent'. Pity them all, so harshly turned into workers but really uneducated. Sister Catherine's idea this weekday was to bring the children to Aylesford to Our Lady, to sing their Mass over the foundations of the old Church of the Assumption and to have a great procession and ceremonies all in the context of history. Their lively minds easily link the present with the past. Bright pictures will remain with them always and they acquire a sense of the timeless Church. They see history here, and, more important, they live in it.

Sister Catherine brought twenty of her Sisters with her and many lay teachers as well. The mediaeval habits of the Dominicans and Carmelites seemed very right in the setting of the old buildings. Yet nobody could accuse any of us of being no more than living relics of the past. It gave one a strange joy to see it all so real and lovely and *present*. Sister herself is a homely, large woman and her beautiful habit falling about her seemed to be the only possible one for such proportions. She is magnificent in her generous kindness and simplicity. By simplicity I mean what St Thomas meant. It is the very opposite of being simple and we can only get back to simplicity by the power of the

Holy Spirit of God who creates it out of the muddle and murk of our natural selves. Sister gave one the impression of a fortress moving or the 'great mill' Chesterton saw in the person and presence of St Thomas Aquinas. Yet she is only one of the great women religious who come here. How rich and varied is the Church in the people she really makes. About them you cannot use the debased language of the present which would mean nothing at all.

There are English nuns and Irish nuns and Polish nuns and there is the young French Mother Prioress and there are German nuns and Italian and our own Spanish Carmelites who have just arrived to be a part of Aylesford. Of all I might say, as Chesterton said of six of his friends: 'He is the best friend in the world'; 'He is certainly the best of friends on earth'; 'There is no friend as good as he is'; 'He is the best of all'; 'He is far better than the rest'; 'He is the most beloved of all friends'; I know a lot more and they are all like that!

Queen Victoria once paid a visit to a convent. She was evidently not impressed. Her comment afterwards was: 'It is a pity these good ladies have not something useful to do.' She would have been even more puzzled by the Carmelites. You cannot broadcast silence and you cannot sell it, so it is useless. To the practical unbeliever the iron grille of a Carmelite Convent is the door of a prison. It is actually the door to the desert for it is not sands that make a desert but silence. Aylesford was founded as a 'Desert House' and has something of the quality of such silent places about it still.

The books of Aldous Huxley were popular best-sellers twenty years ago. He is not a Christian and whether he was ever baptized I do not know; but he is really a Manichean, possibly without knowing it. This philosophy is older than Christianity, in the fifth century it held St Augustine in bondage for many years. Light and darkness, body and spirit, were held to be opposing principles, the body was matter and was bad, the trammelling filth of matter on the spirit. It cropped up in the thirteenth century as the Albigensian Heresy which held that you should get rid of the body as quickly as possible, so that suicide was a virtue, releasing the clean spirit. The modern pagan pampers the body and treats it very delicately, abhorring pain or penance in any form. Strangely enough he loathes it in the end and delivers it over to be cremated, which might be called post-mortem suicide. This philosophy was old two thousand years ago.

One of Huxley's books is called *Grey Eminence*. He has one excellent chapter in it dealing with the coming of the Carmelites from Spain to seventeenth-century France. Most of it was taken from a study by Henri Bremond, the famous Jesuit. Huxley is fascinated by Madame Acarie, Blessed Mary of the Incarnation, who prepared the way for the 'invasion' before becoming a Carmelite lay sister; and his book makes good reading. However, he knows nothing about grace, which is the supernatural life of the soul. He thinks he can achieve union with God without it and lately has been experimenting with the drug Mescalin to attain this end.

It is because of the last chapter in *Grey Eminence* that I mention him at all. In this he mentions the claims of political and economic thinkers to solve the world's problems. He dismisses them at once. Politics is not an exact science and the most it can achieve is a rough and ready balance between opposing policies. Economics has to do only with the production and distribution of goods, the humble necessities of life. But the slave can be economically secure and who wants to be a slave? So having ruled out economics and politics Huxley proposes a solution. He is sure it is the *only* one: governments should subsidize contemplative communities and locate them on the fringes of the great cities so that the life of God could come through them into the whole people. Leaving aside his too innocent notion of the supernatural life, he states quite clearly the justification for our Catholic contemplative communities. We know that God is in everything by his Presence, by his Essence, by his Power; but he is in the human soul by affection and interest. He can be kept out and the door barred and bolted; but 'Behold I stand at the door and knock.' Contemplatives are the open doors for God to come into the world. Life and light and the power of God come out from them to all men; they are ministers of grace and their convents and monasteries are immense power houses of light and life. That is why our contemplative sisters were brought from Holland and established at Blackburn.

Catholics know, or should know, the secret of their immense importance. That is why Thomas Merton says: 'There is no living soul who does not owe something to Carmel. It is also why mystics are so attractive to Aldous Huxley and many others who are on the tracks of truth. The last surprise is the *truth*. Writers like Huxley had glimmerings of it but perhaps they are too conceited to let it possess them, because that is what truth does. They are too full of their worldly wisdom to *be* possessed.'

Early in 1957 Father Malachy went to visit the Carmelite Sisters newly established at Blackburn:

They are not strictly enclosed yet and so their friends and helpers had the great privilege of direct contact and co-operation with the contemplatives. They find them so simple and sincere and it is interesting to note that these two qualities exactly fit the description by Cardinal Gasquet of the pre-Reformation English Carmelites. He said they were, '*Simplices et sinceri*'. Even Catholics sometimes think that contemplatives are bound to be inhuman.

From Blackburn Father went on to the Carmelite Convent at Preston to engage their prayers for the apostolate of Aylesford. When he was there the Mother Prioress allowed him to speak to one of the Sisters he had known years before in Wales:

At that time, during the War, she was a student of London University, part of which had been evacuated to Aberystwyth. She was not then a Catholic but for three years she was constant at Mass every morning. She was constant too at meetings of the University Catholic Society and always brought with her a group of non-Catholics, both Welsh and English. Edna was an enigma within an enigma. An Honours student she was painfully shy yet had great and original initiative. She *displayed* no gifts; she was there; she smiled; she rarely spoke.

On one of the rare occasions when she did speak she told me of an experience during an air raid in London. She was standing in the black-out with her back to a street wall, very still from fear. Somebody felt their way up to her and gave her a sudden poke in the chest. She gave a great squeak out of her; and then she heard a frightened voice saying, 'I thought you were a pillar box'.

Although none of us guessed it at the time, Edna was a contemplative, an open door to God. She became a Catholic and then walked straight into Carmel. Now at her convent she is in charge of the chickens and our conversation was nearly all about them. She had them on 'free range' and told me why. Now at Aylesford we have three hundred and twenty chicks starting life in deep litter in our new chicken house; so I was tempted to argue.

But with such a holy woman it would have been wrong and useless. Instead I listened to her wisdom and advice. She speaks now with authority and without effort. The speech of the Carmelites is always different. It comes out of the silence and is creative as all speech should be. It is clear and bright, not thick with emotion as much worldly speech is. You sometimes hear such speech in the world and when you do it awakens you.

When I hear it I always remember the speech of the 'mountainy men' in Wicklow. To hear it is to see bright images as well. It is all bound up with the Faith of course and certainly with religion. Faith has to do directly with the soul and its faculties of mind and will. And only indirectly with the emotions. It gives light to the mind and a certain splendour of speech. Nowadays speech does not come *out* of people at all, from their innermost selves. They unload words which have collected in their heads: words, words, with no content and no vitality. In Carmel they speak out of silence, from the supernatural life of the spirit which is renewing itself endlessly.

When I was coming out of the Carmel there, over the gateway was a thrush singing on a bare bough, a great cascade of high notes falling from a tree on a February morning. After hard looking my companions spied him, a small brown bird who seemed almost part of a branch. Perhaps his wonderful performance was meant – because it was more than a symbol of the brown Sisters in their bare house of silence.

III

Polished well those Stones Elect

In the three years before the laying of the first stone of the
Church of the Assumption in 1958, foundations of all kinds
were being laid for the great centre Aylesford was to become.
The invisible ranks of the contemplative nuns are of course
Carmel's greatest asset and gradually their prayers and the
prayers of thousands who linked their prayers with the Carmelite intentions were being answered. Through the open doors
of Aylesford and Allington were flowing an ever-increasing
number of people who were instinctively trying to get away
from the formless boredom which lies at the centre of the
comfortable life while from all over the world were coming
the people who had felt and known the horror of living under
Communist rule, whose fears and prayers were as direct as
the others were unformulated.

And reading and hearing the stories of people who have
had to face real persecution makes a nonsense of the movement which seeks to water down the premises of the Faith.
Modern stories of prophetic dreams, of the knowledge of
supernatural protection, even of hearing the Voice of God,
make the Old and New Testaments seem perfectly factual and
reasonable and even rather restrained! Always most conscious
of the Church Suffering, Father wrote that from November
1956 there would be a Novena of Masses for Hungary, ending on 8 December. On that day Polish and Hungarian Pilgrimages would congregate at Aylesford to pray for their
countries. He said:

Darkness had very nearly covered the whole world but already there are gleams of light. For a generation now the stage of this world has been crowded with monstrous shapes whose power for evil is Satanic in its scale; but we can see – even if obscurely – that they are permitted by God to purge the world of sin and indifference. This lack of any fear of God and neglect of him and sometimes the use of him – just as a serving man – is the root evil of our age. We have to be shocked into realization of the greatness of this sin. Indeed we can understand what the Curé d'Ars meant when he said that a time will come when men will be so weary of *men* that they will weep when they hear the name of God. In the tragic events of the past weeks in Hungary we can sense the weariness the people felt for those monsters for whom God does not exist.

But we are not left despairing because already from the horror there has arisen a mighty hope. We had begun to think that Christendom was no more, that the great Catholic nations were in a decline and their faith gone under to the cruel hammering of the infidels. We had begun to think of 'Europe and the Centuries' as no more and that the Catholic States had become mere names in history. A few years ago there was a great Catholic victory over the Reds in Spain. Only a few months ago we were welcoming here a great Polish pilgrimage and on the same day a million and a half Poles had gone to honour Our Lady at Czestokowa, and no power on earth would have stopped them. They were all imploring her for Poland's delivery, something which seemed quite impossible at the time. They had left an empty chair, garlanded, to await the Cardinal's return. In a few weeks Russians were moving out and the great Cardinal was back, counselling charity and forgiveness. It is true that this may only be a beginning; but Our Lady has given them her sign.

Of the old Catholic nations perhaps Hungary was the most forgotten. We had ceased to think of her and yet quite suddenly the name of Hungary is flaming everywhere. Almost a generation has passed since they were enslaved and one would have thought that the young would all have been conditioned by the brutish teaching; and yet it was just these young people and women and even children who fought with their bare hands against those murdering tanks.

Father goes on to prophesy that the disintegration of Christendom which began with the Reformation, was made worse by the French Revolution and the *Risorgimento* and culminated in the depredations of the Communists, may have reached its worst point and that the time is at hand for a great resurgence of the Faith throughout the world.

Our present Holy Father is indeed worthy to usher in this new age of faith. Did he not say a short time ago, that it was a privilege to be alive at this time? It is he surely who by his deep faith and his calm who sustained the cardinals of Hungary and Poland. He has lived to see their return to a precarious liberty; their return with no bitterness or hatred in them but with the forgiving spirit of Christ.

And the Carmelites were continuing calmly to build for a very crowded future: the workshops were ready by May 1956 for their official blessing and dedication by the bishop. After High Mass in the evening of the Feast of St Joseph the Workman, the bishop blessed the workshops. He blessed them all one by one, it was not a hurried blessing but a lingering one, carried out with such a boyish interest that it must have been difficult for him to get on at all with the ritual. He was slow to leave the Carpenter's Shop and slower still to leave the Pottery with its kilns and 'pots'. There was the Printer's Shop and the Laundry and then, since blessings were abundant, a new coach had to be blessed, one of the three which had brought more than a hundred of our Tertiaries from London.

The bishop spoke, inspired as always and with that intimacy which makes him a living part of Aylesford:

'The blessings of the father are strengthened by the blessings of his fathers until the desire of the eternal hills shall come. May it be on the head of Joseph and on the crown of his brothers. . . .' These are the words of the dying Jacob who prayed that his own blessing might be strengthened by the blessings of his fathers before him; an accumulation of blessings on the head of Joseph. Joseph, picked out to be the Prince and Ruler of the House of God. The great St Joseph on whose beautiful feast we have gathered here first to honour him, then to bless these workshops under his protection. . . .

'That evening in the moonlight and in the quiet, the workshops seemed very large – equal to the blessings that had been poured out upon them', wrote Father Malachy. But at that time there was still an urgent need for more brothers and lay workers to man the shops, to provide the future church and pilgrims' rooms with seemly and beautiful furniture, pottery and hangings and to print their own publications.

Gradually and usually 'by indirections', potters, carpenters and weavers came to work there. Two of the Hungarian refugees they were asked to receive after the Rising, turned out to be carpenters and by September 1957 there were nine Choir Brother novices who would do a certain amount of hand-work as part of their 'Rule', and half-a-dozen lay brothers. So by the end of the year, when at last the huge overdraft at the bank had dwindled sufficiently to satisfy the General that they might start building it up again, the rather frightening size of the workshop building gave the impression of having come into a just scale. With the many workers and ceaseless activity they seemed rather to be the normal and necessary 'hives of industry' you would expect to find at any great monastery.

The traditions of good hand-work have always been kept alive in the Church, even during the Industrial Revolution. The floods of bad 'repository art' come from the factories, while the convents and monasteries still turn out work which, whether it is simple or sophisticated, fulfils the Thomist definition of beauty: 'Splendour of mind irradiating proportionate parts of matter.' Care, industry and harmony must, even in the natural order of things, spring from a dedicated life, so it is not in the least surprising that Aylesford Pottery and Printing soon became quite famous and that even with the imposition of 'purchase tax' they were soon more than paying their way. Father once wrote that in the desert St Anthony required nothing in return for his life of prayer but the 'shelter of an old fort with a well and a bag of bread (wholemeal)'; and a Bakery was set up at Aylesford to supply the community and guests with the good wholemeal bread that he felt that they needed.

Father Brocard, with his tremendous knowledge of books, had in the meantime been building up a really good library 'from nothing', in fact it looked as if Our Lady, who 'looks after all parts of the house', was bringing everything together in readiness for the building of the Church of the Assumption.

In a way the thought of further building seemed rather sad at the time. Father Malachy would not agree with this; but to many of us there was a particular beauty about Aylesford that Summer, with the huge and time-worn cedar of Lebanon sheltering the open altar and the lovely open space over the old foundations. He has come up against a fair amount of this English nostalgia for ruins and once wrote, quoting Belloc:

'Have you ever noticed that all the Catholic Church does is thought beautiful and lovable until suddenly she comes out into the open and then suddenly she is found by her enemies to be hateful and grinding? So it is, and it is the fine irony of her present renovation that those who were for ever belauding her pictures and her saints and her architecture, as we praise things dead, are most angered by her appearance on the modern field all armed, just as she always was, with works and art and songs which are sometimes superlative and often vulgar. Note you, she is still careless of art and songs as she has always been. She lays her foundations in something other, which something other our moderns hate. I say to them that it was out of this something other that has come the song and art of Europe and all our past. What songs have they?

'The Church is more than Europe, she is Asia and the Continents and she is returning; *Andiamo*!'

When we first came back here a non-Catholic clergyman used to bring people to see the mediaeval monks among the ruins. For him they were rather lost survivals whom he invested with the romantic atmosphere of Scott's novels. With the ruin that was restored, and the desert that was full of praying people, he does not love us any more.

To look at the present and the future of the Faith is, in any case, ultimately more rewarding than gazing at its past, however glorious. Fatima in Portugal is the great shrine which has been built up, or rather, which has grown up, since Our Lady appeared to three peasant children there on several occasions in 1916. Her last appearance to the three was accompanied by a great phenomenon called 'The Miracle of the Sun', which was witnessed by many thousands of people. At that time Portugal was being attacked by the atheist revolutionary forces within it. Now it is one of the most Catholic countries in Europe and the life of the nation is marked by enormous pilgrimages on foot, on donkey, bicycle, car and bus to the place where Our Lady appeared on 13 May and on the thirteenth day of the rest of the Summer months until 13 October when the Miracle occurred.

For 13 May 1957 Father Malachy had the opportunity of leading a small pilgrimage in an old Wellington 'plane from London to Fatima he; writes:

We were away only a few days but it seemed like many years. We went by plane to Lisbon and from there by coach, arriving at Fatima at midnight. There the coach came to a standstill and we could not go an inch further. There were crowds of people moving in the semi-darkness and cars and coaches parked anyhow, anywhere. Our small party had to find the house of Béato Nuño which the General was having built as a guest house for pilgrims and a Carmelite centre. I was so tired that I thought of sitting on a stone, just where I was, until morning. Then a French Dominican came by, who charitably offered to help us. He must have been born in these mountains for he took the small hills indirectly, very slowly and thoughtfully; or he might have been a sailor on the lookout in the half-light. Under every bush and beside every rock or boulder there were people settling down for the night. As we were to find out the next day there were eight hundred thousand pilgrims and accommodation for less than eight thousand. This great house of Blessed Nuño is being built at the request of Lucy, the survivor of the three children of the 'Apparition', now a nun. Like Aylesford it is a great act of faith.

When we arrived it was after one in the morning. Miss Elizabeth Young, a Tertiary honoured by the title 'Sister' for her years of devoted work at Aylesford, had gone out

to the Beáto Nuño House a week or two before to be hostess
to pilgrimages. By some strange accident we found ourselves blundering about in the darkness in the top floor
of the uncompleted building before we had even seen the
other floors. Everyone had gone to bed but when I heard
Sister Elizabeth's vibrant voice articulating every syllable
perfectly on the corridor below, I knew all was well.

Indeed all was very well. Fatima is not to be described.
When I try to think of those three days, a host of sunlit
scenes are before my eyes and I cannot do anything with
them.

There was the multitude assisting at Mass after a hard
night's Vigil. True it was a great occasion; but there was no
feeling that the Cardinal was trying to rise to an occasion,
nor the bishops. He was a Cardinal, indeed he was, and the
bishops were bishops and the priests were priests and the
peasants were people. All the people, even the smallest
child, were children of God. The bishops wore their copes
as the people wore their clothes – some carelessly, some with
an easy grace. The grand liturgy of the Mass was treated
with great informality; not a precise exercise, because it is
the Mass *itself* that matters. The copes and mitres of the
bishops were all different and some of the tall mitres were
slightly askew and the copes. A face here and there among
the bishops had that kind of architecture that you find in the
old paintings.

Children in the procession were dressed up as miniature
bishops and Madonnas and angels. It all seemed childish but
it was not. It had a strange effect upon one. The peasants
are of low stature and the children seemed like very little
people. Bronzed little bodies, dark eyes, 'shy with secrets',
solemn with a terrible innocence. Many impressions or
glimpses of them I shall never forget: one was of two small
children on their way to school in the morning. They were

loitering a little bit, intent on something between themselves and never once looking back at us. We saw them moving in this way down the road and into the distance, and then they turned off and we lost sight of them. It was like a revelation of the Kingdom of God.

The other was a of peasant woman with a very little girl, or boy. They were in the colonnade of the Basilica and they were following the Stations of the Cross. These ceramic Stations seem to me to be great works of art and much excited me. And there was this woman in black and white with her back to us. There was a beautiful conversation going on between herself and the Stations – a drama of hands and speech. Never have I seen anything so lovely. Occasionally the little eager flashing child was brought in.

I had heard Fatima described as a kind of 'blasted heath'. It is a basin or Cova, with little hills about it and has an intimate and friendly beauty. The part around the Sanctuary is rough and stony and there are winding paths up to Blessed Nuño's House and the other new buildings on the flanks of the Cova. It is not a barren land, there are olive trees on these stony slopes and flowers everywhere: lowly flowers growing out of every cranny and rock, in every shade and colour. The astonishing variety of them makes you gasp or is it strange that this stony desert should bloom for Our Lady?

On our last day there we went to Coimbra to the Carmel where Lucy is now a Carmelite. On the drive, again it was the flowers which were astonishing: geraniums falling over stone walls, flowers that were flaming on the earth. The sun transformed everything and gave that clean sharp outline to the buildings and lit up their colour. The tiled roofs seemed to smoulder on every house. Of everything the sun made beauty: an outstretched hand becomes gold in its light. Beside the road there were olive trees and eucalyptus and on the high ground pine trees with cups fastened to them to collect the resin. And always there were the low vineyards. These Portuguese question the good earth God has given them, and vigorously. She answers them with oil and wheat and wine.

Coimbra is a beautiful city and has the finest university in Portugal. The students, who wear Prince Albert coats with gowns, and the women students who also dress in black, all seem to be part of the pattern of the life of the place. They are simple and dignified; they do not display any conceit of knowledge.

The Carmel at Coimbra is like every other Carmel I know. There is a coolness in it and a quiet which is not just an absence of noise. The Mother Prioress has the unhurried and simple manners, that largeness of spirit which comes only from union with God in prayer. I was not allowed to see Lucy but I was just as glad. As Mother Prioress said, her mission is finished and she has said everything that is to be said. Father Martindale, in his excellent *Portuguese Pilgrimage,* reports her as saying: 'So now, as for me, I remain like a skeleton stripped of everything, even in its own life, and placed in a museum to remind visitors of the misery and nothingness of all transitory things.'

This probably refers to the period before she was cloistered when she had to endure many visitors and much questioning. Now at last she is 'hidden with Christ in God'.

Mother Prioress was pleased to hear tidings of Aylesford and I explained to her the 'Use me to Today' apostolate. She understood at once and said: 'I shall ask Lucy under obedience to pray for the Apostolate of Aylesford. She will have the grace which is given through obedience and Aylesford will have the benefit of her prayers and ours.'

I came away from that Carmel very happy with a sense that a new chapter in the book of The Friars was beginning.

Driving back to Lisbon from Fatima, Portugal and the truth she holds in her way of life was again displayed in flashing scenes:

There were myriad glimpses when we were returning, before the sun was up, from Fatima to Lisbon. There were women with large baskets of flowers on their heads on their way into the town, donkeys and men and women all together; scores of people at sunrise already on the roads, or working in the fields. They work hard from dawn to dusk and yet you would never dream of calling them 'workers'. That is an ugly word – as if men were only for use, created to work in factories, their whole value in what they make to sell.

And then, just near Lisbon, a flashing cavalcade; suddenly there broke upon us the wild clanging of many bells: there must have been fifty horses loose in a fast canter, each with a bell hanging from his neck and all the bells seemed to be of different shapes and each had a different note. Only a neck behind this cavalcade was a young rider, well mounted, colourful, careless – like nature – riding with such grace. With a straight back, smiling, he passed too quickly in the dawn.

We had seen at Fatima a great humility and sheer un worldliness. Could it be otherwise when you see these incredible men and women stumbling on their knees in prayer for long distances to the Sanctuary? And walking on their bare feet with their bundles on their heads for hundreds of miles. Our Lady had asked for prayer and penance and they have answered her call. When I was taking part in the Consecration of Portugal to her I was scared by what they were asking of her. They were actually asking for more penance, for more fortitude, for the gift of prayer – the deep prayer of the spirit which gives the strength to walk the mystic way. Certainly no Carmelite in her Carmel could surpass them in their austere penance nor could have a more sincere desire for holiness. In this country and some others such a consecration might have provoked a purely romantic response; but in that people of God there seemed to be a stark passion for holiness: and they were paying the price of that passion. What is all true sorrow and suffering in a Christian but the desire for perfection? There is no sorrow like the sorrow of not being a saint. There is no sorrow like to this: 'I will arise out of my sins, out of my sloth, and go with her'.

But even such a comparison was not out of context with all that had been going on at The Friars in the years that had passed:

People have died from worry and anxiety and lack of Faith but never from hard work. The craftsman who loves his work or any workman who is in love with God and his holy Will, usually lives to old age. The Cistercian whose life consists entirely of work and prayer, with no recreation, is the most long-living of all. It is usually idle people and self-pitying folk who drag out a weary existence and die young. It is a grace to be in love with work and God sustains us. I say our energy is also from God and we should never be proud of it as though it came from ourselves; but we should accept it and be thankful for it as if it were a kind of present, thanking God for it as a man should thank God for his reason.

There is a great lift of the spirit in work eagerly embraced and done for love. 'Put love in and you will draw love out.' But, even where there is a tireless body the mind sometimes becomes tired and we may have 'days without salt'. As Belloc says: 'This breakdown which comes from time to time over the mind is a very sad thing; but it can be made of great use to us if we will draw from it a lesson that we ourselves are nothing. Perhaps it is a grace. Perhaps in these moments our minds repose.'

I sometimes reflect on the work that has gone into the Restoration so far. It has been an immense labour. The few fine brothers who were here from the beginning grew with the work to great stature. May Our Lady be praised for giving them such spirit and sending us from afar such truly great religious men: 'She is like a Merchant's Ship bringing her treasures from afar.' And may she be forever blessed for mercifully obscuring the appalling size of it, like a mountain in a mist. The mist lifted gradually and we looked back and saw the hard and perilous path. It is her way, the way she lures us up the steep path to heaven; and then the mist lifts for the last time and we are on the summit of God's world.

The Tertiaries who work in the Courtyard would surely have had days 'without salt', and moments of wondering how all the thousands of pilgrims are attended to. They must feel tempted to measure the Niagara of tea and liquid and the mountains of buns and cakes. But that would be only idle and lead to pride. It is better to accept the prodigious energy as a gift from God.

The Summer of 1957, after his return from Fatima, was to present Father Malachy with the pressures of preaching to thousands of pilgrims, often several times a day, of making decisions about the building with its myriad details, of guiding his community so that they could keep some sort of Carmel amidst the flood of pilgrims and sight-seers. Father has an unhurried but decisive way of dealing with every opportunity, every encounter and every demand. But as Belloc admitted, there do come times when body and mind become weary and at the end of September, the Vicar-General put him under

Early days; Fr Malachy looks from the Cloisters to open-air altar

Exterior view of a section of the Courtyard, showing extensive restoration work carried out on the ancient buildings by the Carmelite Friars

Courtyard, showing restoration in progress

View from the air during early stages of restoration

Section of the courtyard, now pilgrim's residence

The site of the shrine, at the east end of the medieval church

The Prior talking to pilgrims informally – first ten years

View from the original cloisters

The way to the upper chapel

The entrance to upper chapel used for the first ten years, and view of the new kitchens

View from medieval refectory. Scraffito by Adam Kossowski

Outdoor gatherin

scapular shrine

On the Rosary Way

Polish procession on the Rosary Way

Medieval refectory, sculpture by Philip Lindsay Clark, painting
by Adam Kossowski

Detail from outdoor shrine by Adam Kossowski

The Annunciation on the Rosary
Way by Adam Kossowski

The Nativity on the Rosary Way
by Adam Kossowski

'The Presentation', one of the
mystery plaques on the Rosary
Way designed and made by
Adam Kossowski

The old cloister chapel before the return of the Carmelites

Altar in chapel of Carmelite Saints – showing antique group of Our Lady of Mount Carmel and Simon Stock, surrounded by ceramics, by Adam Kossowski

St Anne, 15th-century sculpture

St Joseph,
sculpture in wood,
by Michael Clark

Our Lady of the Assumption (Commonwealth prize-winning sculpture
by Michael Clark). Altar and background ceramics by Adam Kossowski

obedience to return to Portugal and stay away for a month
and have a good rest. For all of the Summer, Time must have
had a relative meaning for him; it must have been more a
succession of words and actions, less real than the prayer
which bounded the fields of his work. Going up to London in
the train he tells us that he thought: 'The storm has swept
away the last leaves and cold has come again and winter is
here. The past year seems to have gone like that big sweeping
wind. How quickly it has gone!'

But he was not long alone with his thoughts. He was joined
in the carriage by a middle-aged woman who was immediately
friendly:

She was a Catholic and I was immediately struck by her
very free and happy manner. She had been going every day
for months to see her step-brother who was dying of cancer
in a London hospital. After she had talked to me about him
for a while she said: 'Father, what is Time?'

This startled me a bit because at that moment my mind
was full of this very mystery. She was not trying to be 'intellectual' at all and it seemed as if this question had dawned
upon her for the first time. I gave her the definition I had
learned as a student: 'Time is succession according to before and after', and realized at once that this definition meant
nothing at all. After that it was she who was teaching me
and giving me to wonder again. It was a joy to see how the
Holy Spirit of God, by giving her detachment not only
from time but from all passing things, had rewarded all her
charity to a dying man. She herself was more *outside* Time
than in it.

As one grows older it becomes clear that Time can prove a
great delusion. It is what happens *in* Time which is reality;
many of the saints died young and yet lived a long time.
This is what is implied in the language of Scripture, by

E

'fulfilling time', not merely using it or wasting it. Alas it can flow away from us without our having ever truly known this difference. We are alive and Time will be alive in eternity. Despite the never ending noise and fury of activity in the world, millions never really live because they can never get outside Time in their thoughts. They equate living with being active and being able to run about. Often they seem only to be trying to prove to themselves that they are alive. When do we really live? That is everybody's question. The woman in the train had the answer.

Wise people tell you never to go back to a place which has profoundly impressed you. Only once do you see Rome or the Alps or the sea in storm or the bare grey austere Sierras of Spain. My journey had the virtue of obedience in it, otherwise I might not have dared to go. I had been to Fatima in May and those two days of wondering had seemed like a long lifetime. Now I was going back in the Autumn, tired. It might all have gone dead, but in fact this whole month of the year enclosed so plentiful an experience, so profoundly moving, that it is difficult to write about it.

It is a long way to Portugal. I could not spend much money getting there so I went by train. From Paris to Irun is a day's journey; but I had not been told that a visa was necessary to get into Spain. At Irun I was not allowed to go on any further and no persuasion was of any avail. My passport was given to a gendarme with a revolver in his holster. With my heavy luggage I was put back into the train by which I had come. After an hour's wait it started back to Hendaye, the gendarme and myself the only passengers.

I was full of bitterness at this formality, so costly and so stupid; but there was a momentary compensation, for it was a beautiful evening and looking out of the window I saw two men mowing with scythes and casting shadows on the field. They were following one another with perfect and easy rhythm. It seemed effortless and lovely to watch.

When Father finally reached the Consulate, a few miles away from the station on the coastal road, the Office was closed. The taxi driver said that the Consul was away, 'gallivanting' on the Riviera, and took him back to the Station Hotel:

> There in the entrance was an Irish priest. *He* had been turned back that morning and was either not bitter at all or else had had time to get over it. He had been waiting all day for the Consul with only a sandwich to sustain him. He calmed me down, counselling *Pazienza*. He had been educated in *Pazienza* in Salamanca and was going back to see his old college. We did the only practical thing, we went and had dinner: fish soup which was delicious, chicken and a bottle of wine. Father Cuffe was insistent: 'You will not get away tomorrow.'
>
> The Consulate does not open until nine a.m. and the train from the Frontier, a mile or two away across a long bridge, was at ten minutes past nine. With more faith than hope I got up early next morning and found the church. The Parish Priest was sure that only an act of God could get the Consul out of bed to attend to my passport. Over the altar where I said Mass was a massive statue of St Joseph whom I implored to provide an act of God.
>
> I set off again, this time walking, along the coast to the Consulate. I found a private entrance and rang all the bells I could see. A lady put her head out of the window and bade me in French to go round by the side. I found myself in the Office by a back way – and there was the Consul. I could not believe my eyes. He was making out a visa for somebody in the same predicament as myself. He was an old man, incredibly fine in appearance, who looked like the father of St Teresa. Most certainly he had not been gallivanting

the night before, and he said: 'I will give you a visa at once.'
I caught a passing bus back to the hotel and was out of it
and into a taxi in a matter of minutes. Then there was the
long bridge and the two frontier posts with just ten minutes
in hand; but I was just in time. I had a second-class ticket
but there were only first and third on this train; so third
I went.

A long open compartment had wooden seats and large
windows and was bright and clean. Strangely enough that
day through Spain made up for all the vexations and more.
It was a changing pageant of real and endlessly contrasting
people; there was a stocky woman with hair like a horse's
mane, powerful and loud-voiced. In her care was a small
girl, delicate and well-mannered, who offered me her
sandwich. There were strong young working men, making
their supper of bread and fat bacon and relishing it no end.
There was the woman with the fine face who talked a great
deal, clear-cut Spanish speech. I watched her discreetly,
fascinated. She spoke with her eyes and face and hands:
all movement, all of her speaking. It was superb theatre
and it was life, powerful and spontaneous. The Spanish
man or woman needs nothing. They may go in rags or be
without food, nothing reduces them. They are never less
than men or women.

The end of the journey was at Fatima station at six a.m. I
discovered to my surprise that this is more than twenty
miles from the Cova da Iria. There were taxis outside but no
driver could be found. I walked around for a bit and saw
the town awakening for another day. Returning to the
station I spied a taxi man deep in his taxi and fast asleep.
He was awake in an instant and we were away. Morning
over those hills one could not forget.

Dr Barnsley, his wife and baby Simon and his wife's
mother had gone out to Blessed Nuño's House three weeks

before. The doctor is the novelist who writes under the name of Gabriel Fielding. They received the gift of faith at Aylesford only a few years ago. He had been with me in May and shared all my feelings and despite my cautionings had set off with great hopes of finding Fatima as astonishing as we had found it then. Now he was excited beyond measure by it all and had made many discoveries. He was full of the 'singing mills' and the music of the stone-cutters and the masons, everything.

That same afternoon he had planned a walk through the woods to a fair. We were a small party. The woods of pine trees and eucalyptus were typical of Fatima and of the whole of the North of Portugal. Always the pines are stripped of their lower branches to feed the kilns and have only a tuft left at the top. If you see them in the half-light of the evening they are like dark feathery birds hovering in the sky. Pots are attached to their boles to catch their resin. The eucalyptus tree is tall and straight, dove-coloured and the slightest breeze ruffles the leaves to discover a silver-grey beneath. I was told they 'drank much water'. Their roots have been known to travel a thousand yards in search of it. As you walk through the woods you breathe the pine and eucalyptus. You are not shut in or out by them. You can see through them and the light playing on the rough trunks of the trees.

There are little low walls everywhere, humble like everything in Portugal. They were certainly not built to stop anybody but are just piles of silver-grey boulders all along the way, and in the little enclosures of the clearings there are huge boulders of the same colour carelessly scattered in twos or threes as if by some pre-historic giant. In another country they would have been blasted out of the way long ago. It is wonderful to notice that every tree in Portugal has its uses and ministers to human needs. Eucalyptus gives its oil. When I was at a Dorothean college of five hundred girls near Oporto, there was a great cauldron of eucalyptus boiling and bubbling on the lower floors, filling the whole place with powerful odour to purify the atmosphere and ward off the 'grippe'. Then there are the cork oaks in the South. This is one of Portugal's most valuable exports. The cork that we know is really the bark of this oak and it is beautiful to watch the traditional 'strippers' at work.

There was a great silence in the woods. When we were lost in winding ways three children appeared to point the way. They were native to the woods and were not lost themselves, although no house was to be seen. They were like Lucy and Jacinta and Francisco, the three children of the Miracle, they were quiet and perfectly adjusted and without fear. Their natural senses were awake and not deadened nor their peace shattered by noise.

We were tired walking before we reached the village on the hill. A great church looked down upon a wide-open space. There were houses on each side and the streets were stony and rough. It was a most surprising and interesting sight. Again it was all humility, small oxen and pigs and donkeys and oxen and mules: goats, flocks of geese and every variety of duck and fowl. It was a preview of creation before it became ordered and slick and fat. It all flowed round the church and some of it into it.

Inside the church was a young priest kneeling upright and saying his office and the people of the fair kept coming in and out. You'd see women with a chicken or two in a basket or it might be a turkey or a pigeon or a rabbit or a little pig. There were no seats. These noble women kneeling upright with their baskets on their heads did not need support. Outside on the stalls or booths there was every kind of ware to be had. There were hundreds of beautiful terra-cotta pots from the local kilns spread over a large area with a nimble bright-faced boy, all alert and eager, selling them for the equivalent of sixpence or a shilling. They don't press their wares upon you, but have great dignity and reserve. Men and children are lean as their flocks. They have no flesh on them to hide them and their sombre clothes and long stocking headdresses seemed quite natural. What you see are *people* with steady searching eyes; ascetics who might be saints.

Before we left we had a meal: sardines, bread and wine. The doctor bought enough for six of us for very little money: a kilo of sardines, a litre of wine and a mighty loaf of bread. We broiled the sardines for nothing on a communal charcoal fire; then we sat down on a little wall and had our meal of the cooked fish and there seemed to come about us the light of a morning on a sea-shore and One who stood there: 'They saw hot coals lying and a fish thereon.' Jesus said to them: 'Come and eat.' This is not just an inevitable memory or association. It is a timeless moment, it does not pass: not the fish, nor the sea nor the beckoning Christ nor his communion with the lowly and humble. What a heart-breaking goodness of people and of creatures of God to correct our worldliness and pride.

The wine we could not finish we shared with some men standing by their sheep and goats. They were very pleased and 'obliged'. We came home by the Basilica, foot-sore and tired; and still half the tale of that first day is not told.

I was impatient to see the 'singing mills' and indeed I have never seen any small buildings so beautiful. They are round turrets built of stone with walls three or four feet thick and a diameter of about fifteen feet. They have one door and a stone stairway leading to a floor half-way up where are two mill-stones, a small one for grinding maize and a larger one for flour. Outside the great arms with sails attached give a strange feeling of flight. These little buildings, classical and solid as any temple, have stood along these hilltops for more than a thousand years since the time of the Moors. And yet attached to them are these whirling arms with their canvas sails which make of them something wild and elemental, something of the sea and the sky. Inside, when the wind is blowing up the timbers are creaking and the millstones are turning fast; it is all alive. It gives you the feeling of being on the sea in a good ship creaking and yielding to the wind and yet driven forward on its course. You are alive with the excitement of the ship or the mill.

The wind is the hardest worker in Portugal. It too gives good yield. The farmer comes down the steps with his small pink bag of wholemeal flour; he closes the door and goes down the hill to his home, full of content, to the music of the singing mill. This music is made by bamboo canes attached to the arms with the sails and notched in a clever way so that the wind flutes through them. That is why Doctor Barnsley calls them the 'singing mills'. The music is a practical contrivance to let the farmer at the foot of the hill know if the wind is up and that his mill is turning. If the sails flag he goes and adjusts the set of them to catch the wind. The whole economy of Portugal is like this. Fools will call it primitive and the people backward; but Doctor Salazar has seen the miseries which attend the heedless industrialization of a country and will not allow this to happen too quickly in Portugal. There is poverty in the South of Portugal; but in the North even the sociologists say that the way of life is almost Arcadian. May God preserve it!

When we were coming down the hill the autumn crocus seemed to be everywhere. Even on the trodden paths the crocus had come up in numerous families. My sister-in-law, a Dorothean nun in Portugal these fifty years, tells me the flowers are more numerous than the blades of grass. That is why she knew only a few of their names, Jaqueranda, Bougainvillaea, and Belladonna for the autumn crocus.

Pilgrims of only a day or two miss so much here. You need at least a week around Fatima to make the discoveries for yourself. Only then can you see everything together. You must go to the villages of the Fatima children on foot, through lanes off the main road, saying your rosary. The lanes are stony and may the Lord keep them like that. Dante measures time by the length of prayers: 'In the space of an Ave Maria', so must you. It will take you three rosaries of time to walk to the woods where Our Lady appeared and another one to get you to the Loca where the angel taught the children to pray and to do penance. It is so interesting to note that the children were worn out and exhausted after the angel's appearances. After Our Lady's appearances they were all joy and the threats of being boiled alive did not affright them in the least. After all, an angel is a spirit while Our Lady is one of us.

The place where she appeared in the woods has still got the children's little shrine, still kept up by local children. You have to get very near the ground to look into it. It is more moving than the large shrine with its white marble figure a few yards away. It is good sculpture, but entirely out of place. And now over the great rocks or boulders in the Loca on which the Angel of Portugal seemed to stand, they are putting up white marble figures. Again they are good sculpture by a well-known artist but they will conflict with the dove-grey rocks and break the silence. Silence has been in the woods until now. On every visit we stayed in that place for a long time. You could pray there with the rocks and the silence. You could hear the chirruping of birds in the middle distance and the distant ring of masons' chisels. This only seemed to deepen the silence, giving it depth and mystery. On the rocks were written carelessly –

not cut in the stones – in Portuguese and English the words of the angel's prayer. That seemed right. When it is all ordered and formal it will be very different.

To understand Lucy's relatives you have to see them in the world I am describing. Photographs are no good at all; in fact, except for the ones of her parents, Ti Marto and his wife, whose powerful faces would survive anything, they are positively misleading. Lucy's elder sister remains unchanged by everything; yet she is far from common. In her home you can see the room where Lucy was born in all its clean simplicity, as also the little room with its loom in it and the kitchen with its canopied fireplace and the snug seats on either side. You have to move quietly and with care in these little houses. Lucy's sister is now a plump middle-aged woman, but the distinction which is hers has little to do with a fine figure. She has quiet in her and a great wisdom and as she spoke to Sister Elizabeth, promising to ask Lucy to pray for good masons for Aylesford when she saw her in a few weeks' time, I could see that she was very intelligent.

Then she brought us out to see her two goats. They were eating from a crib in a tiled lean-to at the side of the house. They were friendly animals, full of personality and well cared for. Then we were taken to the garden to see the well, another place where the angel had appeared. We drank cool water and round it were figs on an old fig tree. They could be had for the taking.

These people, relatives and countrymen of Lucy and Jacinta and Francisco, don't envy us our motor-cars and gadgets:

That is surprising to people of this scientific age who only know what they touch and feel and eat. But in fact the early desert saints, and all the subsequent ones, are the greatest scientists the world will ever know because in the light of Grace they explored the vast regions of the human soul. The modern scientist is often a complete extrovert who will die without knowing that he has a soul to explore, let alone to save. When you see hundreds of thousands of pilgrims at Fatima waving good-bye with their handkerchiefs to Our Lady, represented by a very indifferent statue, all decked out with flowers, even we, until we understand more fully, think it is extravagant and 'too much'. It is a mystic who has said, 'Where love is, there is vision'; and to these simple but profound people Our Lady is revealing herself through this simple means. When you understand this you realize that she is as near to their love as she was to the children who saw her over the Cova.

Near Fatima lives Madame Couto. Sister Elizabeth and I were passing her house when two Marymount Sisters we knew were taking leave of her at her gate. She is an elderly lady who speaks several languages and she very graciously asked us in. Her house is beautiful and full of good things. I asked her at once if she were an artist. 'No, no', she said, quite simply. 'I am the help of the poor.'

In Lisbon where she lives during the greater part of the year she has three hundred poor who are greatly dependent on her and in the course of several visits which I made to her she spoke of the devastating humility and goodness of the people. In whatever suffering or adversity they endure they never make reproach to God. She once asked some small children from a poor home what they did. She knew that sometimes in the old days they had only soup to eat. They said, 'You eat your soup in the evening, say your rosary and many thanks to God.'

They told me about the goat woman. Strangers to Portugal profess to be afraid of her. She is always wandering round that free country round Fatima with her goats and keeps up a conversation with them all the time. Her language seemed to me to be poetic and picturesque and Madame Couto confirmed this: 'She is as sane as you or I.' As a matter of fact you don't see or hear of any mad people in these parts. There are odd people and old crones, doting a bit, but they are looked after and cared for by their families, however poor.

Madame Couto had first-hand knowledge of Jacinta. She was there when her body and that of Francisco were exhumed. She saw the body of Jacinta which was incorrupt, with a smile on her face. The story of Jacinta as she told it to me resembles that of Bernadette. She was taken away from her home to the hospital where nobody knew who she was. She knew she was dying and asked the Chaplain for Holy Viaticum. He thought it would be time enough in the morning. But Jacinta died in the night and died alone. There was, about her dying, the same strange desolation of her young life after she had seen Our Lady. She was a very holy little girl. There is now a great cultus for her and many regard her as a saint. You will remember how Bernadette died in a convent far away from Lourdes and how she, who had been the means of healing to so many, was not healed herself. She told somebody who was wondering about this: 'It is my business to be ill.' This is the unworldly wisdom of the saints.

While it is possible, almost literally, to get outside Time at Fatima in the new marble and stone palace built by the Brazilian Province and surrounded by villages in which the houses being built exactly resemble those built a hundred years ago, a fortnight may last a very long time. The hours are marked by a jumpy hymn-tune sounded on the bells of the Basilica which is an exaggerated version of the Moorish-looking village churches. Pilgrims come and go, in groups and singly, all with the purposeful look of business to accomplish or a message to deliver. Only Jacinta's tombstone, with its simple statement: 'Here lies Jacinta Marto to whom Our Lady appeared' acts as a reminder that heaven and earth do not always keep to their appointed places. All is order and rhythm. It is the perfect place for a rest and a retreat, and soon Father set out to explore some more of Portugal and to carry out his roving commission to look for masons for the new church and to gather ideas about building methods from the traditionally minded but inventive Iberians.

In Oporto and Lisbon he was given hospitality at Dorothean convents since one of his sisters-in-law belongs to the Order in Lisbon. Since he was on the look-out for products which could be used at Aylesford he was much excited when the three schoolgirls who had been sent to show him round Oporto kept mentioning a 'smitherie' they were taking him to.

This was the magic word because I thought it had something to do with a forge and wrought iron. We saw the old Franciscan church about which I could write a lot. Then we were taken down into a vast underground full of tombs. The 'smitherie' was a cemetery after all, and what a cemetery! All round the walls of that vast place were tombs with the names of all the famous Franciscans of that famous Friary, for hundreds of years. The guide explained that the bodies were left in the tombs for seventy years. Then he brought us to show us their final resting place.

Shining his light through an iron grille in the floor he showed us the bones of thirty thousand Franciscans. After that we mercifully met an old pupil of the school who offered us a lift in her car. She was a smart woman of thirty and was returning from Mass. She had a Missal and a Meditation book, both of which she used every day.

In Lisbon he met Mother Halpin, his relative. After forty

years in Portugal she had become a fascinating mixture of
Irish and Portuguese:

> She loves the Portuguese [Father writes] and she loves
> the superiors of the Congregation. They can never do
> enough for you. They are deep, deep. You never get to the
> bottom of the Portuguese soul.
>
> She lodged me that night with dear friends of hers. Both
> husband and wife were industrialists with a difference. They
> were living in but not *for* a beautiful apartment. She is a
> convert Jewess who speaks English perfectly, even elo-
> quently. There was about that evening the atmosphere of
> the early Church; her hunger for God had brought her to
> the Faith and she had just come to the Church with the
> directness of a child. Had I been St Paul she could not
> have received me more humbly and kindly.
>
> The industry she was directing had to do with fish and
> sardine canning, one of the great industries of Portugal.
> Since they have no children it is all run for the benefit of the
> workers. I was fascinated by her lucid accounts of the fish,
> the workers, the oil. I shall never be able to see a tin of fish
> again without thinking of her. But all this was only an aside.
> We talked until after midnight about other and more im-
> portant things.

Despite the poverty there is so much of kindness and
welcome and sheer *life* in Spain and Portugal that to return to
the apathy and dull acceptance of the 'civilized' countries is
always a shock. Father travelled from Madrid to Paris by a
Pullman train.

> I was haunted by a strange feeling not unlike death. It
> was like a pervasive atmosphere in this comfortable train.
> The first sitting for lunch was at twelve. I chose the second
> one. At half past one I eventually got to the dining car

after a long and difficult passage. The diners had not yet finished so the head waiter waved us outside to wait. Soon there was a long queue. A false sort of animation among a few gradually subsided into bored waiting. Fortunately I had my rosary beads and standing there in my corner I said two rosaries. In the dining car, while waiting for the liqueurs to pass, I said another. The two hard-faced men opposite knew their liqueurs. The waiter carried five bottles and they just pointed to the one they wanted. Beyond them was a blonde woman who was consuming cognac and showing it.

It was Friday and when I asked for an omelette instead of the chicken a youngish man who was sitting beside me said, 'So you are a Catholic'. He told me he was Jewish but had been educated by the Jesuits and was full of admiration for them: 'But religion is no longer practical or possible.' He admired Catholic priests but he was an industrialist and ninety-nine per cent of his workers were communists. Religion wasn't real to him and when pressed he doubted if anything was real; he said he never prayed and that in any case he did not know how. He asked me what I had been doing in my corner before lunch: 'You were like a statue.' Taken aback, I said I had been saying my rosary. Then I asked abruptly, 'But what were you doing?'

'Just nothing. Why should I be doing anything?'

In the end I said to him: 'If you are not praying you are not alive, and I am trying to talk to a corpse. You've had everything life can give you and you confess that you've had only worry as your reward. If I am to believe what you have told me you are a black pessimist, and a pessimist is one who is tired of good things. Your mood of despair comes not from being weary or suffering but from being weary of joy. We have taken an hour and a half of God's good creature time to get through this lunch. It is indecent. In Portugal there are many living on a crust of bread and a bowl of soup and they are alive. Look at the faces of the people in this dining car. They are practically all empty masks and some are frightening besides. That man over there in the far corner has the most sinister sad face I have ever seen.'

He confessed he never looked at faces or saw anything in them; that he never really saw the faces of his workers. 'It must be terrible to see people like that', he said. 'It is like spying into people's souls.' And then he said, rather maliciously, 'You Catholic priests are good at that sort of thing'. Then, thinking he had hurt me, he added, 'Perhaps it is that *you* can see faces because you are an artist. Are you?'

'Most certainly not.'

Then I told him about the Holy Spirit of God who is the infinitely original artist and how it must be that he gives to us, and particularly to priests, eyes to see his work which is all light.

'It must be so', he said, 'because I cannot see it. To me all people are the same. I only see shapes which I recognize as human beings.'

He made me very sad because he was absolutely sincere in all that he said and, passing along the corridor together, seeing the well-fed men and women taking their ease, he looked into every compartment as we passed and I thought he had eyes to see – at last. When we came to his own compartment he was strangely agitated. He laughed hysterically. He said 'goodbye' and I saw him no more.

So ended Father's journey for that year. He had been able to cross Europe without ever being very far from a Carmel, and always the same saints presided over the altars where he said Mass.

In a memorable poem Harold Munro wrote of those who 'wander the world and never find a home'. Though not so lucky as Carmelites, such people are fortunate in their way because their desires are infinite. In the richer parts of the world, especially in the United States, the circulation is intense. People do not feel successful unless they are for ever touring, travelling and moving house. Most North Americans are the near descendants of pilgrim stock, not necessarily Mayflower founding fathers, but of European exiles who pushed Westward in search of a home in the shadow of heaven.

With motels and caravans and movable houses the urge has become secularized within 'the great American dream', but Europe is not so thorough. At Fatima, Lourdes, Walsingham, Aylesford and Storrington in England, coaches, aeroplanes, shoe leather and bare feet carry crowds to present themselves in place and time before their own formless longings. At a shrine a man may become almost a sacramental being, symbol and bearer of his deepest prayer.

In Holy Russia, the Russia of the Czars, great crowds of pilgrims, a rabble of saints, half-saints and the 'socially unintegrated', used to be given hospitality at all the great houses on their way to or from their shrines. St Benedict Joseph Labre seldom made his long walks to the monasteries unaccompanied. It was always like this in the Church; it is always from the people who are in grace that knowledge comes. There were the pilgrimages and there *are* the pilgrimages. Therefore, these spontaneous movements have authority by their existence. There is no reason, short of the complete triumph of materialism, why the flow of the faithful should ever cease.

IV

The Precious Corner-stone

By 1958 the years of restoration had been fulfilled. Hundreds of feet of fine hand-made oak tables stood in the refectories; the wide-boarded sloping corridors of the guest wings now opened on to decent bathrooms, simply furnished white-walled rooms, central heating and a feeling of home. All the outside elevations had been repointed and the ancient roofs were newly set and snug. It was time to begin rebuilding the Sanctuary Church, to make that act of reparation which was to be both sign and cause of a new surge of the old Faith in England.

Like the sacraments, a well-built church gives line and shape to the intangibles which make up the Faith. Simone Weil said that the principal aim in life is to construct an architecture in the soul; so perhaps there is an affinity between a well-set Christian face and the best of Church architecture.

For people whose life is in the Faith the need to 'localize a presence' in church building seems to be self-apparent and complete. There is no self-doubt in the Newsletters. The only questions for Father are when and how. To the Carmelites it seemed good and sensible to set out with no money to build a perfect church from expensive and scarce materials. Mean-minded questions were irrelevant: to that which asks, 'Wouldn't it have been better to have spent the money abroad on the poor?' there could have been only one answer: 'What money? There is no money.'

Aylesford has a mission to a 'destitute-rich' country half

of whose hospital beds are at the call of the mentally sick, a country still able to do much for the world provided it can regain and keep its spiritual values.

In April 1958 Father wrote:

We are praying for a little miracle that the endless formalities may be completed so that a start may be made on the buildings before May and so that our beloved bishop may lay the foundation stone on May the 18th.

[But on May 1st] something else was happening which looked like the end of what had been begun with high hopes. The Institute of Our Lady of Mount Carmel was leaving Allington Castle on that day and moving to a new foundation at Chislehurst. They had begun their lay apostolate at The Friars in the Gatehouse. For some years they worked with us at the Restoration, and the greatest credit and thanks are due to them for their valiance during that difficult time.

I was under great pressure to advise the General to dispose of Allington but this seemed to me a dreary and unnecessary course; nothing less than horrifying really because it is in the same marvellous pattern of providence as The Friars. It seemed too strange to contemplate that it could be of no further use to Our Lady who was installed in the midst of its towers and battlements on Easter Sunday 1951, the Feast of the Annunciation. She is the one who turns sorrow into joy, not joy into sorrow, and it would have been unthinkable sorrow to have taken her and her Son from that strong place. I am certain that will not happen now, and the General has decided that it will be used as a centre of apostolate for Tertiaries, a thousand of whom regard Allington and Aylesford as their home.

A small team under the direction of our Spanish brother, Nuño, has gone into action and in just over a month the

Castle has been transformed; there is not any part of that large place which is not receiving expert attention. The halls on the ground floors were made ready at once for exhibitions and the Catholic England set is proving an attraction. We have established there 'The Apostolate of the Open Door'.

This was to be a sort of enquiry centre like those they have in some large towns, where people seeking knowledge of the Catholic Faith might find the sort of books and literature they needed. They would also be able to stay there and make informal retreats.

When it was first set up there did seem, however, to be a most grisly air about the Catholic England Exhibition. Somebody had made a too-lifelike model of a nun upon which to display habits. In the half-light from the deep windows this replica made people jump, especially when their nerves had already been slightly stretched by the atmosphere of the mediaeval castle. Other exhibits included a model of a Catholic martyr about to be hanged at Tyburn and a very stark model of a conventual refectory in Pugin Gothic. All of these had originally been made for a London show commemorating the Centenary of the Return of the Hierarchy in the nineteenth century. Fittingly there were large illustrations of bishops, priests and nuns in that gloomily etched black and white preferred by the Victorians. Probably few people were attracted to the Church as a result of viewing all this, though of course there are those who might need a fright!

However, it was not long before the great hall reverted to its function of being a perfect Great Hall, with huge logs burning in the stone fireplaces on special occasions. The Tertiaries worked hard to provide the hospitality needed for Retreats and the kind of genuine welcome which is so rare in our Welfare State. There were nothing like enough Carmelite priests to fulfil the increasing demands, and it would be ten years before the choir novices of 1958 would be ordained, even if they persevered with their vocations. So the Tertiaries simply had to accept more responsibility for the Carmelite apostolate and this centre for their work had come at just the right time.

There was still another great worry which was standing between the Carmelites and the confident and peaceful laying of the Foundation Stone. This was an unpleasant legal action for damages taken against The Friars by two former employees who considered they had been wrongfully dismissed.

These people were described in the High Court as 'Two devout Catholics' [Father Malachy writes]. Actually when they came to us they seemed more than devout. They were Tertiaries of an Order and had turned up at six a.m. on December the 8th to be the first pilgrims of Our Lady's year 1953 to 1954. So devout they seemed that no enquiry was made about them.

For three years the case was pending; this means hanging over or weighing upon. It was continually being postponed, and there were many alarms and legal consultations which had a sinister note in them. But on April the 30th the case was on. It was miserable and it was dangerous. It might have provided headlines for the press at home and abroad, but in actual fact it received very little publicity. In his summing up the Judge said that it had been a 'vindictive action, with no tittle of evidence to support the wild charges which had been made'. He was uncanny in his understanding of the case and was generous and wise in his summing up. His exalted attention was more than the case deserved as it was stupid and boring. His judgement was completely exonerating for us and ended with the words, 'as I would expect'.

I can understand how St Alphonsus gave up the law and became a saint and how St Thomas More stuck to it and became a martyr. The atmosphere of the courts was heavy and bitter. We hear of the great trials, of classic judgements; but usually the matter of the cases is just cheap drama. Whether it is great or petty it is always pathetic and the whole process is tediously slow. This is one of the safeguards of good law as injustice is usually a hasty thing. The Judge takes down all you say in longhand so that giving evidence is like dictating to a learner typist. Mr Justice Pilcher was like a learned and patient headmaster and if the Plaintiff said, 'the defendant was roaring mad' he would write on his tablets, 'he was very angry': or if it was alleged that 'his eyebrows were oscillating in anger' he would write: 'He was somewhat excited'. A snake-charmer would be described as having a pleasant manner and I can imagine how unbearable the whole process might be if the Judge were solemn. Our Judge was not.

I was in the witness box on the first of May. It was a Red-Letter day, of which there are twenty-eight in a year. Most of them are religious feasts and several are feasts of Our Lady.

In former times the Courts rose for the whole of Lent. On the day of our hearing the Judge was wearing a close-fitting scarlet robe with a black sash worn diagonally like a deacon's stole. Indeed he could have been mistaken for a well-groomed bishop. On the other days he is in more sombre robes but on Red-Letter days he is resplendent. This, together with the procedure down to the smallest detail, was obviously ecclesiastic in origin. The Common Law of England was the product of the Catholic Church. The ideal state in Common Law was to be a *liber et legalis homo*, the 'free and law-abiding man', or the man abiding in law with rights not given on sufferance. The Common

Law which has been a long time growing and which has never changed has been transplanted to America, Australia, South Africa and India. There has unfortunately been added a great deal of unpleasant Statute Law, some of it framed in emergencies; but essentially the system of Common Law still obtains in these countries and in England and Ireland.

Lawyers will tell you that it is the Pleadings in the Common Law which mark its great difference from other systems. In a suit the whole case is set out beforehand and all the documents which are discovered and numbered are made available to both sides. No additional evidence or document may be brought into the trial. Except through his own negligence, therefore, Counsel can hardly be taken by surprise and witnesses are very much confined to saying 'yes' or 'no'. A good judge will achieve an understatement, very bare and bleak in the way I have described. In this stupid case there were little asides from the Judge which were a mercy. He affected great surprise at certain pronunciations like 'refectory' and a great ignorance of the meanings of some words. I am sure judges and schoolmasters have been doing this since the world began. I was bewildered in the witness box by the use, or abuse, of some words and felt quite foolish. I turned out to have been causing a great mystery to the court by confusing an 'agreement' with a 'draft' of it – which I had seen months before it was finally dated. Since this draft had not been included among the pleadings, for the purposes of this trial it did not exist.

I was a very poor witness. Being in the witness box was like being in a strait jacket. Actually I was in a black jacket and without my habit or cloak. There was the Judge who looked like a bishop and wasn't one. I was a friar and a Prior and was described officially as a 'Very Reverend' one; but

I was dressed like an undertaker. I was in a kind of pulpit and could hardly say a word. Father Clement was nearly as helpless as myself; but strangely our two lay witnesses from Aylesford, Mrs Yvonne Wallace and Miss Pauline Healy, were entirely admirable. Cross-examining Counsel was unable to shake them and, despite his persona of wig and gown, seemed clumsy and blundering. Air and light seemed to have come back into the morning in that court and suddenly the Judge was in high spirits. The effect of truth is always like that, it is liberating.

I learned a great deal during that trial and afterwards. Some slight knowledge of the Common Law is the greatest help to the understanding of everything that happened in England four centuries ago. The great body of this law was settled in the Catholic centuries before the Reformation. It was a revelation to me to find that government by statute really started with the Tudors. The Magna Carta was not a Statute Law in the strict sense but rather the reduction of Common Law or a declaratory statement of it. But Statute Law was the vile instrument by which a State Religion was imposed upon the people and the *liber et legalis homo* was destroyed. It was not liberation which came in with the Act of Supremacy but enslavement and a crude violation of the rights of man. St Thomas à Becket suffered martyrdom in 1170 because he could not in conscience submit the spiritual to the temporal. He fled the Kingdom and for long lived in exile outside the jurisdiction of the King's Courts: 'Will nobody rid me of this turbulent priest?' Henry II did penance publicly for that crime. Four hundred years later Henry VIII succeeded all too well in ridding the realm of a great and good chancellor and in destroying by Statute the liberty of his subjects. It is a marvel that so much of the forms and appearance of old Catholic times continue.

During the trial, as the Barristers and Judge were

arguing a point of law on Condonation, there came to me a memory of a Scholastic Disputation at which I was present when I was a student in Rome. There were eight hundred students of all nationalities in a great hall. Cardinal Billot, S.J., was presiding and two of the great philosophers and theologians, Professors Hugon, O.P., and De La Taille, S.J., were taking part in the disputation. To be wrong in a definition or slovenly or inexact in the use of words meant sudden slaughter for a disputant. It was in Latin and was as lively and exciting as a football match. Here was a sluggish echo of that disputing.

Inevitably in that court there loomed up in one's memory the great and noble figure, the first layman to be Lord Chancellor of England, St Thomas More. All his predecessors had been clerics. The Lord Chancellor was the Keeper of the King's soul and the Keeper of the King's Seal. The sign of authority is in the Seal and is always carried by the holder of this office. When a Sovereign dies, this Seal remains with the Chancellor and his family and a new one is made. It was the Great Seal of England that James II threw into the Thames before he fled; but it had not the effect he desired because the revolutionaries had a new one made for Dutch William. It was the end of a noble tradition when Thomas More could no longer be the keeper of the King's conscience or of the King's soul. The religious bond that made the Common Law sacred was broken, let us hope not for ever. St Thomas surrendered most nobly to death by the tyrant. He saved his soul, perhaps his sacrifice may have helped Henry too towards salvation. He saved and surely sanctified the Common Law. There is still respect, if not reverence, for religion in the English courts. It may cling to these ecclesiastical robes which the Statute Law has not forced the Lawyers to discard. The Statute Law of the Reformation fills me with disgust. It seems to me only less bad than the Government by Decree under the Communists. Most of the great judges and lawyers are upholders of the Common Law.

Mr Don Harvey was our Counsel. He was an Irish Protestant who went to Trinity College, Dublin and then against all odds became a Catholic. His faith is the faith of the Irish Peasant, or as he would say, of the Irish peasant's wife. He is big and generous and to meet him you would not guess his profession. He is open in his manner and human; I suspect he is a poet. On one of his early visits to The Friars he wandered into the Conference Hall where I was trying to lead an open discussion with a number of enquirers of various religions or of none. Some were hostile. They regarded the 'Road to Rome', particularly that of the Middle Ages, as leading to a very dark and dismal wood or through swamps and unhealthy marshes. One of the most intelligent of the disputants intrigued Don Harvey as if he had seen him before. After the discussion came recognition; it was Doctor Alan Barnsley who had been a friendly rival in the University Philosophical Society. It was Don who had followed Yeats, Parnell and Oscar Wilde into the presidency of that Society. It was strange that he and Alan Barnsley should have met in such circumstances after twenty years. For both their families Aylesford has become a second home and Don undertook the defence only from great love. It gave him a lot of joy and an immense amount of bother and anxiety.

Now all was clear for the start of the building. Planning permission had been given in record time, but there had been delays with the foundations, as Father recounts:

After boring and exploration for weeks the conclusion is that the church and cloisters must be built on piles. This part of the work will cost £3,765. This seems a large figure but the piles must be sunk through twenty feet of mud to reach bedrock. The Foundation Stone will be laid on the Solemnity of the Feast of Carmel on July the 20th.

A non-Catholic engineer has offered his services for nothing and four stone-masons will soon be on their way from Italy. An excellent foreman has been engaged. I have been more than surprised by the offer of several builders from a Building Order in Belgium which now has ten thousand volunteers. In four years they have erected a thousand houses, thirty-one churches, twenty schools, cloisters and youth centres. These splendid builders who begin their every day by offering their sacrifices with the Mass, and live the Mass, will be in the spirit of Aylesford. All these, with our own small band of brothers, will build Our Lady's church. It will jump up.

During that May practically all the foundations of the original Church of the Assumption were uncovered. Father said:

The despoilers did their work well. They left the bones of the dead who were buried in the church but they took away the stones which covered them so that they will now remain for ever the nameless dead. We came upon them as if 'sown in the rich earth', in the old sanctuary. When the digging is over we shall place them all in a common tomb and sculpt upon the covering stone: *Et exultabunt ossa humiliata.* There were many broken floor-tiles and bits of glass which are now part of the Catholic England Exhibition at Allington. There were also some beautiful Gothic window-heads of the fourteenth century, now displayed in the cloisters. That is all they left: no broken image, no broken altar stone, nothing marked with the Sign of the

Cross. 'Proceede to the dissolution and the *defacing*.' That was the decree.

One evening when the digging was finished and the great walls of the tower and its buttresses were showing, the whole manifest like the great limbs of a giant, I was almost overwhelmed. It seemed as if something very sacred, prayer itself perhaps, were coming out of these foundations, released after long centuries, filling the whole place. 'Put love in and you will draw love out', wrote St John of the Cross. Satanic hatred has buried all the vestiges of the love and sacrifice of the early Carmelites. Only love can make them a living force again.

A few years ago the Duke of Northumberland almost decided to give us back the ruins of the old Abbey of Hulne near Alnwick. It was the twin of Aylesford and most venerable, having remained a desert house from the beginning. I remember explaining to His Grace how a bishop had drawn his crozier round that place and had given it to God for ever. Not very pleasant things were said in that rite of any who would dare to defy the dedication. I remember saying that if I were a layman and by some mischance it came into my possession, I should be eager to get rid of it very quickly! The fact of sacrilege is always dreary enough. Everywhere this land is full of it.

But the Church is not only the careful custodian of the past but is presently adding to the new shrines. At Lourdes they had lately added the great City of the Poor where six hundred non-paying guests can be put up at one time. That Summer Father twice led pilgrimages to Lourdes and since the phenomenally wet weather had made a muddy morass of the foundations so that no further work could be carried on, it was a good time to leave Aylesford for a few days.

It was seven hundred years since Our Lady had appeared to

St Simon Stock in England, and the Feast of Mount Carmel that year was to be given over to the Centenary Celebrations of the Scapular Vision. Within a hundred years of the vision the Scapular Devotion was well rooted in the Carmelite calendar and the wearing of the scapular as Our Lady's mantle had become one of the great pieties of Christendom. It later became the burial habit of Catholics everywhere. Father continues:

I heard a Carmelite bishop preaching in Lourdes saying that the choice of this feast was a *véritable revalorisation du scapulaire*; proof, in the Church's own empirical way, of the truth of the vision. Scholars need more proofs however and there is still talk of the scapular 'legend'. One of these dry people remarked to me recently that it is the 'wrong approach', but it was our Lady's approach, so what can we do now?

In the light of the criticism which, in some circles, is now surrounding devotion to the Mother of God, it is interesting to see what Father Malachy was writing on the subject after the Centenary visit to Lourdes in 1958:

I have been to Lourdes often and although in the past I have found myself saying that I preferred Fatima or Aylesford, I do not say it now. Our Lady is not in competition with herself and in the visions of Bernadette or the Children of Fatima there is no particular novelty. We are simply confronted with the Gospel again. Bernadette had a great desire for Holy Communion but she could not learn her Catechism. Her foster-mother at Bartres declared her hopelessly stupid and even when she returned to Lourdes to join the class there in preparation for First Communion on Corpus Christi, she could not learn enough. And it was not because she was stupid. The supernatural wisdom she possessed in such measure had taught her what could not be expressed in phrases or words, although the routine answers meant nothing to her. It is like the difference between eating an apple and having the accurate description of it. You could describe an apple and yet be starving to death. She did know what she wanted and it was pain and desolation to be denied it.

When the bishop came to Lourdes on February the 10th to confirm the other children, she was broken and in tears. Next day, from the poor room of the disused gaol, she set out to gather dry sticks to make a fire and it was then that she met Our Lady. It was after receiving Holy Communion that she was given the desire to go and see her for the last time. Lourdes is not the exaggerated cultus of Our Lady; beyond the spectacle and the singing and the torchlight, beyond Our Lady, is the mystery of the Eucharist and silence.

They pray in Lourdes, regardless. There is great humility there. The maimed and the deformed and the healthy are all one with their immense secrets and their 'secrets to themselves'. Prayer is always prayer, the work of the Holy Spirit in us. By prayer you enter a timeless world: 'The land I love best', said a holy man, 'is the land where I can pray best'. Wherever you can pray or have prayed, that is your native land. That is why many, after hard penance, feel 'lonely' when they leave Lough Derg. It is a wrench and a parting when pilgrims leave Lourdes or Aylesford. By the very act of praying we are being healed in body and spirit. Everybody is healed at Lourdes, it cannot be otherwise. People who don't pray are sick in spirit and are soon sick in body as well. It is very abnormal not to pray. God keeps up a continual creative conversation with all his creatures. With his human creatures it is secret and personal.

Not to answer nor to know how to answer is the worst malady. Suffering and pain would not be permitted if out of our misery we did not cry out to God. Anyhow, in the end we come to the time when the doctors cannot heal our bodies any more and we die.

I always think it is a pity they ever set up a Medical Bureau at Lourdes. Our Lord did not tell those he cured to show themselves to the medical men. On some he imposed silence. Somehow it does not seem like the French to make any concession to atheists or trouble about them at all. Chesterton gives the example of the French atheist who would melt down the church bells and make a statue to Lenin to put in the village square. Next day the Catholics would come and break it into little pieces.

In one of Maurice Baring's essays on Russia there is the story of the Communist instructor on atheism who harangued the inhabitants of a town for hours. At the end he held up a crucifix with a challenge: 'If there is a God let him strike me dead!' He threw down the crucifix and trampled on it. The people looked for a few moments in speechless horror. God did not strike him dead but *they* did. They tore him limb from limb. That could not happen in this country. There is a widespread practical atheism but there is no shape to it and no edge on it. It is blind and very dull. These unbelievers will go on building bigger and better gaols and clinics and schools and homes for the aged. But they will not build churches or schools for believers. They do not recognize the ordered world of charity. They cannot see any connection between crime and irreligion or between atheism and insanity.

Despite the Medical Bureau many of the miracles which happen at Lourdes go unproved and unrecorded. A few people hear of them and that is all. When I was there I heard one lady telling through the microphone how she had come there for resignation to die well from the malignant growth which was killing her. She had two baths and the second one was the signal for her complete cure. Now she was giving her life to the work of the Medical Bureau. Others I heard of, some proved, some merely transforming lives.

Miracles of conversion are numerous at Lourdes as they are at Aylesford. Every true conversion is a miracle of God's grace, having to do with the soul and its eternal destiny. Physical cures are nothing in comparison. I was told the following story of a strong and irresistible conversion during the War: the Polish gentleman who told it to me had himself verified the facts. This one does not involve one of the great shrines, but a convent. It is so boldly cut and definite that it can in some ways stand for the more tenuous lines of most of the conversions that come about.

It is the story of a Jewish officer of the Gestapo. It was an unusual role for a Jew but a Youth Organization had picked him because of his ruthless brutality. One evening he was told by a superior officer that a ghetto was to be liquidated the following night. At last his conscience awoke with a fierce recoil from such a crime against his own people. He went to the ghetto under cover of darkness and gave warning. The old people would not believe him but the young people fled to the forest. After the raid and the killing of the old people the superior officer was waiting for supper and wondering who could have warned them of the raid. The Jewish officer immediately replied, 'I did'.

At first the officer could not believe this because he thought he knew his man; and the Jewish officer, on the pretext of searching for another officer who had not turned up for supper, made his escape. Lying hidden in a turnip field, two sets of S.S. men passed within feet of him and did not see him. He slept and had a dream in which he was told to get up and go to a convent which he was shown. He found it without difficulty, they were the Polish Sisters of the Resurrection. The Reverend Mother said to him, 'You knock on our door in the name of the Lord, I'll take a risk'.

He was brought to an attic where he remained, quiet and patient, for some time. He found a Bible and for want of other reading read it form cover to cover. Then suddenly one day he said: 'I want to be baptized! I know enough. I have full desire.' The Reverend Mother baptized him. Then an order came from the Gestapo: the nuns were to leave the convent at once. They dressed the newly baptized in a nun's habit and give him a nun's bag and so he escaped again.

The young Jews he had saved had organized an underground movement in the forest and he found his way to them. The leader would still not believe in his good faith and condemned him to death. He was able to appeal to their sense of justice, and was reprieved and became one of them. He was an able man with 'full degrees'. After the War he became a Carmelite and is now a priest.

Perhaps the *morbidezza* of the Catholic England Exhibition at Allington was to be of use after all! Father had the great joy of receiving into the Church the first direct convert from the Open Door and he was able to report that several people who had stayed at the Castle during the Summer were 'on their way', which is of course much the same thing. The crowds at Allington and Aylesford were increasing, more than three thousand had passed through the Open Door alone, and Aylesford, as always, was packed on Sundays and all the great Feast Days. But the Italian stone-masons were late in arriving and bad weather was continuing to bedevil the piling opera-

F

tion. So events in the world took precedence in the November Newsletter.

In recent years there has been so much raking over of the political bones of Pope Pius XII that it is refreshing to be reminded of the impression he had left on the world and the faithful at the time of his death. Father said:

> We of the Faith know that the great office of the Pope calls for supernatural help. In the case of Pius it was forthcoming to an astonishing degree. His energy was incredible, that tall frail figure. To those who saw him it seemed as if light came from him with his blessing. In fact the strongest impression one had in his presence was that of great humility and simplicity. All the magnificence which surrounded him, which surrounds any Pope, belongs to the office of the Vicar of Christ and in comparison seems almost irrelevant. Chesterton once said that a Pope cannot just be 'respectable'. He must either come in the rags of St Francis or carry the royalty of Christ. After all, what are these crowns and precious vestments but rags in comparison with the shining apparel of the King of Kings? All this means that the man is swallowed up in his great office. Humanly speaking he is more lonely in the midst of the crowds and the acclaim than anybody upon this earth, and his life is more austere and exacting than the life of the strictest Trappist or Carthusian. This is the Pope's own description of his life:
>
> 'The Pope is never tired, the Pope never rests. The Pope must work until his death and then he passes his work to the next Pope who must also work to the very end.'

There was much speculation about who would be the next Pope. There seemed to be no outstanding claimant so that it looked as if it would be an open issue. Father could not resist another cut at the hardy perennial of St Malachy and his prophecies; but as he says, 'There was a Carmelite mixed up in it too'. Perhaps this made them more than usually apposite.

There are a hundred and eleven of the prophecies of St Malachy about the natures of the successive popes. They begin with Celestine II in 1143. They are said to be forgeries, but a life of St Malachy, 'written by one who boasts that he is the son of St Jarbath', upholds them. I discovered to my great interest that there is a Carmelite mixed up with this too. He was Père Gorgeu. He belonged to the monastery of Our Lady of Mount Carmel in Dieppe and in 1639 published an interpretation of the prophecies up to date. They are a marvellous collection and endlessly intriguing. They all have a poetic flavour and many of them are quite exact. Only a few of them are clear enough to have indicated, before the event, the Pope-to-be: *Fides Intrepida*, Indomitable Faith, rightly described Pius XI who confronted Hitler and the rest of them. He said, 'There has appeared in Rome a Cross which is not a cross', and he added, 'It will all go down in tears and blood'. And what could be more exact for Pius XII than *Pastor Angelus*? Then there is *Pastor et Nauta*, which, with a little stretching fits John XXIII. The next one will be *Flos Florum*, the 'Flower of Flowers'. Perhaps he will be the Cardinal of Florence: I seem to remember that is the city of flowers. After these come four intriguing ones and then comes *Petrus Romanus*, the Second Peter: 'He will reign in the last persecution of the Holy Roman Church. In many tribulations he will feed his flock. Rome will be destroyed. In the midst of these fearful happenings with holy constancy he will preach to his people.' The Latin is curious, really bad, it does not say that Petrus will be the last pope, but another is not given.

These prophecies are doubtfully Malachy's; but about Malachy the saint there is no doubt at all. After the Danish invasion the Irish Church was in a bad way. He was a reformer, or rather a restorer of the liturgy and of the sacraments to the people. He was all for the people, this greatly loving saint. He went to Rome to receive the Pallium and stayed at Clairvaux. He and St Bernard were well met. He called on St Bernard, going and coming, and left four of his companions there to be Cistercians, who were afterwards to found the Abbey of Mellifont in Ireland. That was in 1147 and in 1148 he was on his way to Rome again when he was taken ill and died at Clairvaux. St Bernard preached a glowing and tender panegyric on the saint he loved and afterwards wrote his Life. The whole community were around him when he was dying and in his farewell to them he said: 'Take care of me. I will not forget you if I be allowed; but I doubt it not for I have believed in God and have loved you, and charity will never cease.'

Then he prayed: 'O God, preserve them in thy Name and not these alone but all those who by my word and entreaty have been consecrated to thy service. . . .' All had their eyes fixed on the dying prelate but none perceived that he had breathed his last, so calmly did he fall asleep on the Festival of All Souls 1148. He was fifty-four. His life had burnt out.

It is only decent that I should honour St Malachy, my Patron, in the company of Pius and Bernard. The saint of Clairvaux was the preacher of the Crusades: he was the arbiter of Europe when Christian kings and princes were betraying Christendom to the Infidel. He was called 'the Harpist of Mary' and only she explains Him. There was a mysterious power in his preaching: *raptrix cordium* — ravisher of hearts. He was incredibly noble and attractive. Women used to have to hide their husbands when he came preaching because they would have followed him anywhere. I can say I got to know him through St Malachy:

when I was being received as a novice forty years ago I was terrified of getting the name Moses. The year before, my brother, Murtha, had been given Elias and another Eliseus. The Master of Novices asked me what name I would like. I in my innocence said, 'Malachy' – just because he was Irish and I liked the sound of it. I knew nothing else about him. He said: 'You shall have Brendan.' At the reception the names got mixed up and my habit was labelled 'Malachy' by mistake, so I got the name. But it was only recently that he became more than a name for me: two years ago I was in the Casa Beáto Nuño for October the 13th. It was raining. An American priest had lost his hat so I lent him mine. He was a Father Malachy and asked me if I ever prayed to St Malachy, and I had to say no. 'Neither did I', he said, 'until a few years ago. I was bothered a lot about funds for my church because I had taken on too much. I met a Monsignor whose church was dedicated to our saint. He said, "Try Malachy", and, oh boy, didn't he work! and quick.' Ever since, every day I have prayed to St Bernard and St Malachy. They must have great power with Our Lady.

John XXIII seems homely and kind, as they say in Ireland; he comes from good old stock. His family have owned their land for five hundred years and he belongs to the real nobility, with roots and tradition. A wise Provincial of ours, now dead, used to say about novices: 'Get them from large families and from the land.' And since he was a Wicklow man, he used to add: 'get them from the mountains if you can'. He himself was one of nineteen and, like the Pope, was born under the hills.

But at Aylesford, there in the middle of the twentieth century, in the seemingly leisurely flow of Church history, the work on the Shrine had reached a stage where more workers had to be used. It was simply a question of going over to Belgium to get them, and as always Father had a worthy armiger, named Douglas Smith.

He had been a mechanic in a motor factory and had spent some years doing a single operation; putting one wheel on lorries on an assembly line. Then a strike came and he just got into his car and drove to Aylesford. Since he was a very shy man this must have taken a lot of doing. He drove in, parked his car and was as nervous as could be. He told me at once that he was not a Catholic, not even baptized. In a forlorn way he asked me if he could stay. He would pay for his keep and work as well. I really suspected he was a car bandit which was a very rash judgment. This time he stayed and worked hard and a year later he turned up again. He had given up his job. It was unbearable misery in the factory, nobody contented or happy and everybody behaving like slaves! He had come to stay and to be instructed in the Faith, to work for love and to give the use of his car into the bargain. Now he is a Catholic and happy beyond telling. Perhaps he may stay with us for good.

We were instructed to go to Antwerp. There we were met by the Chaplain of the Building Order who drove at what seemed to be a fearful speed over the cobbled roads to a pretty town near Tongerloo. It was late so we were put into a hotel there for the night. Next morning we were taken for Mass to the Headquarters of the Building Order which was across the road from the Abbey of the Premonstratensian monks.

There are two enormous sheds covering a very large area. There was the chapel in one section, kitchens, dining-rooms and a dozen or more offices. It was mainly a gigantic store. The first sight on entry was a mountain of boots and shoes, all jumbled together and a little man who looked by contrast even smaller than he really was, slowly sorting the mountain. There was another mountain of paper with several workers putting it into baling machines. There were stacks of tinned foods and beds and furniture of all descriptions. The explanation of all this was forthcoming from the Chaplain. It has to do with a remarkable priest, a monk of the Abbey. I heard from other sources that this good priest had been cured of one of the killing diseases. He was shocked by conditions in the Refugee Camps and got permission from his Abbot to go out and preach and appeal for help.

Father Warenfried Van Straaten began his fiery apostolate in 1947. He started in Belgium and Holland: 'an ocean of untold misery and distress, a disgrace to mankind'. The good father knew that the Faith could not possibly survive unless active charity were given and at once. He preached everywhere and at all times. Sometimes he was preaching all day, two hours at a time. At the end of his sermons people gave him nearly everything they had. He was practical; he appealed for money and he got millions and millions of Belgian francs; he appealed for bacon and he literally got tons of it. It is admitted that he has a 'carisma' for this, a special gift of God.

There was an occasion at Fulda when there were twenty thousand Catholics gathered for conferences. It is not far from the Frontier and within a few miles were tens of thousand of refugees in miserable camps and without hope. Father Warenfried preached. Four bishops and a small army of building companions went round to collect. On that occasion they were given millions of francs, enough to buy the land and build a town. This is only one example.

At first his preaching was only to alleviate suffering in the way of an emergency, and than he realized that these many thousands, some of them born in the camps, would never know a home unless active charity was called forth on a large scale. Then it was, in 1953, that the Building Order came into being. It was first organized to help priests with the distressed multitudes they were trying to serve.

The Lay Director of the Building Order is Maurits Nachtergaele. He is a Doctor of Sociology of Louvain University. He is also a physicist and spent two years in the army as a transport officer. He had first-hand knowledge of the terrible living conditions and all this seemingly hopeless misery of his fellow men and women. He was given a terribly vivid sense of his communion with them in the bond of Faith, and it haunted him day and night. He began by giving one year of his life to this work; then he met the 'masterful monk' who swept him along with him.

In the first place he organized 'Chapels on Wheels' to bring spiritual consolation to the destitute. Then he realized that this was not enough and he decided to give his life to building homes. He has a powerful intelligence, hard and objective, yet behind all there is a driving power of love. He takes a modest salary to support his wife and children.

For a whole morning we were with him in his office. He drew diagrams, he gave us statistics of accomplishments which are staggering. During five years twenty-five thousand voluntary workers had been building in a vast network covering Germany, Italy, Holland, Austria, Switzerland, France and the Belgian Congo. Whole towns have been built with thousands of houses. The 'noiseless revolution of love and helpfulness' is directed by this powerful man from his temporary office in the sheds. Most of the talk was highly technical but we kept up somehow. The whole thing is staggering; but with love like that all things are possible. In Western Europe a hundred and sixty million are poorly housed or have no houses at all. In the whole world one family in five lives in houses not fit for animals, let alone human beings. These are the appalling figures which help us to appreciate the vast scale of the charity and the help that are needed.

Belgium was full of the ferment of an apostolic Christianity at that time.

This awakening, this stirring in the hearts of the young, is everywhere now. It is true in the highest sense that 'a terrible beauty is born'. Out of the 'Movement for a Better World' have come what are called 'Oases' – very many young people spontaneously vowing to live lives as perfect as they can make them. Douglas and I stayed for two nights at the Benedictine Abbey of St André near Bruges. There I met a tall frail priest who was a White Father. His health had broken down on the Missions, so he had returned to Belgium to found a movement called 'Sanctifier'. This was in 1949. He lives in the Abbey where the Abbot has allowed him to set up his headquarters. His purpose is to awaken a desire for holiness in the laity and it has been blessed by the late Pope and many bishops everywhere. All that he asks is that people should say one 'Hail Mary' every day that their souls should be awakened to grace. That is *all* he asks. Léon Bloy, so often quoted, has said: 'There is no sorrow but the sorrow of not being a saint.' There is really a deeper sorrow than this: that of not even *desiring* to be. The prevailing spirit of Jansenism makes the mention of spirituality distasteful even to Catholics; yet it is St Augustine who writes: 'The senses have their pleasures, shall the spirit be deprived of its own? Give me one who loves and he will understand what I am saying. Give me

one devoured with desiring and hungering and thirsting
for the living waters of the Eternal Fatherland. Give me
such a one and he will understand what I say'(Hom. St Aug.
Feria IV. Pentecosten).

At home a team of fifteen Brothers and lay workers were
carrying on without a hitch. Floods had delayed the construc-
tion of the foundations but, 'happily, Brother Eugene had
gone to a sale and bought ten Friesian heifers in calf. They are
a beautiful little herd and the General has helped by buying
three of them for us. The whole team set to and built cow
byres and a barn, a dairy and other buildings for the farmyard.
They were up in no time. This is another step towards being
self-supporting.'

There were English, Irish, Italians, Spaniards, Scottish, all
working together, and Brother Nuño with his team were turning out mountains of building blocks with the aid of the
cement mixer which had been freely loaned to them. Practically
all the gear they were going to need had come or had been
promised; and through the Newsletters and other sources,
money had come in as never before. With everything going
well, with, as is so often the case, the only problems being those
of human personality, Father was able occasionally to turn
his mind to reading around the subject. He became much
taken with the ideas of Madame Montessori, with her carefully
charted 'sensitive periods' when a child is best able to explore
the different spheres of experience, and began to alarm us
all about our children's education:

I have been reading a book on Madame Montessori by
E. M. Standing which has been a revelation to me. Every
mother with young children should read it. It is fascinating.
We have all been very badly mishandled and frustrated
from the age of two. I wonder we are not worse than we
are!

But whatever the mistakes in our upbringing, there is always conversion, or the possibility of conversion:

Converts from unbelief, I often think, are most fortunate. To them in maturity comes conversion and the sorrowful realization of St Augustine: 'Too late have I loved thee, O Ancient Beauty, O Truth, ever ancient, ever new! Too late have I known thee.'

Why Catholics should need persuasion to desire perfection is difficult to understand. They are afraid but often it is only fear of the first step. 'One step beyond mediocrity and you are saved.' Father Faber says there are sacraments for sin but none for lukewarmness. Dante, when he was being led by his guide from hell through purgatory to heaven, saw on the outskirts of purgatory a host of pale uninteresting shades of the dead. He asked of his guide, 'Who are these?' His guide, turning to him impatiently, said, '*Non raggianammo di loro ma guarda e passa.*' 'Let us not reason about them but look and pass on.' The damned in hell were terribly, tragically interesting. The light of Mary flamed round the circles of purgatory; but those who were neither hot nor cold were not worth looking at. If young Catholics are not converted a second time they become smug, self-sufficient and full of conceit. Haven't you met them and aren't they awful? That studied conforming to worldliness and respectability! So early! Better the poor beggar man who has not succumbed to that. We must all desire conversion. Don't be afraid of it. Don't slander God no matter what you do. There are sudden conversions and slow and painful ones . . .

And here Father gives one of his many splendid stories of conversions:

This one concerns a lady who is now over eighty. I

hope I do not exaggerate her age. She originally belonged
to Finland and when she was a small baby her nurse
wheeled her from a busy street into a Catholic church.
There she left her – pram and all – in front of Our Lady's
altar, presumably asking the saint to mind her until she
would return from her shopping. The baby was enrap-
tured, gazing at the Madonna all the time the nurse was
away. She cried loudly and long when she was taken home.
Our Lady minded her well. She remained with her all her
life. After a sufficiently long experience of boring religion
the beautiful inviting Madonna of her memory prevailed.
She was received into the Church by Cardinal Canali in
Rome.

Perhaps she saw Our Lady at a 'sensitive period', who
knows? In any case she wrote to Father when she was a very
old woman:

'I have had a bad accident and injured my spine and had
to be flat in bed four weeks when my doctor said, "I have
something to tell you. In my opinion you will never walk
again." I replied, "Thank you". I added, "I have something
to tell you: that I will not see you again and if you come I
will put cotton wool in both ears and shut my eyes and lips.
We have strong wills in my country, Finland, and Our
Lady will help me." Now the miracle has happened. I can
walk and when it does not rain I can, with a stick, go into
the garden.'

Someone has said that the future of literature will have
much to do with cinematic techniques. Certainly that flash
of the shutter on the aristocratic old woman with the stick
in the rain-washed garden states so much so quickly that I
am suddenly struck by the poignant style of these letters, the
flashing insights and the slow deliberations. They are like

'good Catholic talk which though it may begin with potatoes may end with the Most Holy Trinity'. In all of them there is a circular quality: lapidary sayings, images and exhortation complete one another and yet leave gaps which only truth can fill. In the section which follows, most of it written in 1960, I have left in some of the hiatuses in thought, supplying connections only where I was in danger of shortening tenuosities to a breaking point.

Here is Father writing about 'The Mass and Prayer'.

To go to 'follow a Mass' is a common saying in Catholic countries. The ancient ritual of it leads you inevitably to Calvary, to that still point. It leads your life for you for a blessed hour. You have only to surrender. In Irish the word for the Mass comes from the Latin *offertorium*, the offering. In Welsh too it is *yr offeren*, from the same word. In Wales, in the old time, the worship of the Mass was 'seeing God'. This vivid 'seeing' is a Celtic way of worship and of prayer. Faith for the Celts was the light in which they 'saw'. Péguy, whom I so often quote, knew this. In his *St Joan*, Madame Gervaise says to Joan, 'What others know, you *see*. The Catechism, the Church, the Mass, you don't just *know* them, you *see* them; prayer, you don't just say your prayers, you didn't only say them, you saw them.'

Perhaps this is how grace works in the fierce nature of the Celts. St Patrick, who wasn't a Celt now I come to think of it, had this *seeing* prayer. So had the wandering saints from Ireland for six centuries. Dewi Sant in Wales had it and the saints of Britanny and Galacia, that Province of Spain and the northern frontier of Portugal. That is where the Celts came from, so I have read somewhere. They were the 'senseless Galatians' of St Paul, bewitched by too much light. The desert monks had it in the fourth century and now I don't know where my argument has gone.

In the last analysis, perhaps, all our arguments may be widely astray because the Holy Spirit is infinitely original. But the best explanation of it all is that where there is love there is always vision. You can know *what* things are; but you cannot know why they are or what they signify without love. The saints were those who loved and their love gave them the bewildering liberty of the sons of God. Perhaps the best definition of a saint is one for whom God has become real and for whom his creation has become real. It is one thing to know God. Everybody really knows that he *is*, else how could they deny him? But few are *aware* of him, only the saints are fully aware. 'What joy!' exclaimed the Curé d'Ars, 'to be aware of God. United to God, loved by God, wholly with God, wholly to please God. O how splendid! To be a King is a sorry business. A King is only for men! But to belong to God, to be entirely God's without reservation, there is nothing more magnificent than that.'

This reminds us of St Teresa of Avila and her practical common sense. 'Serve God', she says, 'as grandees the King of Spain, for nothing.' For Teresa prayer was 'loving converse with God', for the Curé it was like 'being two good friends together'. And the Curé goes on to tell us of his prayer as a boy. 'When I was alone in the fields I prayed aloud but when I was with others I prayed in a whisper. There was at least some relaxation from work in those days. We rested after our midday meal. I used to lie full length on the ground as the others did: I pretended to sleep and prayed as hard as I could. I did not have to rack my brains as I do nowadays.'

This is reminiscent of St Patrick's Confessions. How difficult it is to put the saints into their proper centuries when they belong to all the centuries.

I started with the idea that this 'seeing' prayer was a Celtic way, only to discover now that it is Carmelite. It is like the prayer of Elias. It cannot be learned in books nor can it be reduced to a system. If a heart is full of the love of God, prayer will come. It is like two good friends together walking along a road – snatches of conversation and silences. Carmelites walk and pray with the Mother of God since she has been given to them by the Holy Spirit of God. There is nothing complicated about *her*. She awakens. What has more power to awaken than love? That is why they call her the Mother of Fair Love.

But there is a way of silent prayer which makes recollection easy. Suppose you were content to be simple and turn over in your mind for the space of fifteen minutes a wordless prayer; short and repeated over and over again. It would ride above the distractions. Before long you would be surprised into praying. It will be your joy. They could be short prayers: 'Lord Jesus Christ, Son of God, have mercy on us. Lord Jesus Christ, Son of God, have mercy on me a sinner. Lord Jesus Christ, by the prayers of Our Lady, have mercy on us. Most Holy Lady, Mother of God, pray for us sinners.' It will be given to you how to pray; you could use any one of these. In a short time you will be able to say the Rosary too without distraction: with this kind of prayer you don't have to 'rack your brains'. . . .

If a man loses God he loses somehow his own presence. You sometimes get the impression that he isn't there at all. If he does not talk to God he loses the faculty of talking to men. There is nothing *in* a man of this sort. He is rooted in nothing and has nothing real to talk about. He has opted out of God's creation. He is in isolation and has nothing, not even the trees, the mountains or the sea or bird song or dawn. He was meant to be a man but isn't. He cannot be an animal: he can only be a monster.

Father has also said that these 'monsters' are 'missing all
the fun'. Looking from the outside at the hardships of the
religious life this may seem an obscure remark; but in the
following passage he does something to clarify it:

A sense of humour is a great gift. Humour is a part of life
whereas caricature or satire or exaggeration are not, though
they may contain truth. St Joseph was surely a quiet man
with no loud noise or explosive laughter in his workshop:
neither was he sad. He certainly was not solemn. And how
difficult charity is: I mean how difficult to use great power
in a happy way even when doing good. There is high
comedy in all almsgiving when you come to think of it.
St Joseph had only his strength and goodness to give; but
I think he did not take them too seriously. We are always
giving away someone else's property, and that someone
else is God.

I once heard or read a story of a priest who was walking
up and down the platform of a very busy city station. While
he was musing, in the midst of crowds, and meditating, a
train arrived. From a first-class carriage descended a youth,
much over-dressed and self-important. There followed him
down the platform a number of trucks piled high with
expensive luggage. The priest was much intrigued to know
who was this flamboyant personage. He discreetly looked at
the labels on the baggage and on every piece was written
'Not yours'. He was shocked that this young prig should
advertise his insolence in this fashion. Then it dawned on
him that these words are written all over the universe.
This great truth is really what underlies all true comedy.
With all reverence we can say that God created the world in
great good humour. You have seen ducks on a pond and
lambs in a field – and you may have read Chesterton's
poem on a donkey! This is why we must not be incredulous

nor hasty but contemplate long and patiently the interventions of St Joseph, the great Patriarch. In them is no implied harsh reproach but a pleasant righting of affairs which we have solemnly bungled and mismanaged. We say: 'O faithful and prudent servant, watch over our weakness and *inexperience*.' We shall always be needing him. We are so sure of ourselves, so solemn and self-sufficient. We shall always be making mistakes until the end. We may never see the joke.

Father tells many stories in his Newsletters about the interventions of St Joseph. It would be impossible to generalize, since in such matters there's always infinite originality and always, too, there is the touch of humour and strong element of 'do it yourself'. This hard-working saint does not seem to be going to give things away on a plate or to make matters *too* easy.

Douglas Hyde reports an Easter sermon by a priest somewhere in Asia to a poor flock. 'Christ was God', he told them. 'But you do not have to look for the Risen Christ in an empty tomb. You need not search for God in the garden. He is in your own hands. As you use those hands tomorrow in your work on the plantation or in the market or the office or wherever you may be, you will be co-operating in, and continuing God's own work of creation. God is in your hands.'

As the preacher said these words an old coolie in a soiled white gown looked at the backs of his thin hands, with their great veins like cords and their broken nails; then he turned them over and picked, meditatively, at the corns across the palms. The preacher continued his sermon, but the old man went on turning his hands this way and that in wonderment. 'God was in his hands.'

So, the quick cinematic flash, the embodied insight and we

are back again, in the same letter, with the Resurrection; which is of course the heart of the gaiety; for with only dead death at the end of everything, what *could* there be to laugh about?

In one of Maurice Baring's books about Russia which I loved, loaned and lost and which I can never find again, he tells the story of an atheist hired by the Government to go into the villages to collect the people around him and prove to them that there is no God. It was his custom to harangue the simple peasants for hours at a time. When he had finished the priest was invited to answer him. On this particular occasion the priest stepped forward on the platform and gave to the people the Resurrection formula of Holy Russia: '*Resurrexit Christus*'. All the peasants rose at once to their feet and gave him back the answer – '*Christus vere resurrexit, Alleluia*'. The priest sat down.

St Paul startled his hearers with the sudden cry: 'If the dead do not rise, then Christ has not risen either; and if Christ has not risen then our preaching is groundless and your faith too is groundless: All your faith is a delusion; you are back in your sins. . . . If the hope we have learned to repose in Christ belongs to this world only, then we are unhappy beyond all other men; but no, Christ has risen from the dead, the first fruits of all those who have fallen asleep.' When astonished people heard this for the first time I am sure there was nobody who argued with St Paul about an empty tomb. They said he was mad. They had to say something; but they must have known very well that he wasn't. It is hard now for us to realize the joy of that good news heard suddenly. The apostles were running to tell it and they are running still. . . . It is not in the thunders, in the shattering triumphs we walk with Christ, but in the sunlit world after the Resurrection when he appeared often and lingered long with his own. To everyone who has the Faith and is wakened he is the Stranger who walked with two sorrowful men one evening on the road to Emmaus and, 'Behold, fire was kindled in them when he spoke'.

It is said that at least once in life each one walks with Christ to Emmaus. As Mauriac says in *The Son of Man*: 'There is no encounter in which we do not encounter him, no solitude in which he does not join us, no silence where his voice is not heard, deepening rather than troubling that silence.'

Of the Four Last Things, Death, Judgement, Heaven and Hell, there is a varying emphasis in the Newsletters. About judgement and hell we hear little, save that, with Dante, Father considers that hell would be *Duro, duro*, 'hard, hard', and cold too. About death, or rather the hope of immortality, there is much; and there is a great deal, too, about heaven, or at least about the inhabitants of heaven. About contemporary 'problems' there is considered comment which is never swayed by the mass movements of opinion which seem to trouble so much of the Church. Here is his opinion, written in 1959, on Birth Control:

A few weeks ago I was visiting a Tertiary Chapter in Manchester on a Sunday. That night I was invited to look at a television programme. Archbishop Heenan was being interviewed about Birth Control, so were half a dozen others. He was given a minute to say that it was not just the Church's law which was being broken, but God's law. The Archbishop of York, the Anglican, was vague and hesitant, saying that in certain circumstances it might be allowed. Sir Julian Huxley was certain that the world was over-populated and becoming increasingly so at the rate of thirty millions a year, and was recommending something more devastating than the atom bomb. Then there was Bertrand Russell, an impressive skeleton of a man over eighty, who looked like an image of pure thought but with a mechanical voice, pitilessly logical and all wrong – on the side of death. These materialists were saying that a woman had diminished chances of life after the sixth child. They had practically all the broadcasting time and spoke last to millions of young married people. I was horrified; they were certainly trying to frighten them into not having children when they could know as scientists that the earth is full of God's plenty; but that half of it is destroyed for gain or wasted, through the wickedness of men. I was horrified that men should seek to take over the providence of God like that; because really that was what they were doing, with their plans and suggestions and calculations, and it was all deadly and decadent. God forgive them. And now the secretary here tells me that according to United Nations statistics the world production of food is increasing faster than the growth of population, so even in their own field these men are wrong.

These scientists always give me the impression that they know nothing whatever about life in its essence. This morning I had a letter from a Tertiary in Canada. She and her husband are living far away from the ordinary amenities of life and have suffered great hardship; but she ends her letter with lyrical praise of God's providence, saying she would not exchange one of her seven children for all the riches in the world.

A few days after that I had the great privilege of receiving at Allington the Spanish Foundress and four of the missionary Sisters of an Order which was founded eleven years ago to send nurses and doctors to India and the Belgian Congo to care for lepers. Already they have more than a hundred members, all young, and I found that they *all* come from large families. The Foundress, herself a very noble woman, told me that her father was one of sixteen and her mother one of fourteen; and from one of these families had come three foundresses of religious congregations. She herself was one of eleven. What dignity and what abounding grace and vitality they had. Meeting them for a few hours redeemed a whole week of fog and misery. Listening to those scientists made one sick!

Although life in our cities is sometimes made confusing by the sudden movements of charity and altruism which disturb the even flow of selfishness, it is still a shock to meet people who are quite simply, good. As Father Malachy once said: 'You never need to diagnose holiness'. And, just to see these nuns, most of whom come from large happy families, is to suffer the pain and self-dislike which their whole acceptance of us brings with it. It is to wonder too, about the 'reasonableness' of the need for smaller families. In a strange way, to see these women is to look back into the centuries, not to that maligned mediaevalism, but to an almost legendary humanity which in the modern world is so attenuated and so rare.

After the War, a German poet was writing: 'The base alone still rule, the noble perished, belief is washed away and love is wilted.' He was cursing the City as 'a pile of smoke and dust and fog'; and he proclaimed the birth of a new nobility: 'not known by shield or crown but by the light within their eyes'.

This is true now. This light divides humanity. They have it or they have it not. There is no gainsaying it, for it is a fact. At Aylesford, when the Sisters come with the children the place is full of light. This light can radiate, can shine on us all and give us a temporary splendour. As Belloc says: 'Holiness has about it a power like none other. It convinces, attracts and confirms. It also reveals. I take it like cold water in a wilderness during the heat of the day.'

Age is the revealing thing. Men who have lived well are better with age and men who have lived ill are much worse with it. But holiness in old age is amazing, it has the hint of paradise! 'Pope Benedict XV had it, although he was not tall or commanding. Once in his private chapel with several students [continued Father Malachy], I assisted at his Mass and received Holy Communion. To me, kneeling, I noticed that he had to reach up, so tiny was he! I saw his face of parchment and that light in his eyes which I have never forgotten. This strange impression is made quite independently of physique or figure.'

And Belloc saw Cardinal Mercier, another saint:

The old man put on his scarlet gown to see the Ambassador, who was standing beside me, but in me he renewed the Faith; and I can assure you that my Faith, to be renewed is like cleaning a sword that has lain out in the mud of fields for years. But all things have a proof consonant to themselves: for measurable things, measurement, and for human things, the common sense of man; but for the Faith, holiness or the distant recognition of it. Whatever produces *that* is *it*.

In the Spring of 1959 Father had been staying at the Esperance Nursing Home at Eastbourne again as his diabetes had been very bad. While there he was reading *Letters from Hilaire Belloc*, edited by Robert Speaight, and he commented:

Hilaire Belloc rose out of the murk and mist of the last century like a portent. He was like a battleship coming out of a fog. He had so many gifts that he could deal on a grand scale with all experience. Whether he is writing of the sea or the mountains or the great plains or peoples, you find clarity and judgement. In his writing it is as if the heroic past of Europe and the Faith, the spirit of Europe and Antiquity were in him or marched behind him. He was a lay figure, a prophet and a sure one; but he stands up in this time as Augustine and Aquinas in theirs. He was powerful, disciplined, clear in style and form. He had such light and clarity that 'fog-mind' in England troubled him unduly.

He had a grievance: he was passed over for a Fellowship at Oxford. He worried about poverty all his life. In great humility he confesses openly to a 'monologue of complaints upon my trials'. All this was to the good. A contented Belloc one cannot imagine. He believed, he had certitude, the Faith was a *command*; but there was no 'sap' in it, no inner consolation. 'Of the higher things I know nothing', he said. He abhorred the sloppy cheer-mongers, with their advice to 'look at the bright side of things', and he says, 'I do tell you that seeing things in the round, as they are, however hard, is worth all the consolations in the world. It is the sacrament of truth.'

Belloc knew all about 'invincible ignorance', but 'invincible impudence' made him furious and fierce. In his later life he could not understand how the world around could pretend to remain ignorant of its principal object, the Church. Hostility he understood; but, 'not knowing anything about it is ridiculous'. His final conclusion after a long lifetime is: 'There are not many disputing for the soul of man; there are but two: the Faith and Nothingness.'

He died on the Feast of Our Lady of Mount Carmel and there are letters written towards the end of his life which show that for him too, 'the fountain flowed'. In one he says, 'I have put into this letter, which I fear is too long,

not one word of enthusiasm. . . . But within myself, when-
ever I touch these things, and that main issue of the Faith,
I hear strong music. And it is the only connection in which I
hear it.'

Belloc's name is always linked with that of Chesterton, at
one time they seemed like twin pillars of the Church. About
Gilbert Keith Chesterton Father reminisced at the end of
1960:

Thirty years ago I met G. K. Chesterton and his wife·
We were travelling in the same third-class carriage from
London to Salisbury. His wife was a frail delicate person.
Sitting beside her he seemed large as a mountain. He was
reading novels. They were dog-eared and occasionally a
chuckle came from the great man – he seemed as if he
were really devouring them. Later it happened that we
were staying in the same hotel in Salisbury. After dinner he
fell into the hands of American tourists and I noticed that
when he was standing he was very tall and had a distinguished grace of movement.

He went out with them and returned at ten p.m. I was
sitting in a corner of the lounge doing some reading in
connection with my visit. He had a great reverence and
was most courteous and had such deference that it made
me, as a young priest, uncomfortable. We talked for two
hours into the night. I remember his saying quite seriously
that if he were a dictator he would suppress all newspapers
and magazines and give the human mind a rest. He said
that the prejudice against the Church and the Faith which
he and Belloc were facing was so blind and unreasonable that
they had no time or opportunity to write about the Catholic
mystics. The writers of his generation, he said, were like
soldiers defending the city. There was no opportunity of
knowing the treasures inside the gates. He was especially

interested in St Teresa of Avila and her Sister of Lisieux. He spoke of them with profound knowledge and veneration. He seemed to be overwhelmed by the riches of the Faith and declared, 'In the matter of fullness, of richness and of variety, the whole advantage is now with the ancient cause'. I noticed his great power and easy way of thinking which was deceptive. When he said: 'It is like this . . .' you had both an argument and an illumination.

In one of his articles Chesterton had said something very germane for the 1960's: 'The moral is that no man should desert that Catholic civilization. It can cure itself but those who leave it cannot cure it. Not Nestorius nor Mahomet nor Calvin nor Lenin have cured, nor will cure, the real evils of Christendom; for the severed hand does not heal the whole body.' Father says that 'you feel, when you have read this, that a thousand questions have been answered and that a great truth has been lighted up in a flash. . . .'

Since Belloc and Chesterton, the defence and exposition of Christian belief seems to have come as much from without-the-walls as from within. Simone Weil, Adolph Reinach, Henri Bergson and Charles Péguy, who were either *créant mais non pratiquant* or unbaptized, and Père Teilhard de Chardin, with his proscribed writings, were great lovers of the Church. But from their positions these people have written most perceptively about the Faith and much of their work has proved relevant to the spirit of *aggiornamento*.

Henri Bergson was a Jew, he died in 1942. He was one of the great names in the history of philosophy, famous as a professor of the Sorbonne and the Collège de France. He has written glowing pages on the mystics. He was humble before a *fact*. The great contemplatives and their experiences were facts, an undeniable part of human knowledge.

Nobody has written more nobly about them, an apologist from without! Jacques Maritain, a Protestant convert to the Faith and now accepted as the greatest lay expert on Thomism, acknowledges his own and his wife, Raïssa's, debt to Bergson. 'The movement of Bergson's thought towards Thomism was the greatest consolation of my life', he says; and Raïssa adds, 'The pity of God caused us to find Henri Bergson'.

Bergson was profoundly influenced in his work on the mystics by his discoveries of the working of the supernatural in their lives. Writing about the human soul, he says: 'Now it is God who, having taken full possession of her, is acting through the soul in the soul. The union is total. The result is an irresistible impulse which hurls her into vast enterprises. A calm exaltation of all her faculties makes her see things on a vast scale only, and in spite of her own weakness, produces only what can be mightily wrought. Above all, she sees things simply, and this simplicity which is equally striking in the words she uses and the conduct she follows, guides her through complications which she apparently does not even perceive. An innate knowledge, or rather an acquired ignorance, suggests to her straightway the step to be taken, the decisive act, the unanswerable word.'

For Bergson, love is like a terrible fire at the very heart of the Universe. He was a believer before he died but he did not become a Catholic because he did not wish to be separated from his own race in their trial. He said: 'I want to remain among those who tomorrow will be persecuted, but I hope that a Catholic priest will be good enough to come, if the Cardinal Archbishop authorizes it, to pray at my funeral. Should this authorization not be granted it would be necessary to approach a Rabbi; but without concealing from him, nor from anyone, my moral adherence to Catholicism as well as my expressed and first desire to have the prayers of a Catholic priest.'

When he died the almost bare walls of his room bore two engravings of great masters, both representing the Assumption of the Blessed Virgin. Very nearly his last testimony to the mystics was: 'They have blazed a trail along which other men have passed.' He was not concerned only with what made the contemplative but he surely sensed what love *does*. Following the Apostle he saw and confessed that the mystics have been raised to the ranks of *adjutores dei* – helpers, co-workers of God. 'The love which consumes is no longer simply the love of man for God, it is the love of God for all men. Through God and in the strength of God, he loves all mankind with a divine love.'

Douglas Smith, the man whom Father had at first taken for a car bandit but who had settled down at Aylesford to work without payment, had been caught on the slippery slope to holiness. He left Aylesford and became a Cistercian monk. John D., another good worker for Aylesford, followed Douglas into the Cistercian Order. Father wrote:

Needless to say, if I had the planning of their lives, they would be here still. I would put them in chains rather than let them go. But this proves all that I am for ever saying. There is no real astonishment, no real excitement, outside the Faith. What unpredictable things can happen to us all. We set out on a seemingly commonplace path and we never know where it will take us.

In a later letter Father Malachy continues this theme:

There is a principle of the theologians that: 'To those who do what in them lies, God will not deny his grace.' As Péguy says: 'Grace is insidious, grace is cunning and

unexpected. It is as obstinate as a woman and like a
woman is as tenacious and clinging. Put it out of the
window and it will enter by the door. The men that God
wants to have he *has*. . . . When grace does not come
directly, it comes indirectly. When it does not come from
the right it is coming from the left. When it does not come
straight it is because it is coming on a curve and when it
does not come on a curve it is because it is coming in bits.
When it wants somebody it has him. It does not take the
same road as we do: it takes its own. It does not even take
its own for it never takes the same road twice. When it
does not come from above it is because it is coming from
below, and when it does not come from the centre it is
because it is coming from the circumference. And the
water from this spring, when it does not come forth as a
gushing fountain, may trickle like the water that oozes
under the dykes of the Loire.'

This is Péguy's way [Father comments]. The way of the
French peasant, a good way, torturing a thought, making
it clear by repetition.

For a real writer it must be a great penance to have to
repeat appeals for money. In 1960, as in 1949, the Newsletters
had to continue their begging. But Father could always alter
his own guise a little:

The last scene of that tremendous mystical drama, *The
Satin Slipper* by Paul Claudel, is most lovely. Roderigo, the
ex-Viceroy of the Indies, is being taken to Majorca to be sold.
The ragpicker nun comes on board the ship, 'to glean the
sea for every convent in Spain'. She bargains with the
soldier for a heap of odds and ends of every kind, the
nun examines and moves the clothes about with her stick.
'What nobody wants, what you throw out; that's what
she spends her time hunting and gathering.' Roderigo,

with only half his complement of legs, appeals to her: 'Mother Gleaner! Mother Gleaner! Since you are a connoisseur, why don't you take me too, with the old flags and the broken pots? You will get me very cheap. I want to live in the shadow of Mother Teresa. God made me to be her poor servant. I want to shell beans at the convent gate. I want to wipe her sandals, all covered with the dust of heaven.' The nun, still bargaining, gets him for nothing, with a cauldron thrown in. 'Take it', says the soldier. 'Take everything! Take my shirt!'

I am becoming more and more like that old rag picker nun [Father Malachy says]. What nobody wants, what you throw out, that is what the Newsletter is gleaning for the Mother of God. Old jewellery, rings, gold! We have had lots of knitted socks and linen and other practical things and we need more. . . .

In 1959 he wrote:

For three weeks we have been in credit with the bank. I had an unexpected letter from the Manager in which he said, 'I feel it is in order not only to congratulate you on your magnificent progress with the building, but also on the very healthy appearance of the banking account'. Strangely enough that gave me a great feeling of disappointment and anticlimax. The implication of prosperous and prospering mendicants was too much and I declare to you that I felt momentarily as if all my Faith had gone, and I had as much consolation as a successful business man or a retired bank manager. Isn't it very strange? But I have recovered Faith again because now at the end of October the bills have been paid and there is ample room again for God's providence.

And by September 1960 the Sanctuary Church was so far

advanced that they were ready for the installation of the great Madonna commissioned from Michael Clark, the son of Philip Lindsey Clark who had done so much of the magnificent sculpture for the Restoration. Michael's work later won an important prize so that when it arrived it was by way of being a 'moment'.

There is an atmosphere about events at Aylesford. It was an event when the great figure of the Glorious Virgin came on the Feast of the Assumption. It did not arrive in a gigantic packing case but was wrapped in two linen sheets. There were instructions from the sculptor that the sheets were to be returned to Katie, his wife. It reminded me of how the small image before which Lucy, Jacinta, and Francisco used to pray in their parish church came here from Fatima wrapped in a clean shirt, and it set me thinking of much else besides. The figure was lifted from the lorry and laid in St Anne's Chapel, a huge parcel. Percy, the foreman, was full of excitement; the next day he set about building a ramp and, before the afternoon, the pedestal for the large figure was in place. On that particular day a big group of Dominican Sisters had come on pilgrimage. We were driven by the rain to say our rosaries in the Tribune in full view of the operation. A dozen voluntary workers carried the great heavy thing up the ramp. We had just finished the Glorious Mysteries when it was perfectly secured into position and Percy unveiled it, no longer a thing but a worthy sister of all the great madonnas in Christendom! It is of wood, nine feet high. Gold leaf has been laid on judiciously and lacquered. It is a great work and inspired, as I knew it would be. After the unveiling a little red-headed boy of nineteen months escaped from his mother and ran up the ramp towards the Glorious Virgin. I am sure it was the sign language again, and prophetic. It was a ceremony that could not have been arranged, it just happened.

Soon after the ceramic 'flames' by Kossowski had been arranged at the head of the new statue, there was a television broadcast from Aylesford. About it Father wrote:

After my part was over I felt as a soul must feel, freshly released from purgatory. Then, as the Mass went on, I had time to reflect. Above us in the Sanctuary were the largest lamps I have ever seen, three on each side and one in the centre, all directed on the altar and on the Glorious Virgin. I was thinking of the Antiphon in the Office of Our Lady, *Qui elucidant me habebunt vitam aeternam*, 'Those who throw light on me shall have eternal life'. The light brought that gold-painted figure into millions of homes. Many non-Catholics wrote to say what a welcome sight it was. They understood her when they did not understand the Mass. But they loved it all the same and sensed its mystery.

So the new Sanctuary was *there*. In some strange way it had acquired validity with the masses by appearing on television. Father fears that many people live their lives at such a remove that they do not believe anything until it has been either reported in the papers or viewed on the screen. But it had also really touched a great many people and letters poured into Aylesford saying so.

So there she was, floating at last, this heavy ship of a place with its golden figure-head, even if she had somehow set sail with the ragpicker nun aboard! Symbolically it seemed right that, facing the high seas at last, Father's end-of-season journey should have been to Dachau. He had been there during the previous year on a pilgrimage of priests and clerics organized by the Hon. Mrs Bower and Group-Captain

Cheshire to make a vigil of reparation in that place of terrible happenings. On that occasion he had written:

It was an experience quite beyond sharing or communicating. I once heard a dramatic recital of Dante's *Inferno* by the greatest living speaker of the Italian language. I shall never forget it. It was twenty years ago and one terrible line of description was stabbed into my memory by the power of the narrator, several adjectives leading up to the last one which was *duro. L'Inferno e duro.* It is not only a hardened heart which can never love or share because for Dante hell is where there is no love, but even in the physical landscape of hell there is hardness, harder than hard. Strange I had not realized the content of that word until we were being conducted round the crematorium and the gas chambers. Massive walls, iron doors, strong as a fortress and even now, the memorials over the mass graves with their lapidary lines of record, hard, everything hard, as hard as hell.

The huts remain in their hard geometry. There are thousands of refugees living in these huts now and yet it seems a city of the dead, even now a strange lost world. There are wide spaces between the interminable rows of buildings but you seldom see an open door. The outsides are dull and deadly in their sameness. The streets are not made and the wind whirls the dust into your face. There is a chapel which has been arranged in part of these long sheds. It is without pretensions but everything in it is good. It has a simplicity and a purity about it. It is well-cared for. Its floors are of wood and scrubbed clean. I discovered afterwards that here the condemned victims were kept before their death.

Dachau is a monument of evil. Few Germans go there it is so shameful. Munich is a Catholic city but Catholics will not go, even to pray. Many say that these terrible camps should be exorcized because evil is in them still. But you cannot exorcize emptiness and nothingness. Dachau is a waste, dry and lifeless as the dust which blows into your eyes and mouth. Never before has the living image of God in man been so venomously attacked by Satan. This is the key to all the horror. Men with immortal souls were reduced to mere numbers. You get tired listening to that fearful count – always thousands mounting up to millions. In Dachau alone more than two thousand priests died; so many priests, consecrated virgins, so many men of genius, the poor common men, all reduced to a common misery, eventually to dust. Death transports, the blood ditch, the mobile scaffolds, the progressive butchery, the killings and beatings and millions starved and made to work until they fell, a lost world without pity or mercy!

These with all the additions of cruelty! There is only one explanation and it is simple. These men were possessed by devils. Many believe Hitler was possessed. The devils attack God in man. They betray themselves by a mysticism of evil. It is not ordinary. There is a glint of hell in it. It is always the same pattern because the devil is monotonous. The only difference is in the tremendous modern apparatus of evil in the hands of men possessed. It was the same in Spain, in Mexico. It could happen anywhere. The devils cannot enter or possess human souls. They can possess the bodies of men. Their world is on the fringe of the soul, in the world of the senses. Their action is in the seat of emotions and morbid states. The body is the way to the soul which they cannot enter. They explore it with a fierce inquisitiveness. We must not say it is in the nature of Germans to be cruel and abominable. If we leave out Satan and his angels that is the only conclusion. We would

G

be very wrong. 'I saw Satan like lightning falling from heaven.' And of Judas it was said, 'Satan entered into him'.

He, the evil one, is not a new invention. Our Lord commanded devils, drove them headlong from the bodies of men. The Church which is Christ to us does not forget or ignore Satan, 'and all wicked spirits'. The prayer which is said after Mass every day is an exorcism calling upon Blessed Michael the Archangel. The Church is not play-acting. These prayers and exorcisms are in her ritual, to be *used*. [The prayers after Mass are now no longer said.—E.F.]

Places can be *obsessed* by Satan, *men* can be *possessed*. There is only one way to redeem Dachau and that is by the Mass and prayer. People will not forget it even if the bleak buildings are wiped out. It will go on breeding hatred and revenge. The Germans themselves have their martyrs there. Nearly every country can claim martyrs in these camps. We have the witness of those who were there that all of those victims who were there came to know God. There was a community, not just of men in the same misery, but of charity. Satan's triumph was empty as always. He only delivered millions into the merciful hands of God. Knowing God's terrible love it is unthinkable that any could be lost.

I had a special reason for going to Dachau. Father Titus Brandsma, the Dutch Carmelite, died in that camp. I knew him well. He was a frail scholar. As a student he was sent home from Rome to die but he survived and became Rector Magnificus of the University of Nijmegen. He was head of a Faculty for research on the mystics of Holland and the Low Countries.

In his study he was surrounded by great tomes and worked at his typewriter all day. He smoked many cigars. He told me his father always lit up in the mornings when he awoke. It was his way of 'offering incense' to the Lord, first thing. He was no Jansenist, and liked all good things. He was very simple, very happy in his ways and lively; so frail that he seemed to be living by will-power all his life.

He was taken with many others and his life ended in Dachau. He was a saint in the camp. He suffered grotesque humiliations of every kind, never a word of complaint. The nurse who killed him with a final injection was a terrible woman. She was overcome by his holiness. Grace worked in her cruel heart. She became a Catholic. The cause of Father Titus was introduced last year. Uninvited she came forward to testify to his holiness. When Father Titus is beatified perhaps there will be a memorial church in his honour. He would be the voice of all the others, to pray forgiveness for the enemies of God.

Another Carmelite in another camp was Edith Stein. She was a Jewess who found peace and fulfilment in the Faith. From her baptism her life was one of prayer. She said the Breviary every day and was a philosopher. She was taken from a Carmel in Holland and Father Oesterreicher, himself a Jewish convert, writes of her: 'There in Auschwitz a creature who had never willingly injured a human creature was tossed into torment; a woman pure as morning air was smothered as are vermin, a thinker of truth and lover of the Word was made to die a wordless death; fearlessly Christian, she was, and yet her witness had to go unwitnessed, the blood of her testimony speak in silence.'

Now in 1960 during the Eucharistic Congress in Munich we are back again for another vigil. On this occasion the Bishop of Munich met us at Dachau on the Wednesday afternoon of our arrival. A Memorial Church had been built and dedicated to the Passion of Christ. Over the entrance is a crown of thorns. The Bishop spoke to us in

English in front of the church and said that it was entirely due to our first vigil that the church had been built. Before last year it was an evil place, very few Munich Catholics ever went there, nor could you blame them. This year many thousands of German youth went cross-carrying from Munich for the dedication. On Friday, the official day of reparation, there were many thousands gathered there to pray and do penance. Contrition's work is not with the soul alone; it has a historic task as well. We kept the Vigil in St Paul's Church in the city. The vigils are always hard and I am always saying I will never do another. But I cannot tell you how much I believe in them. Only by prayer and penance can we confront Satan.

Back at Aylesford the winter of 1961 was wet and stormy. Father said it would always remain in his mind under the three R's: rains, roof, roads:

> Floods tore up both drives to the Castle and worst of all, the rain came dripping through the roof of one of the main wings into several rooms. Water is wonderful, but when you wake up to the drip, drip, drip of it beside your bed it is different.

Since expensive repairs were needed for both roads and roof, they tried without success to get help from the Historic Buildings Council. Lord Cornwallis, Lord Lieutenant of the County, and the Architect, Mr Adrian Gilbert Scott, supported the application. They pointed out that The Friars had been independently restored, that Lord Conway had already spent £70,000 on the restoration of Allington and that the Council might well be expected to do its bit towards the preservation of these precious historic buildings.

> They pleaded lack of funds; they have not one but a hundred ways of delay and frustration. The knowledge and

authority and enthusiasm of all those who appealed availed nothing. . . . We have had little success in dealing with public bodies.

Aylesford too had had its share of the floods again:

The Medway is a tidal river as far as Allington Lock. When the tide is out it is a dirty puddle, fouled with effluent from the factories. At full tide it is still impressive. When the floods came it was mighty and fast-flowing and very frightening: an irresistible scavenger bearing with it a harvest of apples from the orchards, tin cans, great logs and every conceivable burden. It overflowed into the Great Court and did considerable damage but only weeks before, our insurance broker who had The Friars covered against storm and tempest, woke one morning with a sudden fear. Next day, without consulting us, she insured against flooding. That was a blessed inspiration and the Insurance Company paid out generously.

Within a few weeks our force of masons and tilers had laid down new floors and there was no loss at all. Fire and water breed elemental fears – a fearful detachment and loneliness. You are completely helpless. We can never be proof against calamity.

A non-Catholic film director, a good friend of Aylesford, telephoned to ask Father to go with him to stay with a family with the intriguing name of Tobias at Lisieux. They lived next door to Les Buissonets, the home of St Thérèse. Father said:

'So it was to be neither a pilgrimage nor a visit. With so much work on hand I was really wondering why I was being dragged off in the middle of winter.' And the film director's friends were surprised too. A silly story about him was evolved in London and was much repeated:

'I hear Brian has gone on Pilgrimage to Lisieux.'

'No, not really! Is he walking?'

'Well, not exactly, but they do say he's kneeling up in the back of the Rolls-Royce.'

Father arrived at the Tobiases' house by an indirect route, having had to return to London to fetch his passport which he had forgotten. He came up a narrow lane past Les Buissonets through a common door in an old wall opening on spacious gardens; and with its back to the lane and overlooking the town was a beautiful house.

Here he was received with the 'uncommon courtesy and hospitality of a Catholic home'. There were three little daughters, the youngest of whom was six and made great friends with Father:

Claudia, the youngest, is a dynamic little girl and very surprising. She is bilingual and was able to make for me such innocent fresh translations from the French. She translated into English St Patrick's Breastplate which was in her 'book'. She was proving to me all the time the marvellous discoveries of Madame Montessori. She also demonstrated for me the complete nonsense of most of what we hear about children. Here was a mind exploring and more daring than her parents'. She had quite definitely in her mind the whole world of God. I mean she had it in view. With adults this fresh world of God sinks into the unconscious or subconscious very soon. She talked to me, a little timidly, of heaven and hell. She was not too sure about getting to heaven and showed surprising humility. There was no fear at all, though. It was the Faith she had and no make-believe or nonsense. Children of her age are theologians and can bear the truth.

She brought me to the Carmel one day and chattered all the way. 'I *like* God', she said, and told me very clearly why. Before I left I enrolled the three children in the scapular, explaining it as simply as I could, telling them to say each morning to Our Lady: '*Servez vous de moi comme vous voudriez aujourd'hui*'. Indeed they understood very well, and the little one best of all. The Curé d'Ars was once asked by a fussy woman how to get to God. He said to her, 'Straight, like a cannon ball'. That is the way of children.

Father was able to offer Mass on the altar near the grille in the chapel where the saint lies in effigy. Near the altar is a marble slab with the inscription which asks St Thérèse to hurry up the conversion of England and to intercede for France, the mother of saints.

That chapel has no kind of distinction but there is about it a great silence which receives your prayer. That is distinctly felt. My friend kept saying in a strong voice at unexpected moments: 'You will get everything you are praying for.'

One night at dinner with the Tobiases there were other guests, one of whom was a very interesting and lively priest from a near-by parish. His work has also to do with the 'problem' of industrial relationships between employers and employees. He apologized for mentioning the word 'problem' to describe his work. It is said that a rational, nimble-minded Frenchman reduces everything to a problem. There may be problems to do with the physical world, involving research and finding the answer: for a Catholic there should be no moral problems at all. Why not get rid of the word? People are now obsessed by it. Why not call problems 'sins' or the results of sins and get on with our penance? God did not create problems, and I dislike the wicked word. Faith is not a problem but is always a victory. And the Providence of God! It is always there beforehand, adequate and sufficient, before we start manufacturing problems.

Father's forgetful mood at that time was causing some changes of plan for him, not problems of course; opportunities would be the better word:

Due to my forgetfulness instead of arriving in Le Havre on that Tuesday morning, I arrived in Paris. I went to the Marymount Sisters in Neuilly for Mass. Afterwards the Reverend Mother spoke to me of an apostolate inspired by the Archbishop of Versailles similar to that which we are trying to achieve at Allington; and she presented me with the latest literature on it. I began to see why I might have forgotten my passport, and in the Métro in the early morning I saw something which has haunted me ever since.

At some of the stations, if not all, were poor men getting up from the hard seats and shuffling into another day. These stations serve as shelter for the night. The poor men fade away in the morning and are somehow hidden, as they are forced to be by their poverty. The sight is quite alarming even for one with a vow of poverty, but it is quite certain we cannot get to heaven except in the company of the poor. Dom Primo Mazolari, an Italian priest, writes about the Italian poor: 'Comfort makes us dizzy, it steals our eyes; we have to avoid seeing. He who has little love sees few poor people around. He who has much love sees many poor people in all places. A strange virtue, love. Between the poor and God there is a close resemblance, a continuous encounter. They live so closely bound up with him that in the minds of men the same things happen to the poor and to God.'

Only love can *see* the poor. Love that has first *seen* God. The Abbé Pierre saw them and cried shame. Perhaps that is why they have a tax now in France on *les signes extérieures de la richesse*: the outward parade of wealth: great houses, great motor-cars, servants and all that goes with them. Dom Primo ends his reflections in a painful and personal way: 'On every road there comes a bend sometimes; suddenly, rising out of my inmost self comes the realization that God is there, that pain has got hold of me, that death is on the way – and the poor man appears in front of my face.'

[Father continues] It is really those who have the world's wealth who are most to be pitied. We see about us the strange poverty of the rich. A starving man can be so far gone as to lose his taste for food. Now men have lost 'a taste for God'. When you think of it, there is nothing more horrifying than a world of men without God, a world without civility, without mystery.

At one of the week-end retreats at Allington there was a Hindu lady. Father wrote about her:

I became aware of her when, in one of the Conferences, I was talking about God. She was not just passive but intent and eager and her face glowing. Afterwards we had hours of conversation about her family, about the Hindu religion, about God.

She had been married at seventeen and had two children. After the children came she had a desire for knowledge. She attended a university and acquired an M.A. and an Honours Degree in Music. She had none of the 'conceit of knowledge' and she soon came to regard her degrees as a screen for real knowledge, 'Whatsoever that is – security, oneness'.

The Hindus have strict fasts. A fast means taking neither food nor drink. She fasts every Tuesday. They fast for the dead from Full Moon to New Moon. They have great respect for dead people and always observe their 'days'. After a three days' fast she always feels 'secure and light and happy, floating in the air'. Parents fast on behalf of their children until they are twelve years old: 'We redeem them.' From our conversation I learned much about the Hindus. They are mostly vegetarian and dislike to eat flesh: 'Our daily duty: offer to God first.' They have a rosary of beads made from very special plants from which come 'Tulsi', very powerful spiritual vibrations which are purifying. Hindus also have 'the Mother Lady', which for them is both an aspect of God and God's aspect of motherhood. They have a firm belief in God's providence. She told me, to illustrate this, that 'We are like pieces in a game of chess and we are never the player. For instance by coming to London I met you and now we are talking together of God's ways.'

London had made her feel stifled and smothered: 'In India they are very poor but there is no poverty like there is here – the poverty of the spirit. London is very mad. People there are ashamed of speaking of God.'

Father comments:

In the West people are planned and conditioned. They have progressed they know not where, but it is only from one meal to another, from one holiday to another, from one flash of *experience* to another. They arrive at nothing and even Catholic parents encourage their children to accept illusion for reality especially at Christmas time. Everywhere people are over-worked and weary to create the illusion of joy. Alas for the poor rich; alas for all who have to live on illusion. Every man, no matter how sunk in materialism, has Augustine's 'restless heart for God': 'My Lord and my God, my one hope, hear me lest in my lassitude I no longer wish to seek you; but let me always search for you *ardently*.'

Cardinal Merry del Val, a near-saint, wrote his own epitaph: *Da mihi animas, cetera tolle!* 'Give me souls, take away everything else.' Give God back to souls, give souls back to God. This is the only adequate purpose of all our prayer and work.

When Father did finally get back from Lisieux the Aylesford finances were looking as depressing as ever:

On a Sunday afternoon the Bishop and I had a long unhurried chat discussing ways and means. Then there was a telephone call: someone wanted to see me urgently at The Friars. We were at Allington but the Bishop was able to bring me to Aylesford on his way home. A very dear benefactress of eighty-eight had come some distance in this midwinter. She was all goodness and compliments and then she said, quite simply: 'I can let you have £5,000, or perhaps £7,000, if you need it to clear the overdraft, it must be a great worry to you.'

And that was not all. On looking through the post I saw that $3,980 had come from Mr Sensenbrenner, an American, a constant and persevering friend of 'the Blessed Mother' – as he and his countrymen so often call her.

At that moment I recollected the strong voice saying, 'You will get everything you ask for'. But it was for other things that I had prayed to St Thérèse. It must have been St Joseph. But where did the sense of motherliness come from if not from Our Lady? I suspect they were all in it together and I am telling this good news because it would be mean of me not to tell you. Besides, you have a right to know because Our Lady's Building Company is also yours.

Father Malachy was now living at Allington. Diabetes, the raw Kentish winter in the cold Castle, together with long hours of work and some worry had combined to depress him. Spinoza thinks that those who seek holiness should not expect heaven and the sight of God; for him, virtue should be its own reward. Surely he must have forgotten those endless cold cloisters in which so much virtue has had its being: Dante visualized a hell of freezing cold.

But that heavy stonework does have some compensations. There is a way in which sunlight falls on those rough surfaces that is really exciting.

In February Father wrote:

It is good counsel not to surrender completely to moods. This has been a strange winter for me. The work and responsibility have grown. Diabetes produces every mood there is without the help of rain or common miseries. You can never be sure that the mood has not come to stay and you are mortally afraid. Then after the clammy wet days comes the sun.

In the first days of February I was sitting dictating letters by a window in an office at The Friars. Suddenly the court-yard was lit up by bright sunlight which remained for the whole morning. There is hardly anything more beautiful than sunshine on ragstone. It acted like magic on me. In a moment the heavy alarmist mood had gone. And now there is sunshine on ragstone walls nearly every day at Allington.

By April the long winter had finally gone:

The spring has come suddenly to make amends. Now we have had a month of sunshine and so far no east wind. Through the slits in this tower room I can see the dovecote and the grey walls of the tilting yard hung with white alyssum, wind sown or bird sown; unnoticed before, it is suddenly in full flower, and the white against the grey walls is the loveliest note of Spring. The daffodils are thick and stately on the bank above the moat and the willows fall in a golden spray to the surface of the water.

The wild duck reared here come back to the moat most nights and there is the most resonant quacking and to-do under our windows. In the morning, before six, there is an even livelier leave-taking. In competition the ducks have it against the thousands of singing and whistling birds in the trees round about. The dawn of the day is theirs and no mistake. The birds remain but the duck will have gone undaunted and, after a long day, return at top speed. They are so full of living that you wonder how they could ever stop and be dead.

Over at The Friars the work has reached an exciting stage. Brother Elias and Brother Hugh, with a Portuguese voluntary worker, have made many thousands of flags for the paving of the piazza of the Sanctuary. The old foundations are marked and can be traced by flags laid down in a different colour. The plastering of the great Sanctuary is finished. The gold colour plastering on the ceiling and the purplish plaster on the walls are entirely successful – as the builders say. Even now it looks right and has grandeur. In a few weeks' time the altar will be re-erected and the ceramics which have been made for it, in place.

The candlesticks are being fired in our own kiln.

In one of his commentaries on the Psalms, St Augustine gives us a vivid picture of the Christian life of the Africa of his day:

People rouse one another, 'Let us go, let us go!' 'Where are we to go?' 'To such-and-such a place, a holy place.' By their mutual talking they set one another on fire and their fire makes one blaze: they hurry on to the holy place and the holy idea goes to make them holy.

Father says that by our mutual talking we can spread the apostolate of Aylesford. But to most English people today the idea of a holy place is Greek, or at best, Latin. In 1962 he reported:

The Times conducted an enquiry in July. It was headed, 'The Pulse of England'. I quote from no. 8 of the series where the correspondent is observing and enquiring about life in the Home Counties.

He writes: 'Here in the Home Counties is good living in a super setting. Here the advertisements for armouries of barbecue equipment, the pictures of sleek women leaning against potent sports cars, make sense. These dream people really exist. They live here. . . . They are friendly, co-operative and highly competent at doing things about the house. They do not really see the relevance of things like religion, nor do they think much about it except when they have little flurries of grief or bereavements. . . . There are, I suppose, about 100 or 200 people in the town who are doing all the voluntary work for 55,000. I doubt whether most people here ask for anything from life that would not be requested by a talking pig. I am afraid that it would be possible to look upon the place as a chromium-plated pig-sty' (*The Times*, 26 July).

This desolate picture of the affluent society brings us back to the question of poverty and why God allows it.

There is a great mystery in it. The Greeks and even more ancient peoples had a true perception of it. The poor man, deprived by the gods of everything, became a *suppliant*, and that man was great. This revelation found in Greek thought and tragedy inspired Péguy:

'The suppliant represents. He is no longer only himself. He is not concerned, and that is why the other man must look out. Stripped of everything by this same occurrence which brought about the dangerous good fortune of the man to whom supplication is made, he is a citizen with no city, a head with no sight, a child fatherless, a belly with no bread, a back with no bed to lie on, a head without a roof, a man with no goods, he no longer exists as himself. And that is what makes him fearful. It is the *suppliant* whoever he may be, the beggar along the roads, the miserable blind man, the man proscribed or crushed. . . . It is always the suppliant who in reality holds the upper hand . . . commands the situation. The fortunate man, for the Greeks, is to be pitied, the man to whom supplication has to be made can speak only in the name of good fortune. It is not much. It is not much. It is nothing. Less than nothing.'

This throws some light on the mysterious role of the poor man at all times. Our Lord said the poor would always be with us and he blessed them and threatened the rich. The painful contrasts of rich and poor in India and in many countries! The poor suffering and dying of hunger in the streets without reproach to God! Stripped as they are, the Good Lord must truly have them in his Kingdom. Even as they live they are suppliants. When we understand this we are not tempted to ask why does God allow poverty.

And it was poverty in the first place which taught Father Malachy what he knows about the design of churches. Despite the large sums, all donated by rich or poor, which have been spent at Aylesford, it was the small church at Lampeter which might be called the dress-rehearsal for The Friars Restoration. When this Whitefriars Church was dedicated and it became known that the whole place with its furnishings had cost no more than £5,000, Father was asked to write about the spirit of Carmel in our churches and in the newly dedicated church,

for an American Liturgical review. This is what he wrote at
the time, 1939:

I did not set out to express the spirit of Carmel in the
church at Lampeter; but the very limitations and the
poverty of means achieved it. The barn on which it is
modelled is a simple building, mellowed with age. I have
seen this barn many times and in all lights and seasons
it is beautiful, it never fails. Our architect is an artist;
humble before beauty; he submitted to it and followed its
lines.

You can build a church of any material; but let it be
honest: stone, brick or wood. Use it intelligently and according to its nature and the result will be good. Why should
wood be painted to masquerade as marble? That is not
truth.

A church should have good and generous proportions.
If these are good you need little decoration, and you have
architectural quality. The sanctuary should be a large place
with the altar in the midst. Everything in a church should
have spiritual significance. A church is not a bazaar.
Statues are not just church furniture. Let them, for the
love of the saints, be made by hand and have the mark of
personality upon them. Let them be on proper pillars,
growing out of the foundations, integral in the church,
one with Christ, not accidental decoration. All things good
can worship God.

Use colour, light, gold, silver, according to its nature.
Let it honour God. The village dressmaker can make good
vestments, the joiner good furniture, the smith good
iron-work.

Once I thought all this just an ideal. Poverty made it
possible at Lampeter. Blessed be poverty! Before you begin
to build in a missionary country you must have faith

enough to move mountains! Then all the means I mention will be added to you and your church will be beautiful in sincerity and truth.

And now even the great task of the Aylesford sanctuary church, with its chapels and sacristies, was nearly completed. In June 1961 Father was at last able to write:

The last months have been spent in tidying up and finishing a thousand odd jobs. It was not spectacular in the doing but the result is indeed impressive as you can see. It is always exciting to see a plan realized: the Sanctuary is paved and the altar finished and permanent. Great wrought-iron gates are being made at a local forge for St Anne's Chapel and the Relic Chapel. They will cost £250 each and we would welcome a donor or donors for them. Work is starting again on the Relic Chapel.

V

In their Places now compacted

Among the Carmelites, as in many orders of the Church, a Prior is elected for a term of three years only. He may be re-elected but not indefinitely; so in 1961 Father Patrick Russell, the ex-Provincial of the American Province of New York, was the Prior of Aylesford, and Father Malachy was in charge of pilgrimages. He was asked by Father Killian Lynch, the Prior-General, who had been for seventeen years Professor of Philosophy at Marymount College outside New York, to make a tour of America, to appeal for funds for Aylesford and the Carmelite centres, and to further the apostolate of 'Use me today' and the Scapular Devotion.

But, as he said later, his trip was just too 'innocent', not planned ahead, and although he had the opportunity to talk about Aylesford in many places and to get a wonderful idea of the vastness, vitality and scope of the United States with its highly organized Catholic communities, he was running the risk of the loneliness, waste of time and humiliation which is the lot of the haphazard traveller in such a tightly run place; and it was only the timely intervention of the Marymount Sisters of Tarrytown who got him in the first place to address all their schools in New York and the kindness and interest of such good friends as John and Dorothy Cunningham, who later made an extensive 'schedule' for him, that made a success at all of the project.

In January 1962 he wrote:

When I was told about going to the States to appeal for

Aylesford, I was dismayed. It came as a complete surprise. The Father General had written to the two Provincials of the Carmelite Provinces based on New York and Chicago, and they, in turn, had written to me assuring me of a warm welcome and every help. I still felt hopeless and lost and inadequate. I have no illusions about the largeness of the continent – the vast distances and differences. I did not appreciate the need for a *schedule*. In America it is all important, it is your passport. Months beforehand everything is fixed to the day and hour. For the past twelve years at Aylesford things have just been *happening*. Insofar as there was planning it was quite wild and reckless.

Father thinks that a Catholic should be at home in all the Christian centuries and to live at Aylesford with its vast historical context and to enjoy the company of community and pilgrims whose customs and outlook are all 'God-directed', is to reinforce the idea. It was only when he was precipitated into the shifting kaleidoscope of life in the States, that he 'felt' his 'big world shrinking'. 'However,' he says, 'despite my not having any schedule, things began to happen which had not been arranged or thought of by anybody.'

And before he had been long in America he had become fond of the angular pattern of life there, where Carmelite priests were all embarked on their busy days by five o'clock in the morning and the intent, scurrying, uninvolved crowds at the air terminals seemed to show up the lonely destiny of each individual. Meetings there were, sudden epiphanies of mutual help and knowledge, and then the affectionate faces were lost again in the crowd: *happenings*, Father called them. They were the mark of his entire American journey: for instance, here he is on his way to stay with John and Dorothy Cunningham who had invited him to Kansas City for Christmas:

I left New York by 'plane on the Saturday afternoon before Christmas via St Louis to Kansas City. Every seat was taken. I had been travelling in the forenoon from Alantic City and making connections with only minutes to spare. I thought I would finish my Office and relax. The young man sitting next to me in a dark suit was reading the Acts of the Apostles. When I had finished my Office he asked me very abruptly what I was reading. He wasn't a young preacher, as I had suspected, but a student of electronics. He had discovered the Bible and was very busy; but nobody had told him that the Catholic Church existed before a word of the New Testament was written, that the Bible is guaranteed by the authority of the Church. He was a big serious lad with noble intentions. He carried my bag from the 'plane and I did not see him again.

At the Terminal of St Louis I realized that I had come to the Middle West. It was crowded with people travelling over Christmas from far-off states. The weather had upset all time-tables and many were stranded. All were loaded with Christmas gifts; one good man had a lobster packed nicely in a gift box. Everybody was friendly. There were many young soldiers, very innocent-looking, in greatcoats, going home on leave. At that meandering airport you were confronted with America in all its rich variety.

The plane for Kansas City took off, surprisingly, on time. It encircled Kansas City for over an hour and returned to St Louis with its passengers.

But it set off again later and among the passengers Father met a Carmelite Tertiary, enthusiastic and alive. He was delighted with her little girl:

She is a quaint little girl and has the most alluring ways. She taught me how to draw tulips. She was a wonderful little mimic and gave generously to me of all the praise and encouragement she had herself received. Without knowing it she was demonstrating to me – with her left hand, all the principles of Montessori.

Going round the Catholic colleges and universities it was this direct and childlike quality of giving, of the urge to give back in some way the imagined riches of an austere society, which seemed to be the mark of the new culture:

There is no conceit of knowledge in the Carmelite colleges. I have the impression that learning is treated just as a tool with which to do a job of work. On the subways in New York droves of Sisters may be seen on Saturday evenings returning from courses – some young, some not so young. They are for ever sharpening and polishing their tools. Critics would say that this specialized knowledge will never ferment into a Catholic culture; but since it is people informed by prayer who make up a culture, there *is* a Catholic culture in the United States even though it is not yet expressed adequately except in its prayer. . . .

And within the sophistication and the high standard of living I have met Catholics whose simplicity of outlook and faith remind one of what the early Christians must have been. There was the dear old cook in one of our houses who insisted on showing me the 'fridge'. It was her pride because there was always the making of a meal in it. 'This is your home', she very kindly assured me. Her great regret was that she had not the chance to receive Holy Communion often, '*Oh, Father, it takes the pain out of everything*'.

At Middletown, outside New York, where Father made his first appeal of the trip, there is a Carmelite pastor who has built a parish school for 500 children:

It is a most impressive one-storey building, planned to the last detail. The kitchen is a marvel of stainless steel and *clinically clean*. The Dominican Sisters have charge of it and they admitted to me that the convent and school were materially perfect. The Chinese philosophers have always rightly held that perfection in material things is imprisoning, you cannot get any further. The Chinese saying is that it is 'like a stoppered jar'. They used to leave an unfinished bit in finished manuscripts. The Book of Kells, that eighth-century marvel, has a small section left unfinished. This, the scholars say, was the bit left for escape. The Reverend Mother was becoming uneasy in our conversation until her eye fell on a crack in the floor of her perfect convent. . . .

These geometric functional buildings are relieved by the lavish use of wood. There is a great variety of timber near at hand all over the States and there is beautiful well-made furniture in schools and homes. The old Colonial furniture was fine too and in all these practical things the Americans must be unsurpassed. These objects everywhere are a delight to the eye though it is a very different matter where the higher arts are concerned.

I was discussing this perfection of material things and the high standard of living unimagined in other countries, with Father Roland Murphy at Washington. 'Where do you go from there? Into the desert?' He did not know the answer but it is significant that the Cistercians and the Contemplative orders have waiting lists.

In England the Carmelite priests and nuns could be counted very quickly. It was wonderful therefore for Father to be able to visit great numbers of Carmelite houses and colleges: within sight of the spray of Niagara Falls, for instance, is the Mount Carmel College:

Nowhere, outside of Rome, have I seen so many Carmelite priests and professed students. There is also a college and a high school for those preparing to be Carmelites. I was very busy with them all the time I was there and they could not hear enough of Aylesford and Allington.

And there were the Carmelite nuns as well:

Our Lady's Schedule has brought me to Germantown. It is a prosaic name for a most beautiful locality. St Teresa's Convent at Avila on the Hudson is the Motherhouse of the Carmelite Sisters. They are a comparatively new branch of Carmel. Mother M. Angeline Teresa is the Foundress. A small group were asked in 1929 by the late Cardinal Hayes to found Homes, not for the destitute poor who are already being looked after, but for the not-so-rich about whom nobody was thinking at the time.

Father Flanagan, about whom I will tell you more later, recognized a kindred spirit in Mother Angeline and gave her much help in the beginning; and Father Magennis, the truly great Prior-General of the Order at the time, gave the affiliation to the Order of Carmel. So they are Carmelites, active contemplatives. If the spirit of Carmel means the spirit of Our Lady, they have it. They are simple, sincere and radiate happiness. There are now about thirty homes in this foundation, and four hundred Sisters, caring for five thousand people.

During his journey Father visited a very great number of convents:

It seems that all the old Catholic countries have given of their best to the Church in America. There is a Polish congregation, the Felicians, which is very numerous. I have also met Indian Carmelite Sister students in many places, Chinese too and many from Hong Kong. Perhaps the most charming and innocent of all are the Sisters from the Philippines. The sisterhoods of America have been referred to as a modern phenomenon, as indeed they are.

In England since the Reformation, religion and learning have drifted apart. There should be no such thing as *secular* learning; only atheists can have such a barren thing because for Christians, 'the sum of it all is, God is all'.

Most of the teaching in Catholic schools is done by Sisters. Last year 168,527 United States Sisters taught five million elementary, secondary and college students in thirteen thousand schools, nursed thirteen million patients in nine hundred and twenty-five hospitals and sanatoria, cared for twenty-six thousand dependent children and thirty-one thousand aged people. They are an army of God-invincible. No wonder the Catholic people make great sacrifices for the schools. It knits them all together as nothing else. Having been generously schooled they are now generous by instinct to every good cause.

Among these orders, in their strength of course, are those which have been founded in America. Through his friends John and Dorothy Cunningham, with whom he stayed in Kansas City, Father was able to meet, either in legend or in fact, most of the great figures of the American women's orders: it would be hard to put them into any order, except perhaps geographically for they are all great women. In Louisiana there was Mother Dolores, a Carmelite Mother-General whose predecessors, active Carmelites, were driven from France a hundred years ago. 'A few came to New Orleans and began again. You can break an *organization,* you cannot really break a religious family. We are always coming back from under the centuries.' They have fifteen convents in Louisiana now.

Then there was Mother Seton. Staying in the Cunningham home with him *happened* to be Monsignor Code, who is a writer and historian and who was forwarding the cause of

Mother Seton who became the Foundress of the Daughters of Charity which now number more than ten thousand.

The story of how this very womanly woman with five children of her own came to achieve this, is strange and wonderful: it comes from the very roots of American Catholic history. Her father, who was a famous physician and scientist, was entirely given to fighting disease, especially yellow fever. He was devoted to his daughter whose mother had died when she was three years old. Elizabeth was born in 1774 and grew up in the first years of American Independence. Her husband died in 1803 and in 1805 she was received into the Church.

She was a spirited and adventurous woman, often ill. She loved Eternity but she loved the poor and suffering too, mixing heaven and earth and retaining her youth throughout her life. Experience had given her a profound faith in the Providence of God so she was afraid of nothing. The good Lord was God and Elizabeth was Elizabeth. She is a saint with a difference.

Sister Catherine Sullivan was the creator of the great Marillac College in Normandy, St Louis. This is really a university for Sisters.

It is all new and extensive, with a large campus and equipped regardlessly. This is possibly unique and well ahead of our time. The Faculty is composed of Charity Sisters and Sisters from all the other groups. The object of it is the integration of knowledge and religion and a sharing of the riches which these great sisterhoods have from the Old World.

Happily, Sister Catherine has lived to be the architect of her own vision. She is greatly loved by her own and by all who know her; for she herself is an example of her aims. At seventy-five her mind is clear and her intelligence as keen as when she began. She has a prodigious power of grasping great ideas and details, too. She is one of the great ones. She is selfless, a woman lost and wondering in the providence of God.

At the Motherhouse of the Sisters of Charity at Leavenworth, a great Georgian-style building standing in a large park, Father met hundreds of the Sisters living there: 'The Mother-General of these Sisters, and others I have had the privilege of meeting, made me wonder if convents and monasteries would be the last refuge of the great people of the world.'

Catherine Drexel was an influential woman who became one of these great ones: Father met *her* via an order of coloured Sisters whom Mother Dolores had asked him to address:

The large chapel was full of Sisters. I was distracted while I talked to them: by the chapel in such fine taste, evidently the work of a first-class architect, and by the Stations of the Cross high up on the walls: most beautiful they seemed. The Sisters themselves seemed to have a desolating humility and to carry with them the sorrow of their race. There is a University for the coloured in New Orleans and many of these Sisters are on the Faculty. The buildings, which are said to be the finest in the country, are reminders of the great woman who built them.

Catherine Drexel was an heiress. She inherited from her father fifteen million dollars – the equivalent of four or five times that amount today. She was obsessed with pity for the coloured peoples and the Indians. There were a quarter of a million Indians and nine million coloured people – everywhere neglected. Processions of these used to go to her house three times a week. She had 'holes in her hands'. When her father died, with the help of Bishops O'Connor of Omaha and Ryan of Philadelphia, she formed a new congregation of religious women devoted to missionary work among these races. Mother Drexel herself lived a life of extreme poverty. She walked where she could and took public transport where she could. She wore her shoes to the uppers. Her Sisters used to go in at night to her cell when she slept especially to replace her worn-out shoes and clothes with new ones. She used to say that 'the salvation of souls is worth more than all riches'. She was active up to a few moments before her death. Nobody could have guessed she was ninety-four years of age. What an example for millionaires!

John and Dorothy Cunningham brought Father a hundred and thirty miles out into the frightening vast prairie land which stretches West from Kansas City, to visit a monastery of Benedictine Sisters at a place called Clyde:

They have the full monastic office and discipline, with the addition of perpetual adoration of the Blessed Sacrament. Day and night for fifty years this has gone on without a break. There are nearly two hundred Sisters. The monastery is like a great fort and can be seen for miles. It is full of prayer and silence. There are five or six monasteries with this rule, all of them depending on Clyde. One of them is a shrine in Kansas City. Mother Carmelita is the Superior of all the monasteries and is regarded as a Foundress. There is no quick summary possible of these truly great women one meets in these communities. They are all different.

Mother Carmelita has a radiant happiness about her. Her courtesy and grace are what one remembers. It is not mannered but is something extended to all God's creatures. This physically frail woman has staggering achievements to her credit. She is a rare blending of a Benedictine and a Carmelite. Her Irish mother and father had great devotion to Our Lady of Mount Carmel and the Scapular. After her mother's death she became a Sister and her father went to the monastery every month to persuade her to leave. In the end he gave his consent on condition she would be called, in religion: 'Carmelita.'

Father Malachy was reading the works of Gabriel Marcel at the time. While he was continually meeting such people there was little chance for the doctrines they contained to touch or even interest him; although he had a fright in New Orleans where there is a great lake with a bridge across it, twenty-five miles long. With his hosts he had 'occasions to cross and re-cross it. It is a weird experience. It is like being caught up in infinity. Nobody is ready for an experience like that.'

From the Mid-West Father went on to Los Angeles and Santa Barbara. From Brian Desmond Hurst, the film producer, he had an introduction to John Ford, the millionaire film maker, whom he hoped to interest in helping Aylesford:

A young student, three-quarters Mexican, brought me out to Belair where John Ford lives. My driver lost his bearings and we found ourselves motoring round in circles in a maze of hills in the most wealthy and beautiful district of California. This nice boy, of some culture and refinement, was scared of the exotic show of wealth and was afraid to knock at doors to ask directions. John's dwelling was big but not pretentious. It was furnished in good taste and there were many good prints and some originals by Irish painters on the wall and a large autographed photo of Mr de Valera from far-off days. On the mantelpiece were many 'Oscars'.

It was late afternoon when I called. In the States there is no afternoon tea and dinner is late. I wanted a glass of milk for my diabetes. The housekeeper asked if I preferred but-termilk and buttermilk it was – two glasses of it. I had never had buttermilk since hay-making in my long-lost youth in Wicklow. In that sophisticated place my youth came back with that marvellous buttermilk – and in an instant, so everlasting is memory.

There was a long talk with Mrs Ford, a quiet lady with a soothing voice. Eventually John came; he certainly is impressive, has a powerful personality and presence. He does not apologize for his existence. He is a big man, spare and angular, and his talk is angular too. He is a religious man in a blunt way and his words are battling. He told me he receives only ten cents in every dollar he earns. I think twenty per cent of his income may go to charity, tax free. I am told he is a millionaire over and over again; but he has his own charities. I was disarmed before I began!

When John Ford said goodbye to me in that place on that lovely evening everything seemed as unreal as the cinema. Here in this magic place is an ultimate of human achievement with everything material that one could desire. Yet I came away from it as if I had had a great fright. In the midst of wealth I realized more than in any place else what Gabriel Marcel calls 'the absurdity of living'.

Marcel had inherited from his aunt an 'accurate and implacable sense of the absurdity of life'. Man may achieve the ultimate in good living but is still subject to that last incurable disease. On the material plane there is no escape from the absurd except into sordid indulgence or suicide. This Christian Existentialist philosopher had progressed from the sense of absurdity to a philosophy of love. Love is the key to everything and takes you to mysteries far beyond reason or nature. Love gives knowledge of others, and in the knowledge of others we know ourselves. Without love people are strangers to God, strangers to one another. This kind of love is a gift of God and Marcel says enigmatically: 'Prayer is the only way to think about God.'

All this is readily translated into the language we Catholics are using every day, which has become weary and not startling any more. After all, what redeems our lives from absurdity is the subtle over-riding providence of a good God weaving a most delicate pattern of the supernatural, always unexpected, always unpredictable. In *The Broken World*, Marcel dramatizes his thought about the possibility of final absurdity in a frightening way:

'Don't you feel sometimes that we are living – if you can call it living – in a broken world? Yes, broken like a broken watch. Just to look at it nothing has changed, everything is in place. But put the watch to your ear and you don't hear any ticking. You know what I am talking about; the world, what we call the world, the world of human creatures. It seems to me it must have had a heart at one time, but today you would say the heart had stopped beating.'

[Father Malachy goes on] The final absurdity would be, of course, if we were not destined to live for ever. Like the Existentialists he is impatient of abstractions. Marcel says that the creative relationship between man and man and man and God is something lived rather than stated. This is why *being* is so much more important than saying, it is why the thousands of statements, *living* statements, who are the religious, the nuns, monks and priests of the world, are so much more impressive than Catholic journalism.

In this connection there is an apt quotation from F. H. Heinemann's abstract of Marcel's works: 'An increasing socialization of life and the growing powers of the State are invading the privacy of the person and destroying the brotherhood of men and the fertile soil in which creativeness, imagination and reflection can flourish. In a world in which human beings tend to become "fonctionnaires", exercising a specific function in human society, they are reduced to statistical numbers, and are no longer free agents in their own right. In a society dominated by technology everything becomes a "problem" to be solved by reasoning and calculation. "Having" is here more important than "being". Everybody *has* employment, *has* possessions and has certain functions to fulfil.

'In an original analysis Marcel distinguishes between "possessing-having", e.g. to have a house or a motor-car; and "implicit-having", to have a specific quality such as pleasure or pain. "Having is a source of alienation. Objects which we possess; houses, books, factories, gardens; or ideas and opinions which we regard as our 'possessions', in a specific sense 'have' us! We are in danger of being imprisoned or devoured by them. People concentrating on having are in danger of becoming captive souls cut off from other persons and not responding to their presence. They suffer a loss of *creative being* – the ability to give of themselves". They are, Marcel would say, "absent". They talk and talk about what they will do for you but in an hour of peril they are not there, not "present", i.e. not at your disposal.

'Here Marcel sheds new light on a specific feature in human relationship: "There may be persons in the same room with me and nevertheless they may be absent. On the other hand, a friend in another continent may be 'present' to me. 'To be present' is to be in immediate contact with, to respond to, to be at the disposal of. If we scrutinize our experience we find to our surprise that only a very few of our contemporaries are present with us in this sense. 'Absence' should be replaced by 'presence', 'betrayal' by 'fidelity', denial by faith and despair by hope." This is Marcel's message and the basis of his Christian message of hope.'

Father's experiences in America seem to underline the truth of Marcel's conclusions. Though he is not scornful of anybody, to someone accustomed to seeing the outlines of people's spirits, there is a great sadness in the amorphousness of those who have become swamped by possessions. There is, too, a corresponding exultation in the recognition of those who have put aside things in exchange for their own growth:

These Sisters have a certain something about them belonging to the centuries, they are not intimidated or overwhelmed by progress or modernity. This indefinable spirit of theirs must come to them from Mary Ward, their Foundress. Great women like her are always contemporary and everlasting. . . .

That was what he said about the Loretto Sisters, and, speaking of Mother Moira, Mother-General of the Sisters of St Joseph, he said: 'She is endless, a dozen interesting fascinating people all in one; and you cannot say that about too many. . . .'

At Williamstown I met Father Laurence Flanagan. He is just on eighty years of age. A Sister had just described him to me: 'He looks majestic, like a great prophet. He must be six foot six, straight and commanding – yet with the most kindly presence. Still alert and ready waiting for the bell of office. It was his habit of a lifetime. . . .'

At the Carmelite Theological Seminary, Father Roland Murphy and the rest are a Faculty of scholars and yet you are not overwhelmed or diminished by them. There is a simplicity and carefree gaiety that comes from integrity.

Two of the Carmelites in the College in Los Angeles were novices of mine thirty years ago. The Prior, too, belonged to that period in my memory. The pastor in the Parish of St Raphael was a fellow-student. I knew them as I could never know the other fathers of that large community. Their mannerisms, even the colour of their thoughts had not changed. I suppose they could say the same of me but I had the advantage of them. As a Master you only know students by your own detached interest in them. There is no other way. There comes a time in the space of life between childhood and age when everyone must accept himself, the inevitable self. People who have accepted themselves are always interesting. There is no pretence any more, only truth.

So Father had not, in the main, exchanged his large world of Aylesford for a wizened material world, the America he had feared and sometimes met. It's there all right: somebody has said that America contains more junk than any other country and, to follow Marcel, one might almost imagine that the inhabitants had not only leaked much of their vitality into their possessions, but that they had then *thrown them away*. It would be possible, for instance, in looking at one of the vast sprawling car dumps which litter the States to think of all the energy, pride and narcissism represented by this abandoned investment. These things, more an atmosphere than a fact, are inclined to hit Father suddenly and unexpectedly. On his way home he spent some days in New York:

> My last days there were strangely different. Although I made two appeals on the remaining Sundays, one in the Church of St Simon Stock in the Bronx, the most successful one I made, the other in Tanafly in New Jersey, which also had a good result, I felt that something had gone. It was a mood hard to describe except by borrowing from Maurice Baring's whimsical attempt at describing that city:
> 'I am in New York, tall buildings rise wistful and white in the pale milky sky. They are tall those buildings and they affect me with a strange longing to go away, to be somewhere else; not here; there, where, elsewhere.'

H

Actually I had tried the direct approach to some Catholic millionaires and it is all wrong. There is a ceremonial for that. In two attempts I was frightened by the gleam of wealth and ran away. You have to recover from that and it takes time. . . .

But for the most part Father Malachy's tour was a chain of kind welcomes. By the nuns he was passed from Motherhouse to Motherhouse and the Carmelite houses, so many of them strung across the States, vied with each other for his company, as did secular friends, notably the Cunninghams and the Arthur Mangels who entertained him delightfully *and* put him in touch with many religious houses which might otherwise have been ignorant of his presence in the States. Events meshed. Had he had a 'proper schedule' it is unlikely he would have seen the great section of Catholic America that he actually did. It has been difficult to convey, without inserting the relevant Newsletters verbatim, the scope of his journey; and in any case, Father is not the most concise of diarists. But here is a passage which shows how he was practically passed from hand to hand:

I was persuaded by the nice, friendly, charming voice of Father Howard Rafferty of the New Aylesford, on a long distance call, to give the Keynote address at the National Tertiary Congress in Detroit. I had no script at all and no time nor inclination to concoct one. I told him so but I do not think he believed me. The address turned out to be something like the Newsletters, spoken. I never had such a good listening audience; 'they were with me all the way'. I do believe they would have gone on listening all night, not because of me but because of something to do with Our Lady. Later, at a big rally of Tertiaries and others in a Chicago hotel, it was the same. There were two Tertiaries from Canada at the Congress in Detroit. I knew at once they were Tertiaries with a difference. They belonged to a Community centred at Combermere. Several of its members are Carmelite Tertiaries and the Centre there is called Madonna House.

The whole work or movement to which they belong began in the slums of Harlem, New York. It was all started by a refugee baroness from Russia with a few others like herself. In the most appalling conditions, with no money and in extreme poverty they set out to feed and house the hungry, and to feed the hunger in their hearts. Again, as so often happens, I went to Combermere by indirections. A pressing invitation by these Tertiaries and an invitation from the Motherhouse of the Sisters of Loretto in Toronto decided for me. It was only a diversion of six hundred miles.

Combermere: a wet evening after a coach drive of two hundred miles; for the first hundred, vast plains, mostly empty and nothing but pine trees. I thought we were climbing most of the time until a little wizened man at the first stop said, 'Here we are exactly eight inches above sea level'. The rest of the journey was uphill to the tree line and it was fast and furious, past two big towns and lots of scatters of houses – one called Maynooth, another New Carlow.

Combermere lies in a hollow in the mountains with pine forests all about, interlaced with silver birch. It is a large timber house in the Colonial style, extensively added to by other timber houses in good taste. There is a wooden footbridge to an island on which there are log cabins and landscaped gardens. Inside there is order everywhere, books everywhere, cleanliness everywhere. It is wholesome. There are men on the farm and in the forests, and women at home. There's a newspaper, a lending library and a depot for distributing clothing to the poor. The methods are up to date and the chapel is in a loft. The priests are very intelligent and spiritual. It is rather like finding yourself with St Augustine at the end of the fourth century; the freshness, newness, endless hope and charity. Rather it is like Christ, living in men and women, manifest, and there is an old Celtic rune which fits:

> I saw a stranger yester'een.
> I put food in the eating place;
> Drink in the drinking place;
> Music in the listening place. And in the Blessed
>   Name of the Triune
> He blessed myself and my house, my cattle and my
>   dear ones:
> And the lark said in her song:
> Often, often, often,
> Goes the Christ in the stranger's guise.
> Often, often, often,
> Goes the Christ in the stranger's guise.

Father Emile Brière, who is the spiritual director, has rare insight. He is not just a book of rules, but analytical. He is a French Canadian, full of charity for maladies of the mind and spirit.

On the south and west of the great Union of States there were the old Catholic missionaries from Spain to follow up:

Fra Junipero Serra and his Franciscans came up from Mexico on the Mission trails of the eighteenth century, in 1769, and their trails are marked by a Litany of Saints and Christian mysteries. These are a revelation of the Faith. They went on foot, these poor men of St Francis, or they may have had mules or donkeys, but not horses. They named their stopping places after the Saints or Mystery of the day's Feast. The Spaniards have always been intense realists. The Communion of Saints was translated on to this earth with a terrible and startling intimacy. No wonder the Baroque saints and angels are so dramatic and often so beautiful. I am thinking of Spain with all her majestic madonnas, with costly robes and jewels in scale in so far as human genius can translate these realities.

Father Brendan Gilmore, the Provincial, brought me to see a Mission church in the desert outside Tucson. These Mission churches were all alike in style and are not easily distinguished. They seem to be a mixture of Indian, Mexican and Spanish. The interior of this one was dark and cool but shone with splendours. Even now, in semi-decay it is alive. They are alive as no modern church I have seen is alive. I remember now two Baroque angels and several beautiful figures of Our Lady and the saints. It's a strange thing that many of our modern churches and their furnishings seem to be still-born, whereas these old churches in decay with their saints and angels are still alive in a startling way.

These Franciscans did a splendid thing. Not only did they baptize and preach, but they Christianized the villages and settlements and gave them indelible names. There are names and titles that seem to glow all along the coast to San Francisco. They are a shining Litany laid down upon the earth. They are a catechism and a history. The Virgin herself, La Purissima Conception, Santa Maria, Carmel, Santa Monica, Sacramento, Santa Cruz, San José, Santa Clara, Santa Barbara, San Simeon. It is a Litany embracing all the centuries and no mystery is omitted. And the great archangels are there too: San Gabriel, San Rafael and San Miguel. The very first Mass in California was offered by a Carmelite Friar.

No people have been more conscious than the Spaniards of the angels and the whole world of God. The Missionaries faced the same perils as the Conquistadores; and not only for the King of Spain, but chiefly for the King of Heaven.

In practice, the interests of the King of Heaven and the King of Spain did not always coincide. But the Missionaries engaged all the resources of the 'Immovable Armies of Heaven'. It was a Spaniard, Suarez, who wrote three-quarters of a million words on the angels. When he was dying his room seemed full of angels and he was heard to say, 'I never knew it could be so sweet to die'.

Theologians tell us the number of the angels is only less than infinite. More numerous they are than all the grains of sand on all the seashores of the world, than all the blades of grass upon the earth. An angel's mind is a whole world of pure knowledge radiated from God. There can be no ignorance in it. The great mystics like St John of the Cross have seen the angels as filtering knowledge down from God to our poor intelligences upon this earth. An angel is a mighty being. It is said that they are all different and keep their ranks in the hierarchy of heaven. An angel *is* where it acts. All its world of pure knowledge is at its disposal. In talking and writing of the angels the saints have always been in scale. Many of them have had splendid visions of angels, visions of God's *whole* world. It is not so much an open book to them as a vision of splendours. . . .

Some years ago I knew of a house infested or obsessed by evil spirits. It is a well-documented story from beginning to end. The end of the evil spirits – poltergeists – was an exorcism. I knew the people and the house. It was frightening, but most interesting because it revealed a pitched battle between good spirits and bad; and the good spirits won, with the help of God. As a consequence all the family except one had the gift of faith, and one of the sons became a priest.

The good Sisters I visited in Los Angeles knew all about the battle which is always going on between the evil and good spirits in the 'city of the Angels'. It is going on all the time everywhere. What a pity we do not acknowledge the angels more and pray with them and join with them against evil. The Devil is not an abstraction but *someone*.

Before I began to write this Newsletter I had a long discussion with a friend about the angels. He had done a deal of research on them for a talk for the B.B.C. for Christmas. He was full of the lore and the love of the angels. He told me of Isaac of Nineveh, who said the angels often showed themselves to the Fathers of the Desert, and 'brought them warm bread and olives'. 'You can always get at them through the Queen of the Angels', he said. Now you know why these wonderful Kossowski angels are being planted about the statue of Our Lady at Aylesford.

Returning home to England, Father did not much care for his journey in one of those huge transatlantic liners:

It was rough on the sea but not rough enough to be exciting. It was cold and forbidding on deck; not a sea-bird to be seen. Tourist Class on this ship is needlessly bad. A professor of mathematics calculated that we walked one seventh of a mile to and from our meals. This journey was by confusing passageways through the crew's quarters and in sight and smell of the engines. The food was stale and most of the waiters had a new way of being dull. But after the bright courtesy of the States it came as a shock. Over there in restaurants and for any public service, if you say, 'Thank you', there is always the lilting reply, 'You are welcome'.

They came from Allington to meet the boat at Southampton. The Spring was full in, extravagant and fresh and rich and rounded. It was like seeing the English countryside for the first time. Memory does not narrate or record one impression after another in mounting intensity; but in effect

I do believe we do see everything once only. Last year, coming from the burning sun of Spain to Dover through Kent I saw that county. I do not think I shall ever see it again. Coming from bigness and buildings and landscapes, England seemed an island as it truly is – and intimate.

It was midnight when we arrived at Aylesford. The Great Court was mysterious and timeless in the moonlight and the new buildings unexpected yet quite inevitable, blending perfectly with the old. Only next day did I see Adam Kossowski's angels. My heart jumped up when I saw them. They are not only great works of art but meditation. They have repose in them and wondering reverence. They have a certain quality which seems to relate them to Our Lady and to our poor humanity and to their own function. I have never seen angels like these. They are all different in gesture, and various. There is a heavenly grace and calm about them, reminding one that the Old Testament is full of the bustle of angels; the traffic on Jacob's ladder, angels coming down and going up.

Their appearances were always at first terrifying and then reassuring. Only the good angels seem to have taken on human forms. The evil spirits most often appear in the lower forms. The good Lord does not allow them the dignity of human shapes. It is the supreme test of an artist to make an angel truly an angel and yet endearing. Angels by their *nature* belong to an unspeakably noble family; but it is said that our guardian angels have some kinship with those they guard. They are our first and earliest friends, pure spirits. Jacob wrestled with an angel all night and was terribly out-matched. The children of Fatima were worn out and worn down and made heavy by the visit of an angel. After the visions of Our Lady they were light and gay and joyous. This we would expect. Our Lady is one of us.

But on that moonlit night of his return there were, besides the angels, many other changes for Father to see:

> The walls of the Relic Chapel have gone up to the roof, and the landscaping at the back, facing the Rosary Way, seemed right and certain too. Then there is Michael Clark's St Joseph already installed in his chapel. I was most anxious to see the figure because photographs do not do it justice. It is strong and powerful and entirely worthy. Alas, I could only see him in the midst of chairs: two hundred at least in his small chapel! He is so strong that he needs room and contrast.

The Summer after Father's return from the United States was a great time for *finishing,* because there was more than ever the feeling that every part of the place was destined for great use. In August the Triennial meeting of all the Provincials of the Carmelite Order was held there:

> The Prior-General and his Curia came. All the Provinces of the Order were represented with the exception of Poland, and their deliberations went on for a whole week. All were astonished beyond measure. After the initial cost in 1949 no further appeal has been made to the Provinces for help except in my attempt recently in the States. That was just too 'innocent' and, relatively speaking, did not yield too much. Practically all the money, means and labour for the Restoration has come from the Friends of Aylesford – the Members of Our Lady's Building Company. Many of the Provincials did not know what to expect. The Australian Provincial had seen Aylesford some years before we had it back and now he could not believe it was the same place. I am not surprised they were astonished. From day to day I am astonished myself.
>
> Some weeks before the meeting there was great activity.

All the voluntary workers were concentrated round the Relic Chapel. Percy Kitchen, the foreman, was intent and unrelenting. Roger Brown was putting on the last thousand tiles, seemingly without hurry. Then, one evening, a message was sent to me at Allington that all the scaffolding had been taken down. I could not wait to see the finished building. I was taken over in the late evening and with some others, equally curious and expectant, viewed it from the Rosary Way gardens at the back. The effect on me was of something massive and timeless – quite unexpected too – but right, as if it could not have been otherwise.

By the river, there was a long vista of buildings with distance in it. The buildings are important and cover a large area. It was a very big project and we did not know this until we had finished it. The roofs, all at different heights, are very impressive. Roger, with an occasional helper or two, has done all the tiling: over a hundred thousand old peg tiles, a hundred tons, have been laid on these roofs. He had given three years of his life to this work for Our Lady. He is a craftsman in the old tradition: humble but very knowing because he was launched very early into his craft. At the age of seventeen he was given two roofs to tile: a year later he was in charge of the roofing of a hundred and twenty. Roger and Percy are alike in this: they are undismayed by size. Time does not seem to enter into their calculations. They would start again on a job as big or bigger.

The old peg tiles and the ragstone make for continuity. In a decade or two it will be difficult to distinguish between the old and the new at The Friars. Much of the ragstone came by indirections from the old buildings; some from secular buildings which had been built from the churches pulled down by the despoilers. To procure enough ragstone was a hunt in which the angels must have led.

Because of our urgent need I had acquired an eye for

ragstone. In Maidstone, in a street of drab houses, was an oast house. It was large and finely built but its chief interest for me was its circular wall of ragstone. With the faint hope of acquiring it and then selling the site, I had enquiries made. A friend of Aylesford frequented a near-by pub in the hope of finding out something about it and its owner. Not a scrap of information could he glean. That was most strange.

I had had my eye on it for eight years when one day as I was passing in a car I saw that the roof had gone. The people in the adjoining house told me that there had been a fire and directed me to the owner, a farmer some miles away. He was a prosperous farmer and lived and had his office in a large period house. He was away but his secretary was most courteous and charming. Later he spoke to me on the telephone. He said immediately, 'I know what you are after. The oast house is a Public Monument and I may have to restore it as it was. But if I can get permission to demolish what remains of it I will let you have the stone. I know what wonderful work you people are doing.'

Some months passed; but only an hour before I left for the States he telephoned to say that the stones could be ours at a reasonable valuation. That was a good-sized miracle. What a wonderful fire! It injured nobody, benefited the farmer greatly and gave the stones to their final destiny – let us hope – in the Temple of God.

So now most of those stones were in place and the great years of building were over. There remained only the finishing and decoration and even that was nearly complete. The angels were already there, set in amidst the stone; signs of the Church which, like an angel, '*is* where it acts'; but which also in its permanence and scale gives significance to Place and delimits Time:

I was in the Sanctuary one Sunday evening trying to listen to a sermon which was completely out of context – and I was distracted. I was sitting underneath and in full view of Kossowski's great angels, looking as if they had just arrived from paradise. They are always a comfort but an oblique glance from where I was sitting caught the sun on the walls of the Choir Chapel. The stones were dancing. This is the effect of random ragstone building since the stones are not laid in straight courses, but anyhow. Without intending to do so the mason works a pattern of incomplete circles which is the result of rhythmic movement in the mason himself. You would expect this to be all wrong. You would say a wall should be solid in appearance. Who would ever want to build a dancing wall? And yet there it is. What might be heavy and solemn is lively and gay. Leave the mason to his instinct and he will make poetry of the stones. Now this is a consolation I would not have expected. The world in which we live seems to be organized in straight lines. What is more terrible than the long straight line of a road? What more terrible than the geometric houses in which millions are now condemned to live? No wonder so many people go mad.

And in the same Newsletter, September 1963, Father had to announce the death of the fine architect who had planned the new buildings at The Friars:

Mr Adrian Gilbert Scott, the Architect, died recently. He was monumental in stature and fine-looking. He was eighty-one when he died. He told me often that his work was his recreation. His life was what the mystics call, 'playing before God' – certainly working before God. He seemed to have come straight out of the last century, out of the many churches and public buildings he had designed. Gothic was the idiom in which he revelled. He was a young man at the beginning of this century and it seemed to be more that past century which he finely represented. It was said that nobody could handle stone better than he. He was a deeply religious man, a great gentleman always and most patient, having great humility. His work at Aylesford proved disconcerting to him but adventurous. Actually he had drawn at least a dozen sketch plans and had almost decided we did not know what we wanted. I must confess we didn't; but he never showed impatience. The site was restricted and difficult and getting foundations under forty feet of mud of the Medway was a nightmare. He had all his life been dealing with contractors who knew their job; but we started our work with voluntary labour, most of it unskilled. I remember very well his surprise when I told him there was no other way. He was such a man, so dynamic that at last I had come to think he would never find time to die. May God rest his soul, though I cannot imagine him at rest at all.

But although the building was started in an atmosphere of haphazard endeavour, Adrian had not been left long without competent help.

At a critical moment, and by indirections, Percy Kitchen our foreman came. He it was who saved the situation. He had to train the Italian masons in laying random ragstone, and the rest of the voluntary workers as well.

Of course there were others. There was Mr Ashenden who brought Percy to the site in the beginning. He it was who laid out the foundations of the Open Sanctuary. There was Mr Laws the architect who organized a drawing office with a couple of assistants. He was elderly but not old; that is why he had what amounted to a veneration for Adrian, for he too was young and adventurous in spirit. On one occasion he gave me a slogan which I shall always remember, 'Boldness be our guide'. Then there was Anthony Scott, son of the architect, who is very much with us still; but it was Percy who was really matched with his destiny. He was probably the only foreman in England who could have done this work. He had that feeling, now so rare, for ragstone. He had authority too. It could not have been done without him and it is his monument. No wonder he received the Gift of Faith in return for his great labours and care for Our Lady's Shrine.

Claudel, whom Father considers to be a universal genius, comparable to Dante, and whom he often quotes, wrote an essay on an underground church in his *Ways and Crossways*, which gave Father some illumination on the subject of the Entrance to the Shrine. Material for his Newsletters comes sifting into his hands from various sources: from reading, through the post, from friends, usually only in the nick of time:

A fortnight before I began to write this Newsletter I felt dull and uninspired. Perhaps I was tired. There are times when you can be persuaded that your good is evil. I felt in the mood of Yeats in *Adam's Curse*: 'Better go down upon your marrow bones and scrub a kitchen pavement or break stones, like an old pauper in all kinds of weather.' But don't pity me. I am head over heels in love with living and with being used. Now I am half way through this Newsletter and I don't know what to do with all the material that is coming so plentifully out of my fingers. The last thing I want to do now is to break stones like the old pauper. It is Our Lady again, contriving situations, drawing people in here who are spiritually alive, putting relevant books into my hands or getting them to me through the post.

Now Claudel had suggested that since the Door to Our Father's House can be so forbidding, that even one step up to it is too much for people nowadays, conditioned as they are in body and soul, therefore it should require no effort to enter. New churches should be built underground and the entrance would be a trap beneath the feet of passers-by so that they could fall in bulk like grain into the bottom of a silo.

When I was reading this I was thinking of Aylesford. Very many, perhaps thousands, come in off the main road who never set out to come. You enter The Friars from this road down which you come by force of gravity. It is an alluring way. There are no gates, no obstacles at all. From the road you have sight of the great thatched barns, restored at enormous expense by Messrs Reed's Paper Mills and which now by their most generous gesture belong to The Friars. On a plinth near the road is a stone figure of Our Lady and Child by Michael Clark. Her open hand is by her side in a gesture of welcome. It is really the gesture of abandon, as in Michelangelo's Piéta. She is saying, 'I want you all, all to come in'.

Very near is a pillar of a gateway with a painted sign inset. We were in trouble over this. The authorities protested that a 'development' had taken place without permission too near the public road. I explained that it was a fine sculpture by a great sculptor, worthy of any highway in the world, as it truly is. That did not help. Eventually Adrian Gilbert Scott came to the rescue. He described the sculpture as a garden ornament which may legally be erected within twelve feet of a street or highway. The pillar with the sign he described as 'a glorified gatepost'. Everybody was satisfied. At the bottom of this drive, bordered by the old garden wall, by great elms and lombardy poplars, is Michael Clark's translation in stone of the old Seal of the Priors of Aylesford.

Turning in from this is the main entrance, again by the

old wall through the Gatehouse arch. Over the archway of this old building is another stone figure by Michael. It is of Our Lady and Child and she is holding out her great cloak to pilgrims. It is a fine work not seen by many. Practically all the pilgrims enter by the other two main drives. As you turn by the Seal the view is sudden and startling. You have come into a spacious and beautiful land of orchards and gardens. The roads may be said to sweep in. Too soon you come upon the open Sanctuary of the Glorious Virgin and other buildings on the left, and on the right the old Fishpond with the stones from the ancient ford laid about it. A quick look gives you a glimpse of the Great Court. Relatively this is all miniature and all the better for it – effective in the suggestion of the beyond, as are the slashed faces and houses and trees on the edges of great paintings.

There had been many pilgrimages during that Summer of 1963, but still Father said:

I don't think I shall ever be satisfied. When I think of the three hundred thousand or more Catholics within thirty miles of us, I feel we have not begun. For the Solemnity of Carmel there were many pilgrims. There is a Tertiary, Mrs Chapman, who actually *is* 'Aylesford Tours and Pilgrimages'. She brings many pilgrims in the course of the year. There is also Mrs Bailey whose main endeavour is for the vigils. It was a united effort for the Feast of Carmel. The weather this year reminded me of the glorious days of the Return of the Relics in 1951.

The Castle also had been full all Summer, the Eight-Day Pilgrimages having been a great success. A fine reconstruction of the original mediaeval castle, this place is still ill-adapted for the housing of guests in large numbers as the bedrooms are stately, with great cold bathrooms equipped with mahogany and porcelain fittings and claw-footed bathtubs with enormous taps from which gush cascades of tepid water – boiling if the furnaces are full on. The Castle is difficult of access too; so usually the community there are in the grip of some sort of domestic crisis:

In the early Summer we have had crisis after crisis mainly to do with the kitchen. After a few intriguing try-outs and experiments we found that the cook was here all the time. She is Maria del Amparo, whom we call 'Ampy' for short. She is the wife of Vincente. From doing other work she took over the kitchen, very modestly and with many apologies. She is good in every sense and typical of the fine women of Spain. She is pleasant, always smiling and most intelligent and serene.

A lady who was staying here, and who was on the verge of collapse, suffering from a very great shock, offered to help the young staff to clean up and bring order out of chaos. She was wonderful, like a strong commander who knew how to get things done. By the time the action was finished, so distracting and absorbing was it, she was nearly normal again.

There were many light moments. One day one of the girls, who seemed to her to be slow, threw the broth from the boiling of six chickens down the sink. 'Were you sorry?' asked the lady cook in great anger.

The reply was unexpected: 'No I was not! What's the use? It's gone.'

After that she went right up in the cook's estimation and now, in a quiet way, she is a very good cook's help.

Vincente is a ragstone mason but he can do almost anything. We have in him the nucleus of a building team. In June and July we had six boys from Dublin who worked well under his command. During August three others came, so young-looking that they seemed to have come almost out of their mother's lap. Two of them were fifteen. One of the younger ones was the son of a builder. They were splendid boys, doing the work of strong men. They made hundreds of building blocks and paving flags. At times there were two French students, a Portuguese and an English one. The Chapel was full for Mass every morning.

In addition there was an energetic working party setting the Tilting Yard to rights, and Roger Brown was finishing off the tiling of the big barn which was to be used as a 'Unity Centre' with other buildings. Father was delighted: he had managed to get a hundred yards more ragstone from a demolished church in Gravesend. . . .

In October there was the Unity Week-end, larger than the usual discussion and week-end retreats because it had been sponsored by the League of Christ the King:

Taking the leading parts were a monk of Downside and an Anglican Canon from Canterbury. There was a group of Anglicans belonging to a society with similar aims to L.O.C.K. The Canon was particularly stimulating and an aside about sheep-stealing produced great laughter. Anglicans and Catholics should laugh more, but with the Church, not at the Church, their Mother and ours. It makes apostolic frankness easier. This encounter wasn't solemn at all; but it was most revealing just the same. The most bitter of the grievances of the Anglican Church it seems had to do with mixed marriage regulations and the re-baptizing of converts. Another grievance touched on by the Canon was concerned with our making a morality out of Canon Law. He thought that the grave obligation to go to Mass on Sundays and days of Obligation, and the Precepts of the Church generally, seemed unjustified.

It is not a question of Canon Law or the Pope or the Church *making* new sins, as if there were not enough already! The Church did not make the natural law. It is built into us by our Creator. Our obligation to go to Mass on Sundays is only a definition of the natural law. As a matter of fact it's always surprising to me that we are not obliged to give formal worship to God every day. The Eastern peoples give more time to God and are more religious than we are in this respect. They certainly would not regard half an hour or an hour a week in formal worship as anything but a paltry gesture to the good God.

In the years which followed that first Unity Week-end there was still more building to be done. Eventually it might even involve Father's great dream of a City of Mary: comfortable houses big enough for large families built in the Castle grounds. But in the immediate future there was all that ragstone to be used for extra accommodation round the Barn courtyard at Allington.

From now on it would be the lives, the people, the living stones of the Church which would be ever more prominent in the minds, plans and prayers of the Carmelites.

VI

All that Dedicated City

In September 1965 Father gave a full account of the ceremonies
for the Feast of Our Lady of Mount Carmel at which the new
altars had been consecrated. People had realized that these
celebrations, following the pattern of the days on which the
relics of St Simon had been brought from Bordeaux, were a
mark of the end of the beginning, a chance to catch that
usually imperceptible moment when a dream becomes reality.
So they would not be contented until he had written a full
account of all that had happened during those significant
three days. But, as is usual, there is so much involved in every
statement of his writing that there are no flat and finite sentences. To quote Boethius, Father's facts are like that eternity
'from which none of the future is absent and from which
nothing of the past has drained away'. As Father himself says:

> For me reporting a past event just as an event, with facts
> and figures, is a sorry business. Perhaps it is because I
> am a Carmelite and the Carmelite Order is prophetic. I do
> not mean that in the ordinary sense of foretelling the
> future, but in the sense that it is the clarification of the
> present. We see the future in the way we expect to see the
> plant or the flower issue when the seed is sown on the
> ground. This event, splendid as it was, was in the nature of
> a prophecy, a looking forward, something still unfinished.
> Never have I felt so impersonal as during those days.
>
> Aylesford is not my achievement. I was sent under
> obedience to do this work, against my natural inclinations.

It meant pulling up my roots after thirteen years in Wales. Prayer was all I brought with me, and there were and are so many people involved in Aylesford. Nearly twenty thousand came for the 'great day'; yet they are only a token number of all those, living and dead, who have poured their love and desire into it. 'The heart's earnest and pure desire is always fulfilled.' It was not even a Christian who said this; but how eagerly and urgently so many have looked for the fulfilment of their desires to Aylesford. So many poor widows have given their life savings; the small alms of so many and the big alms of some! And there were so many who have given their hands to build Our Lady's House and Shrine again. Surely it was *their* day; and surely this accounted for the happiness and serenity on the faces of those who came.

Major O'Connell Hewitt was there with his wife for the great Sunday, looking happily bewildered. Ten years ago he acted as guide and guestmaster at The Friars and was known to many thousands of pilgrims. He gave some years of his life to this work when we were a very small community. On one occasion he was taking a party of pilgrims round the Cloisters. He was telling them of our church to be and of our dreams for the complete restoration of the Shrine. A venerable lady, who seemed to be on her last legs, said to him, 'Alas! I shall not live to see it.' He said to her, 'You will, you will. It will jump up.'

She proved to be a most generous benefactor and the Major's prophecy was fulfilled. That great lady is now living in the Courtyard of The Friars and is completing her ninety-fourth year. She is younger-looking now and more sprightly than ten years ago. She is not really growing old at all.

There had been much prophecy connected with Aylesford.

Archbishop Cowderoy had prophesied on his first visit, when it was a desolated ruin, it would become one of the great shrines of Christendom. Father Cyril Plummer, parish priest of Uckfield, had been praying since 1929 for something to happen there in the way of a return. It must have been in 1929 too that Father Peter Elias Magennis, the first Irish Prior-General, and Father Elias with him, paid a visit to The Friars when the Copley Hewitts were tenants.

On that day there was a Girl Guide Jamboree going on and the Archbishop of Canterbury was a guest. Mrs Copley Hewitt gave a great welcome to the Prior-General:

Despite the other distinguished guests present she clung to him eagerly and they got on very well together. This was not surprising. He was a personality with the gift of bringing people to life wherever he went. I remember Mrs Hewitt as a spiritual woman, gentle and wistful, and aware of the timelessness of prayer and spiritual things. The Father General became a legend and as so often happens he was greater than the legend. He spent the last years of his life climbing stairs to visit the poor living in tenements, and was greatly revered.

When the fire in 1930 destroyed a great part of The Friars we Carmelites thought it was the end of our hopes; but again in the end was a beginning. The Earl of Aylesford sold the ruined property to the tenants. It must have been Mrs Hewitt's great love of the place which inspired the restoration they themselves undertook although it meant incurring a heavy mortgage on the property. When we returned in 1949 the big chapel with its beautiful roof, constructed from the timbers of the old Arethusa Training Ship, was all ready for Mass and served us well until the new chapels were ready. Mrs Hewitt did not live to see the Carmelites return though I am sure that she still cares about the place she so greatly loved. And the two great Carmelites are in heaven long since.

It is interesting that the Prior-General at the time of James II petitioned the King for the return of Aylesford to the Carmelites. Another forerunner and prophet of the Return was Father John of the Cross Cogan, a former Provincial. He was Prior of an important priory when he volunteered to come to Kent in order to be near Aylesford. Recalling all this, I can see now that there was about the Carmelites of those days an indefinable chivalry which could only have come from Our Blessed Lady. . . .

Then there were the ghosts who seemed to be the heralds of our return. An Anglican lady, at that time a tenant of the old Dower House near the village, had a very special reason for welcoming back the friars. She wrote her interesting ghost stories for me but they are now lost in a mass of records. There were many strange happenings in her house: ghostly figures were seen kneeling in the basement where she believed there might be an altar stone or something sacred from the old Priory. They were pleasant ghosts and not evil.

A former Vicar of the place, I think the father of Dame Sybil Thorndike, the actress, went out late one evening to post an urgent letter and ghost figures brushed him in the half-light. When this lady saw us on the bridge on the historic afternoon on the Vigil of All Saints 1949, she was suddenly able to identify the white habits of the ghosts that had been seen. She is sane and indeed matter-of-fact about spiritual realities. She loves The Friars and often comes. When she left the Dower House some years ago she gave us a good painting of the Annunciation for remembrance. It hangs in the Reception Room and I never see it but I think of her and the pleasant ghosts.

But to return to the Ceremonies:

Three days' ceremonies followed the pattern of the 1949 celebrations. There were nearly a hundred Carmelites for the Father General's Mass on the Friday. They were from all over the world, most of them returning from the General Chapter in Rome. There was one Provincial from Poland, the first to emerge from behind the Iron Curtain for twenty years. He had already served his purgatory in Auschwitz and Dachau. To have so many Carmelites together and to be able to accommodate them all would have seemed a fantastic happening not so many years ago. The majority of the priests were gathered round the Carmelite Bishop of Arezzo for a Concelebration Mass in the large chapel restored by the Hewitts.

The Ordinations were on Saturday evening and the evening itself added a sense of mystery. All the Carmelites and the considerable congregation were gathered around the Archbishop to see two Carmelite priests being made on the open Sanctuary. The power of the priesthood being handed down in solemn and unhurried ritual is always full of mighty promise and prophecy. And then the great day itself was there.

To have three fine days in succession in the worst July anybody can remember was not the least of the mircales. So many prayers went up to Our Lady and St Elias that I never doubted it would be fine. A triumph would not be the word to describe it all, a 'shewing' is a mediaeval word and better. The Consecration of the Altars was a long ceremony. At one point in it I was startled by a moment of sheer beauty. I was happy to be looking on: the huge bare stone, thirty hundredweight of it, had the Relics buried in it and had been anointed. Four small candles were placed on each of the four corners and lighted.

A slow and beautiful chant was sung as the candles burned down. I didn't know what they were symbolizing; but the Sanctuary was filled with an ancient mystery. It stays in the memory and was so overwhelming that one felt no urge to enquire or ask what it meant, for fear it might vanish and escape for ever.

The Cardinal is a familiar figure to almost everybody now. He is tall with an easy dignity and smiling presence. He has a good face and a voice which is soft and very clear. He has an easy manner and was at home at once. His motto is, *Sub Umbra Carmeli*, which could be translated variously 'under the shadow of Carmel' or might also be rendered, 'under the mantle of Carmel'. He could hardly fail to be at home as he walked to his throne over the foundations of the old Church of the Assumption of the Glorious Virgin. To the many who awaited him he was very obviously a beloved figure. He congratulated the Archbishop, the first of the new Metropolitan See of Southwark, and after that was easily in context:

'Saint Simon Stock was known by a simple title throughout Christendom in the thirteenth century. He was known simply as "The Englishman", because in those days England was so celebrated for its devotion to Mary. . . . We all know that the Anglo-Saxon King Alfred founded the Royal Navy and, of course, burned the cakes; but a lesser-known fact is that he made the Feast of the Assumption a public holiday: and yet there are those who talk of the Assumption as being a new-fangled Popish doctrine!'

He pointed out that attacks on the Faith were always centred on the two points of the Holy Sacrifice of the Mass and devotion to the Mother of God. But he said that it would be quite untrue to say that Protestants could be won back to Catholic allegiance by denying the Sacrifice of the Mass and the glories of Mary. Rather would it be

true to say that in the new spirit of ecumenism, Mary can
be the means of unity through whom we can lead others to
a knowledge of her Son. Since fewer than one in ten of the
population of Great Britain were even occasional church-
goers, the need for the conversion of England was most
urgent. Unless the country were returned to Our Lady's
Dowry it looked as if most would soon have lost their
faith in God altogether.

The Archbishop, in his Pastoral from Aylesford, took up
the same theme when he depicted Our Lady as 'looking
forward to the return of her children for whom she has prayed
throughout her earthly life and whom she will welcome home
when we have passed through the dark shadow of death and
lead us to the feet of her divine Son; her God and our God'.

Father says:

> The Archbishop is simple and uncomplicated in his
> devotion to Our Blessed Lady. Always he takes me back to
> fourteenth-century England, to Julian of Norwich and the
> 'marvellous great homeliness of the Incarnation'. This is
> truly in the spirit of mediaeval devotion. It is Julian of
> Norwich who writes of Our Blessed Lord with great
> courtesy at the end of life receiving us into his great house
> and thanking us one by one.

The B.B.C. had not mentioned the celebrations as an item
of news, nor had the national press; but the Catholic press
had given great coverage to them, so in a way it turned out
that the great majority of people there were Catholics, most
of whom had provided The Friars in one way or another with
help. So it was fitting that they should be thanked in 'His
Great House', by his representatives on earth.

Now that his great task was completed, Father's role was
still unique. As writer of the Newsletters, as priest-in-charge

of pilgrimages, as the personal friend of innumerable people in all walks of life, he was able to present the fruits of his Catholic judgement to a most catholic array of subjects. Bearing within him his own *clausura* he is able to cut through to truth in a way which is extremely rare. The man with a foot in two camps seldom has balance; he veers either to one side or the other; he is brashly worldly or coldly cloistered. In a world where 'the best lack all conviction' Father's insights are sure and definite, his balance perfect. With the peasant's wife it might be boldly asserted that even when he is wrong he is right.

In January 1964, writing on the death of President Kennedy he wrote:

There is no true summary of the late President possible if we leave out the Providence of the good Lord. Neither his genius nor his drive explain him. He had all the gifts and he used them, every one. I would say that as far as his natural endowment was concerned it was 'in his blood'. We have leave of the psychologists now to go back to his ancestry. Mauriac, the great French novelist, in his Memoirs, has this reflection: 'At the source of a man's being lies not himself but the swarming life of a whole race.' A man like the dead President didn't just *happen*. He had in him the unbroken generations of the Faith, he was the *Catholicus homo*, the Catholic man of St Augustine, and surely in him this tremendous thing derived from the contemporary of St Augustine, St Patrick himself. In him too was a passion for freedom. For him liberty was sacred as a sacrament. We know where that comes from yet we know it did not begin from his grandfather who was driven from his homeland in the 'hungry Forties'. There is a residue of something from the long past which every man carries with him. What is this which stirs in the blood of the old peoples, this ancient thing, ancient as God? It is a right instinct in the Irish-Americans to trace their ancestry and to be proud of their family name. What a pair of names the dead President had! It is not the beginning of an aristocracy of wealth and power that we have known. There is no title at all compared to the ancient title of the blood.

The dead President was not a pious Catholic. He had the Faith and went to Mass. He went to Mass in the same way as any ordinary Catholic does. He did not have what is called a Catholic education. What he had in him was something other. He had in him, in common with many other Irish people, the Faith as a command: word to keep and give back to God. It was almost entirely without emotion. When I was in the States I saw and heard him often on television. He knew the hammering power of words and his short sentences were reinforced by a mannerism of his jabbing fingers. It was dry and too much in the style of a traditional rhetoric. This style did not suit his personality at all. He was most revealing in informal interviews, sitting in his rocking chair with no eloquence, hesitating but not uncertain, innocently out to change the world into one of families like his own, enjoying the amenities of freedom from fear and freedom from want.

There has been a great deal of writing, and indeed of fine inspired writing about his death; but it sometimes happens that a stray remark or observation by some quite ordinary person reveals more than many pages. And so it was the description of the President's last moments by an English nurse, Diana Hamilton Bowron, of the hospital staff which received him after the accident, that impressed me most.

'When we brought in the President he was covered with petals from the flowers which Mrs Kennedy was carrying, and as we worked on him they were scattered all over the floor of the room. Mrs Kennedy came in there with a trolley and stayed until it became too crowded. The hospital staff tried to persuade her to come outside but she came back in just as he died. After he died she kissed his hand: then she took off her wedding ring and slipped it on to his wedding finger. It came just up to the knuckle.'

If I knew the pieties of the Kennedy family I might guess the secret of that lovely happening and the renewal of the Sacrament. It would have been natural to be hysterical at such a moment. We can only say that it was something instinctive and in the blood, in the memory that goes back and becomes automatic at a terrible moment; as if all the generations of her Catholic ancestors were awaiting it, completing this gesture.

When my mother was dying and getting weaker, just a few days before she died, she told me deliberately of my father who died when most of the family were young and she was left to carry on almost alone. She spoke slowly and without any emotion. She told me how he said goodbye to her and then kissed the wedding ring on her finger. Again, where on earth did this gesture come from? She told me that in all difficulties which followed that he was near and that she was without fear. Many other things she told me which were hard to bear because I knew she was saying goodbye while she could.

In February 1964 we are given two other glimpses of life at the Castle:

The Castle has truly become the Open Door we have intended it to be. The Unity discussions, which have been held every week in Lent, were most friendly and helpful. There were several denominations and they all asked for the meetings to be continued. A non-Catholic wrote to say,

'What a wonderful, kind and reasonable House she keeps. I wish the whole world were like it.'

One day an ex-Buddhist came to be a voluntary worker. He began life as a Catholic but allured by the mystery of the East went to Thailand. He wanted perfection at any cost and carried out all the exercises designed to get rid of all consciousness of self. At the end of it all he found nothingness and was scared out of his wits.

One night he bolted to the nearest Catholic Mission. The American priest was surprised to see this saffron-robed monk on his doorstep. 'Gee!' he said, 'I dunno what to do with you. I must look at my Faculty Papers.' The Buddhist came back with a wallop, he says, and has never done thanking God for what has come to him since.

Also to the Open Door last Sunday came His Holiness Swami Bhola Nath with his Maharanee and their son. His Holiness wore a simple white robe with a scarlet turban, the sign of a holy man in India. He is a mystic and writer and well known all over India as a religious philospher and has addressed mass meetings everywhere. When he speaks of God he lights up and is most eloquent and his language sheer poetry. 'Where God is,' he says, 'time does not exist.' He uses Christian words like *Grace* and knows that the life of God is in him to be given endlessly. He must be baptized by his great desire for God and his great love.

The friend who introduced him said that his outlook was exactly like mine! 'I want to deliver a man to you. And what a man! The Maharajah has powerful "Desinturbulating" powers, meaning giving people back their souls which they have lost in the "rat race". He has a spiritual power of breaking up atheists.'

On a Sunday afternoon at Christmas there occurred one of those situations that happen so plentifully when we practise the 'Use me Today' apostolate. In the Castle we were sitting round the stove having tea. It was a cold afternoon. Somebody looked out and said there was a man, all muffled up, coming in. Then he corrected himself, saying, 'It is not a man at all but a priest'. We were all laughing. The priest had seen us through the window and he was laughing too when he came in. He was a priest with a difference, having all the appearance of a lively Commando, light-hearted and free. He was on his way back to Switzerland and was craving a lodging for the night. We talked all evening and after supper and it was a blessed evening for us all. It was one of those conversations which go on for ever in your mind afterwards. I think that all conversations should be like that, creating all the time, and yet they are so rare in this world of tumult and noise.

He was a monk belonging to a celebrated abbey in Switzerland. Before he joined it he had been a missionary priest in China and had been working there for nine years when the Communists came. They began by proscribing all meetings: one person visiting another in his home was a *meeting*. It was death by shooting for being anti-Communist. Five million Chinese were shot for nothing else. The tribunals were just fact-finding, cold and impersonal and sentence of death was automatic.

The Father was arrested with other priests and kept in solitary confinement for nine months. There were the usual investigations and examinations which were diabolical – cold, evil, subtle brain-washing all the time. Father had little doubt but that they were all possessed. There was evil in their eyes and voice, in every action. Always he pleaded guilty of being anti-Communist and expected death at any moment.

In his account he never mentioned suffering or torture. When he had no defence and no friends at all he found that God was with him in a way that he had never known

before. God for him was a *discovery* and he not only felt
but *was* as strong as God, not just defiant and enduring. He
was saying that you can talk on God and lecture on him
and be a learned professor and yet not know him in this
way. It is Our Lord's command, 'Have no fear, even if you
walk through the valley of death, God is with you'.

We are taught this as children but because we are hardly
ever completely dependent on God's direct help, our faith
in God's Providence is not put to the test. And Father has a
very simple way of explaining this. He says, 'It is like having
a complete catechism in electricity; and having had it
installed you turn on the switches and nothing happens –
until you need it'. The hours during which he talked to us
seemed like minutes and one of the things which was
impressive was the way in which the good Lord was concerned for the prisoners' relatively small needs. They had a
needle between them which was very useful when they
unravelled old garments and knitted others. And then this
needle was either captured or lost when they were moved
from one prison to another. The priests were sad indeed
at the grievous loss.

The guards were kind and they were allowed a certain
amount of liberty at the stations. Our priest wandered
aimlessly along to where there was a newspaper stall.
There was a bundle of papers and he lifted up the first paper
he saw. Underneath was a needle. This needle was later
used by all of them until it was discovered and taken away.
On the train a guard recognized him as a priest. He held out
his hand to him with a rosary and said, 'We will keep Faith'.

Of these small interventions there seemed to be no end
and of St Thérèse he said, 'She is absolutely sure'. He told
us of how a large Catholic community survived in Japan
for three hundred years. Both the sacraments of Baptism
and Marriage can be administered by lay people. That was

how it was possible. They were given signs by which they would recognize the True Faith and know the priests when they would return. One of the signs was Our Lady.

Father has the greatest admiration and love for the real character of the Chinese. They will never be Communists. They are very deep and mature and patient and serene. They are certainly not an upstart people; the ancient wisdom of Confucius still prevails. Confucian doctrine is the sum of the wisdom of the ancient kings going back three thousand years before Christ. All their sayings and precepts were collected and collated by Confucius in the sixth century B.C. They are based on family life from which derives reverence for parents and ancestors. It is said that Confucianism is not a philosophy but the religion of a gentleman. It is the highest natural wisdom in living and behaviour that has ever been realized. From it came the elaborate courtesy and mutual respect and serenity of the Chinese. The whole of life constituted the pursuit of wisdom and since it was the highest possible attainment there was a warning against vainglory in the saying of the ancients: 'The man who discovers wisdom in the morning may die in the evening.' Three great emperors, 3000 B.C., were contemporaries of Abraham, Isaac and Jacob; there is a description of the emperor Choen. 'He was indeed a sovereign. He had abandoned the empire without more regrets than if he were discarding an old pair of shoes. He was great in dignity.'

This continuing tradition has helped the missionaries of our day. Every home has a 'holy corner', and Catholic homes have an altar. The priests used to offer Mass in the homes as a matter of course. All the family gathered for Mass round the holy place. The home for the Chinese is sacred, the temple of the Lord of Heaven.

The home and the family were the bedrock of Eastern

I

wisdom. The following is quoted from *Ways of Confucius and of Christ* by Dom Pierre Celestin Lou Tseng-Tsiang – Chinese diplomat. He became a Benedictine and Titular Abbot in the Abbey of St André near Bruges.

'In the family we possess the pattern of the whole of society. The family is the soil whence we are sprung; whence our children are born and will be born, and in which is sown the seed of all the human race. How could we rate too highly the importance and nobility of the fact of the family . . . the bond of family life is filial piety . . . filial piety discloses to us, then, in the serene light, the human wealth which God has given us and which he does not cease to give us. Through it we bind ourselves to all the generations which have preceded us. . . . The man who neglects it breaks himself away from his own roots. He is an anonymity (a nobody). Without filial piety the individual is no longer a filial being; he is no longer a social being, he is disintegrated . . . he who frees himself from filial piety is a dead man. . . . Civilizations and cultures which were the very brilliant contemporaries of Chinese civilization and culture have barely bequeathed to us their pyramids and tombs. Filial piety is the principle which conditions all the spiritual and moral life of mankind from its most distant past to its uttermost future.'

China has had many tyrannies like the present one and for long periods. Yet missionaries who have suffered and known the ruin of the external Church there by no means counsel despair. They say the Chinese are deep and loyal and trustworthy: they are hard-working and honest, long-suffering, patient and serene. They are most lovable. The three million Chinese will keep the faith even though the external Church be destroyed. One of the missionaries who suffered much told me surprisingly that a time would come when men would be grateful for the six hundred million Chinese. The saintly Abbot I have been quoting from, who died not long ago, wrote towards the end of his book. 'The ways of God are mysterious. And that is why, in our faith and in the charity which God gives us, we have a filial confidence in His Providence. That confidence fills us with an audacious and invincible hope.'

All this makes one wonder if we don't 'have it too good', in the West, if we couldn't do with a few trials in order to come to some kind of knowledge of the dimensions of the human soul and the reaches of the personality. In a sheltered society people seem to be living in just a few rooms of the possible vast mansions they might have. Many have cut themselves off from the roots of Faith which have nourished their families for generations of hardship and find they have become what the Abbot at St André would have called 'nobodies'.

Under the heading, 'Seeking Identity', Father Malachy had earlier discussed this very question:

During the Summer (of 1962) two young people came to stay at the Castle at different times. Both were under the care of psychiatrists, both were graduates of famous universities and very brilliant. Neither had any religious convictions. One could talk of the Catholic Faith more brilliantly and convincingly than I could. I was taken because there seemed to be nothing I could do or say to help her. Both spoke the same kind of language. They were trying to *find their identity*. They had divested themselves or had been divested of any faith they ever had and of the natural knowledge of God and his Purpose for Creation, which should be uppermost in every human being. I realized at once that this identity seeking is not empty jargon – but a tragic fact. Here were two people, liberated from the moral law and every restraint, and in the end not knowing who they are or what they are for or where or if they are going anywhere. Insecure is not the word, they are just lost. They are rooted in nothing, waking up to nothing. Everything had become unreal to them, even people. They say they converse but they do not communicate. There are millions of sophisticated and highly intellectual people who are now failing to have any *communion* with their fellows. How can anyone bear a loneliness like this? Gabriel Fielding said a striking thing about them: 'The more they penetrate such illusions as they have, the more life becomes a series of unrelated dreams. Without God they are walking out of life.'

What gives security to Catholic people is the Faith. It is operative in our prayer in the Mass. *Per ipsum et cum ipso et in ipso*, 'Through him and with him and *in* him'. This is complete identity. St Paul many times uses the words '*In Christo*' to express this. A Christian can find identity in nothing else upon this earth. It is a vain search. How strong it is and secure it is to be *in* God's will. You will find the freshness that comes from this and the innocence everywhere in the Catholic world: in the Wicklow Mountains – the Spanish girls now with us in the Castle have it, and the girls from the Tyrol and from Portugal who have come here in other years have had it too. It creates an atmosphere which is so happy and reassuring. If you want to know what the Faith really is and does, look at them, observe them, for that is *it*. Education or a higher standard of living doesn't produce it. And the moral is, as Chesterton wrote, that 'no man should desert that Catholic civilization. It can cure itself but those who leave it cannot cure it.'

But of course ecumenism is here to stay. Now, as the Pope has said, it is a straight dispute between those who believe in God and the forces of atheistic materialism. One of his friends persuaded Father Malachy to go on one of the ecumenical tours of the Holy Land which had 'come in' in support of the movement. So on Easter Monday 1964 he set out with a hopeful heart and his journey is described fully in Newsletter no. 73.

The party followed very much the usual 'Classical-Academic' itinerary – Malta, Knossos in Crete, Beirut, Baalbek, Damascus, Jericho. It was not until Father was able to go down and touch the waters of the Jordan that he felt he was truly 'in the steps of the Master'.

We caught up with the main party at the Dead Sea. Then with no great delay we were on our way to Jerusalem.

The light was failing but from some miles out we could see the golden dome of the Rock, not, alas, the sight the pilgrims of old saw when they sighted Sion from afar. The driver showed us the Mount of Olives. The shadows of night had begun to fall on Gethsemane. I was glad to see it in the half light as we sped up and up. Then we halted suddenly outside the Ambassador Hotel. I was very tired but after the violence of the driving, glad to be alive.

After dinner in the crowded lounge there were several clergy and a bishop. My first instinct was to escape for I was in no mood for solemnities but almost as I sighted him the bishop came forward with a most friendly greeting. As Canon Fyson of Rochester he had been a frequent visitor to Aylesford in the desolate days, always friendly and encouraging. We didn't talk of Unity at all but of the human soul and I don't know what, for an hour or more. Then I met the Greek Orthodox bishop from London in the same party. It was all very unexpected and happy. It was a 'situation'.

Really Father quite enjoyed the mixture of clergy and

denominations in his party. He was slightly surprised to meet a deaconess from the Methodist Church and he found the perpetual reciting of the Lord's Prayer, which was considered to be the only 'safe' communal prayer for the party, rather monotonous, used as he was to the great treasury of Litanies and prayers to Our Lady and the saints which the Church has collected over the centuries. When asked 'Was this Journey successful?' he answered:

> Of course it was, if it did nothing else it helped to allay prejudice. When I worked in Wales years ago I usually met people who thought a priest had horns under his hat. I encountered nothing like that on the journey; but there *is* prejudice. It is a fixation not about the present but about the Reformation and the Inquisition and Satan knows what. This prejudice is sometimes stated like this: 'The Catholic Church will have to clean herself up a lot before I join her.' This always reminds me of a story of M. Jacques Maritain when he and his wife Raïssa were compelled by conviction to ask for Baptism. He was a Protestant, she was Jewish, they had a burning desire for Truth. Jacques finally said to Raïssa, 'If Truth is on a dunghill, it is there we must go to find it', and they lived to become ardent lovers of the Church.

And one of his expectations on starting out had been to find Elias:

> When he was taken away from the earth a company of 'Sons of the Prophet' set out to look for him. They came back to Jericho to report their failure to Eliseus. He just said, 'I told you so'.
>
> I was hoping to find evidence of a cultus of Elias and I did. Archbishop Hakim of Galilee told me that forty churches in his See are dedicated under the title of Elias.

I spent a vivid hour with a monk on the very top of the Monastery of St John on Patmos. He spoke Italian and was most dramatic. We had just seen a most beautiful eikon of Elias in their museum, which was full of lovely things. We were looking across to a higher mountain with a church on top of it. It was the church of Elias. He told me that his mother used to climb up every day to offer incense to the prophet. That was her prayer. One day, coming down, she was caught in a tempest of rain. Not a drop fell on her. *'Che fede, la madre!'* 'What faith my mother had!'

At Aylesford we are always desperately invoking him against rain. Because of what happened on Carmel Elias is always invoked in the East and in Russia for rain and against it. We want to restore the cultus of the prophet at Aylesford. Carmel without Elias is hardly relevant; without Our Lady of Mount Carmel it is nothing at all. I always think of Carmel as being where the West ends and the East begins. We can invoke her for the unity of East and West – so long overdue – and she is using Aylesford and Allington most powerfully for Unity.

Of St Elias St James says he was a man *'passibilis, similis nobis,'* a man subject to weakness and to moods and yet confessing his zeal for the Lord. 'With zeal have I been zealous for the Lord God of Hosts.' This is a Hebrewism which has become the motto of the Carmelite Order. If people realize fully the moods and despairs the prophet had had to contend with, his cultus would not be long in coming! The Cult of Mood most certainly came into Europe with the Romantic movement and it seems that it is only Zeal for God which will shift it!

And with the aid of Elias, Father was bearing up well to all the sightseeing:

The only place I could arrange for Mass next morning

was at the Franciscan Church on Calvary. Mrs B, an energetic widow in her sixties who spent most of her time translating books into braille, and I took a taxi, not all the way, for there was a stiff climb from a square through narrow passage ways. The church was large and clean and cool. The Franciscan guardian was Italian and as friendly as could be. We got back late for breakfast and the other pilgrims had gone so we had a taxi again and went back to Calvary and did the Way of the Cross. Down many steps we went to the original pavement of the Lithostratos, the place of the Judgement. Cut out on the flags is a Basilikos game – the King Game – which the soldiers played with Our Lord in horrible realism on the first Good Friday.

The Holy Way is narrow and sordid. It is certainly not nice, which is just as well. It smelled indescribably – the smell of humanity, smells of all kinds coming from dark dens and doorways. Passing up this Holy Way we encountered something which I shall never forget. There was a butcher's shop reeking with smells because it was also a slaughter-house. Taking up half the street were two men with two tall, short-woolled patient unresisting sheep. They were bargaining with the rough butcher who was feeling the sheep for fatness. With an instant sharp pain one thought of him who was led along that way like a lamb to the slaughter. It was easy enough at that hour to say our prayers and to get along. This was the only serious obstacle we met.

Gethsemane they visited and Bethlehem:

From Gethsemane we went to Bethlehem along the sides of little hills – it seemed to me. They were bright with flowers, small flowers you might find anywhere, buttercups and daisies. Lots of rocks and stones were showing in the sloping fields. . . . Down in the crypt was the cave about which every Christian knows, about which all the songs are sung. Here in this cave-dwelling was all that was essential for *wholeness*, a roof, a shelter, the Blessed Mother and St Joseph. These caves were larger than we realized. We cannot imagine Our Lord in a palace or in soft garments or in the middle class or even in that poverty usually confused with destitution. He fits into no category. . . . Our Lord comes *whole* to us out of a cave. What he was wearing did not matter at all. He had no house – he died without a place on which to lay his head. It was what he was. This is the revelation of Bethlehem.

And such a place, simple, adequate, classless, is, by inference, the most fortunate niche in which to be born and brought up. Father is never tired of writing about his home village in County Wicklow which has this in common with all the reasonably poor villages of Christendom; that they are the cradles of giants. In a Newsletter of 1962 he gave news of his home:

My sister Margaret has just written to tell me of the death of one of the pilgrims who came with the Irish Pilgrimage in June. She was from Aughrim in Co. Wicklow. I was born three miles further up, at Ballymanus on one of the foothills of Lugnaquilla, the second highest mountain in Ireland. We called it a town but Aughrim is really a huddle of houses on both sides of a river at a point where there is a bridge.

So selective is my memory that I remember still the lights of the village seen from afar as we came down the dark roads on winter evenings, and I remember the peculiar smell of hardware in one of the shops. The bridge itself is as fine and beautiful as any in that valley. The river is crystal clear and can become a torrent in the rainy season. There is a small waterfall by the bridge made by the water overflowing the containing wall of the millrace which turned the large mill further down. The mill is a tall building, built of granite as is the fine parish church and the priest's house. The finest granite in the world is quarried only a mile away. . . .

And very good granite it had to be; as strong as Father's purpose in writing the Newsletters. Reading those of the last few years it is a hard shock to see how much he suffered all the time from exacerbations of his diabetes and other illnesses. Several times he was in hospital or under constant treatment at the Castle. In December 1964 he wrote:

In the middle of the high Summer I was bedevilled by sciatica. After weeks of pain I had to surrender to the plank bed. Then there were X-rays which showed no slipped disc nor any spinal deformity. The doctors told me that since the sciatic nerve is hidden by muscle no external treatment can get at it at all. I had many remedies sent by friends, ointments and lotions of all kinds. One good friend sent me a herbal mixture with the comment: 'There is no real evidence that it ever cured anybody'. It was a horrible drench. Eventually I was persuaded that the only cure was to rest and to be out of circulation for a considerable time. Reluctantly I went to hospital, fearing the change of food might upset my diabetes which had been behaving well for two years. What I had feared happened. The pain-killers failed and all the functions of the body seemed to go out of order. Two days and nights were dramatic after a purge supposed to be mild. Perspiration rolled off me and in the mornings it was like being in a tepid bath and yet there was no high temperature. I lost seven pounds in a week.

This sciatic pain is quite savage. I feel that in these weeks I have done my dying. However, on the last Friday I was there the diabetes at least had returned nearly to normal. On Tuesdays and Fridays the specialist visited the hospital but since he was going on holiday the next day he did not have time to see all his patients. That evening I was desperate with pain. They had given up even trying the pain-killers. I said dozens of rosaries, each one worse than an all-night vigil. I offered them for people whom I knew needed prayer and somehow the rosaries seemed to get into the pain and grapple with it. I was surprised I could pray at all with recollection. It really did make sense of pain like this. 'Blessed are they who suffer and know why.' I offered rosaries with Our Lady, with St Joseph and with St Jude. In desperation I went round the rosary beads saying the jingle prayer, 'Little Flower, in this hour, show thy power'. In the morning my mind was made up and very firmly: the young house doctor came in and began to explain the programme for the next weeks. I said that I was going to return to the Castle that afternoon. 'In the middle of treatment?' he asked, surprised.

As he went out an innocent looking letter was handed to me. Two rose petals were enclosed in it. Someone had sent the petals from the first rose on a new rose tree called Stella. A great peace and reassurance came with it. It was a bold decision and seemed rude and ungrateful to break the treatment. For the good sisters and the nurses I had qualms, for the specialist I had none at all. When I came back to the Castle there were rose petals awaiting, sent from Lisieux, and roses in abundance on my desk.

The Curé d'Ars has described pain as 'an austere interview with God' and there is a French saying, 'To suffer passes, to have suffered never passes'. To suffer pain, as Father says, is only to get in touch with the world's pain, to acquire a touch faculty for all who suffer. But to get back to the village:

Those Irish quarries are not worked now, alas, and the activity of the mill has been diminished, I fear; it is not worked now any more by the great water-wheel which used to be such a great object of wonder to us, as was the miller.

Down by the river at one corner of the bridge was the forge. The smiths, powerful brawny men, would work hard for hours, ding-dong, with a ringing rhythm. There would be a run of alternating blows on the iron and then two taps on the anvil. Every now and again the smiths would come up and sit on the bridge, always at the same place, and talk to passers-by. I remember the ding-dong even now just as all the country sounds from one's youth come back from the deeps of memory. Not only the sounds of animals and birds and cocks come back, but the sounds of water falling and swishing and rippling and a million others. They are truly *in* one and they are a possession forever.

At the other end of the village was a Post Office. Mrs M. B. Phelan was the Postmistress and much else besides. After the priest she was the most important person, and she was that by virtue of who she *was*. Mass every morning was the order of her day. She was the kind of woman to whom everybody went in trouble. She needed no organization into doing good, her charity was sudden and spontaneous and practical. There were many sorrows of her own and of others which she knew and in knowing, bore. There was never fuss or panic and never did she try to by-pass sorrow or sickness by merely human alleviations. I cannot describe goodness like this; but in this woman it was translated delicately and sensitively into action.

When my mother died she was in our home; maudlin grief she could not understand, nor did she show any. During my mother's illness we had the privilege of a private oratory in the house. There was a Wake. This is an old institution and was edifying and unforgettable to me, prayer going on all the time, informal and homely; no insincerity or solemnity. My mother was laid out in the brown habit of Carmel. Many generations of the people have been clothed in the same way, it was normal and not fancy. Since the fourteenth century at least men and women of our race and Faith have been laid to rest in that way. It made death and its griefs appear most natural.

On the Sunday morning Father Elias and I offered our Masses at home. The Parish Church was three miles away. All the people of the household, tired and exhausted, availed themselves of the opportunity of 'getting Mass'. Some knowing person questioned whether they fulfilled their obligation in a private oratory. It was typical that the question was referred to Mrs M. B. and not to us priests. Very clearly and like a Judge summing up and giving judgement she said: 'If I myself were involved, I would not go to Mass again for the Pope himself.'

The youngest of her four children was Lal, a bonny girl, gay and lively. You would say that she, particularly, was made for happiness as indeed we all are. She remained at home, got married and had children. Occasionally she wrote to me and asked for prayers. Her husband had a serious illness and she herself had contracted creeping paralysis and long desired to come on pilgrimage to Aylesford.

After what proved to be the lapse of her lifetime she came with the Irish Pilgrims and I saw her – a woman. She seemed tall but wasn't. She was erect and walking with a limp. She was slim and seemed to me to be very elegantly dressed. She had a suffering face. She talked fast and well and seemed to grip everything keenly with her mind. Pain had made her like that. There was no trace of self-pity or weakness and she seemed secure and serene. She had her mother's speech and all her reverence and courtesy and Faith. I am not writing about a famous woman or a singular one. She was typical of the many of that place in the

mountains. In the Chapel of the Relics I gave her the
Blessing for the Sick. I do not think I saw her again. And
now my sister writes, 'Lal Phelan died yesterday. She was
very happy at the end saying she could not see anything in
front of her except the Shrine of the Glorious Virgin at
Aylesford.'

She is typical of the people who were all round me in my
youth. I did not really see them then but now I see them
and know they belong to the unbroken generations of the
Faith. If only one could linger to remember them and de-
rive security and sanity and wisdom from them. How often
have I heard said of the old people, 'They are all dead and
gone now!' with infinite regret. They have always known
that death was going somewhere. Parting was heart-breaking but only *au revoir*. Death is a mighty summoner of the
abyss of memory.

And in 1966 Father had to write the obituary of a man
who had entered the world of the giants through the doorway
of Aylesford:

During the past year Percy Kitchen has died at his home
in Folkestone. He was the foreman to whom more than
anybody else the Restoration at Aylesford owes a debt
beyond repaying.

In the beginning Percy was only *lent* to us and there was
a dangerous moment when he was being taken away to
build a small chapel or some such building. Percy was a
working foreman. He had a rough exterior and seemed on
occasions tough, but he was the heart and soul of courtesy.
He would never speak to me or to any priest without taking
off his cap and holding it in his hand all the time. To him
was due the organization and training of a very mixed body
of workers and masons. He had real authority which
showed itself very quickly; and he had a real knowledge,

which he gave to the masons, most of whom were Italians and did not understand a word of English in the beginning. What he achieved was quite as miraculous as anything that happened at Aylesford. He must have been Our Lady's choice. For himself he would never have sought such a distinguished role, to work under a London architect of the eminence of Mr Adrian Gilbert Scott and to leave such a monument after him. Another builder, congratulating him on the work, said that it was an utterly professional job and that he was quite certain that no contractor in the country could have done it for love or money.

I am sure we shall never see his like again. He was very orderly and hard-working. Every morning he walked to the village just before seven and after he had become a Catholic he was invariably at Holy Communion. There is no mark on the buildings to perpetuate his name.

Perhaps it is just as well that this shrine should be entirely anonymous and built by loving and dedicated hands. It was the fashion in old times to put the image of the master builder outside on the façade of the old cathedrals. Once I was in Strasbourg and a priest brought me round to show me the glories of glass, etc. All the time he was exclaiming '*Magnifique*'. He brought me to the lower crypt of the cathedral and there in the furthest corner was a small image of the master builder built into the wall, only three inches high. He had to strike a match that we might see it. This attracted the notice of a guard who immediately pounced upon us. But that little image, when I recall it, stands in its humility for those who have restored Aylesford.

Again I am sure we have given a hostage to heaven. How could Our Lady not welcome that rugged man? What an unexpected and what a blessed historic role he anonymously fulfilled....

There are some the news of whose death would put you

off your breakfast; but there are some the news of whose death would break your heart. We all feel that way about the news of Betty Chapman's death. Betty was greatly beloved, not only by the community but by all pilgrims whom she brought to Aylesford and Allington.

She was a Jewish convert. When she became a Catholic she seemed to possess a totality of faith, very difficult to describe but often met with a Jewish converts, and strangely enough in Welsh people also. Her conversion was extraordinary enough. She seemed in those early days, before she became a Catholic, to possess a kind of hunger or appetite for God. It did not leave her any peace until it was satisfied. After trying chapels and churches of various religions she found herself in hospital. The patient beside her was a Catholic, a very fervent woman. After some talks Betty was quite certain that she had got the Faith. She was very frightened and was wondering what her husband would say to her and was prepared for the worst.

While Betty was in hospital a good Catholic neighbour helped her husband with his meals and they also began to talk about religion with the result that Eric also got the Faith. When next he went to see his wife she said to him, 'I am afraid you will not like what I am going to say to you now. I have got the Faith.' Eric was greatly surprised because that was exactly what he had been going to tell her about himself.

In a world which to Gabriel Marcel seemed to be heartless and broken, Aylesford with its conversions and spiritual renewals seems to be the affirmation for which the despairing ones are crying. In the nineteenth century Nietzsche seemed to be craving contradiction when he wrote:

Have you ever heard of the madman who on a bright morning lighted a lantern and ran to the market place calling out unceasingly: 'I seek God!' I seek God!' As there were many people standing about who did not believe in God he caused a great deal of amusement. 'Why! Is he lost'? asked one. 'Has he strayed away like a child?' said another, 'or does he keep himself hidden? Is he afraid of us? Has he taken a sea voyage?' The people cried out laughingly, all in a hubbub.

The insane man jumped into their midst and transfixed them with his glances, 'Where is God gone?' he called out. 'I mean to tell you. We have killed him, you and I. We are all his murderers. But how have we done it? How were we able to drink up the sea? Who gave us the sponge to wipe away the whole horizon? What did we do when we loosened the earth from its sun? Whither does it now move? Whither do *we* move?'

It is further stated that the madman made his way into different churches on the same day and there intoned his *Requiem Aeternam Deo*. When led out and called to account, he always gave the reply: 'What are these churches now if they are not the tombs and monuments of God?'

With the new Shrine risen on the foundations of the old, with Nietzsche's philosophy entombed with his follower, Adolf Hitler, in the rubble of the Führerbunker, Father Malachy is more alive to the utterances of the Woman of Samaria:

There are tales of conversions in the Old and New Testaments; some slow, some violent and sudden, but here we have a conversion in slow motion. The account bears the stamp of truth and of true reporting: Our Lord is tired. All his disciples have gone into the town and left him alone at the well. It was a town they didn't like, nor did they like the people of it. The Jews always tried to bypass this particular town. I imagine that the Samaritan woman

was tall and stately and had a fine carriage from her habit
of carrying water pots on her head. In Portugal today, even
in the cities, you see such women carrying their burdens
on their heads. In this instance what you see is a convert
being made: she was indeed a very unlikely one, being
somewhat saucy and brazen in her approach to the stranger.
She was very good at heart and humble. She was sur-
pised that a Jew should speak to her at all or ask her for
any service. We can see in this vivid account with what
subtlety Our Lord summons the great good that lies in her,
how he leads her from the waters of the well of Jacob to
the waters of eternal life which he was already giving her
and for which she was asking. 'Then, Sir,' said the woman,
'give me water such as that, that I may never be thirsty and
have to come here again.'

Only then does Our Lord speak to her about her husband
who is not her husband and the five husbands she has
already had. It was a confession, very gently extracted, and
then he completes the instruction. The disciples then came
back and were very surprised to see him recovered from
his tiredness and talking to this strange woman. They came
to the conclusion that someone had given him something
to eat, and when they offered him food, he showed no
desire for it but gave them instead a vision of the harvest
to be reaped. Meanwhile grace was working in the Samaritan woman and so she left in such excitement that she
forgot the water pot. She went in a hurry into the town and
told everybody she met. She didn't attempt to explain or to
talk of the living water but summoned them all to come
and hear the Prophet and judge for themselves. Many did
come and were likewise converted from hearing him, and
she must have been glad when they confessed that they now
believed for themselves what she had told them; that he
was indeed the Saviour of the World. All this happened

because a woman, touched by grace, went and did what any woman, or a man for that matter, could do at any time and at any place. The Church was never meant to be a secret society.

With Paul Claudel, Charles Péguy, François Mauriac, 'for the first time for centuries the sap of Catholic life in its fullness began to rise in French literature. Since France had so largely been given over to atheistic systems of thought by despair and desolation, much of their writing is the literature of conversion.'

In his letter of January 1965, Father quotes from Claudel's *Letters to a Doubter,* which eventually helped to convert Jacques Rivière to whom they were addressed:

Conversions are always the result, not of some great pitched battle, but of a long series of little efforts carried to a successful conclusion; in other words, the machine that is functioning amiss must be made to function aright... learn your religion, probably you are completely ignorant of it, and acquire the habit of speaking to God every day if it is only for a few moments, if it is only to tell him that you do not believe in him and that he bores you. Above all, practise almsgiving and visit the poor. This will soften your heart. Have patience.

If possible go to daily Mass, follow for one year at least the cycle of worship of the Church, wear a scapular, recite your rosary and make the Way of the Cross. When you fall, don't lose courage. Have an imperturbable faith in God's love. Remember it is not the sins of which we are most ashamed that do us the most harm. The only thing God really hates is pride.

And Péguy. In April 1966, not by any means for the first time, Father talks about him. He was a pilgrim. His pilgrimage to Chartres in 1912 was a turning point in his life. In a letter Péguy said:

I did the hundred and forty-four kilometres in three days. From the moment I saw Chartres it was ecstasy. All my iniquities fell from me at once. I was a different man. I have prayed for an hour in the Cathedral on Sunday morning before High Mass. I didn't assist at Mass, I was afraid of the crowds; but I prayed as I have never prayed before. And my boy is safe. I gave them all three to Our Lady. My children are not baptized so it is up to the Blessed Virgin to look after them. I am a sinner and not a saint. Sanctity can be recognized at once. I am a sinner, a good sinner.

In 1914 [Father continues] Péguy was called up to the War which was to end all wars. For him it was a holy crusade. Although he had been estranged from the Church and had not been able to receive the Sacraments, he went to Mass on 15 August, the Feast of the Assumption. The night before he was killed he bivouacked in an old barn which had for long been a place of pilgrimage. It had been a monastery which had been destroyed during the Revolution; but a statue of the Virgin, greatly venerated by pilgrims, had been hidden in the hay in this same barn which was consecrated and turned into a chapel. All the details were set out on a notice placed on the door and assuredly read by Péguy word for word. The building was all so simple. The old beams were there and whitewash on the walls and it seemed to suit exactly Péguy's type of inspiration – with the statue of the Virgin, a delightful piece of mediaeval workmanship, on the wall to the left.

The War for him had taken the colour and shape of an immense pilgrimage with the Virgin at the end. It was a most hallowed and truly peasant setting, nothing like it in all France. It was the unwritten poem of Péguy, all the elements gathered by an invisible hand. He picked some flowers and brought them to the consecrated barn and when his men were peacefully at rest he came back to the chapel for a night of prayer. It was his last night. Next day as he led his men forth to the attack, he was shot.

Although there was a great Cultus of Péguy after the War and his writings were widely disseminated, his heroic death did look at the time like a frustration, as if all his prayers and writings and labours had gone for nothing. But, as we know, all prayer is answered, and how marvellously beyond his own expectations Péguy's prayers were answered. His wife became an ardent Catholic, his children were baptized and I think one of them became a priest; and so many thousands of students followed in his footsteps on pilgrimage to Our Lady of Chartres. And he is remembered today and the very memory of him recalls heroism and the spirit of old France.

In Catholic books we often come across the phrase 'Devotion to Mary' without realizing its implication. Until it is translated into life it is an abstraction and this is where the spiritual genius of Péguy comes in. In one of his grand poems he has an image of a woodcutter in the forest. He is striking the wood with his axe. It is very cold and the cold is congealing the breath in his beard; but the woodcutter goes on striking the wood. Meanwhile he is talking to himself and we overhear what he says. He is thinking of his children, his wife, his love and his cares. He is kept a prisoner in this forest and sees very little of his family, which worries him. What is happening to them, what are they doing? All of a sudden he thinks of Our Lady Mary and with one swift joyful lift of the heart he hands his little family over to her and puts them all in her arms:

'So quietly he puts them there,

By prayer he puts them there
So quietly in the arms of her whose part it is to
Bear all the sorrows of the world.
And whose arms are already so laden.'

There were times when Péguy's heart was full of bitterness. He wrote to his friend, Lotte, 'Would you believe that for eighteen months I could not say "Our Father, Thy will be done"? It was quite impossible to say. Can you understand it? I could not accept his will. It is terrifying. Prayer isn't a matter of trickling off a few prayers. You have really to mean what you say. I could not really mean "Thy will be done". It was an impossibility. It was still more impossible to say: "Forgive me my trespasses as I forgive." ' The words for forgiving someone called Lavisse would have stuck in his throat. He would have had a liver attack, he declared. 'So I prayed to Mary. Prayers to Mary are reserve prayers. There is not one in the whole liturgy, you see, not one single one, that the most miserable sinner cannot say and mean. In the machinery of salvation the *Ave Maria* is our last resource. With that you cannot be lost, not with these humble words to the rescue; less a prayer than a belief and entreaty, a cry of a speechless child to his mother.'

What puzzled Péguy and what puzzled Claudel when these men suddenly became alive, was how can God be possessed. Only by a miracle, there is no other way. Man cannot find Faith alone, his nature won't let him; but if he is looking for Faith it can find *him*!

An old manuscript, quoted in the Aylesford Guide Book, says:

We read how King Louis of France was freed from a danger of the sea by the merits of the glorious Virgin Mary and how from the affection that he had for the Blessed

Virgin he secretly wore the habit of the order and died in it
and how he brought the brethren from Mount Carmel to
France and settled them at Paris, building a beautiful
cloister.

St Simon's relics were in Bordeaux for six hundred years:
St Thérèse seems to cross the Channel so often to Aylesford
—the French connection, the connection with Lourdes and
Lisieux is really strong.

In December 1964 Father wrote:

A very prominent Catholic lady who was very fussy said
to me once: 'Why don't you get St Thérèse to help you?
Have you ever heard of the twenty-four days' prayer?'
I had not and she explained that this devotion consisted in
saying twenty-four 'Glory-be-to-the-Fathers' in thanksgiving to the Holy Spirit for St Thérèse's sanctification,
for twenty-four days, each day representing one of the
years of her life. At the end of that time, or during that
time, a rose will be given to you.

I thought this was all rather far-fetched but later the
same day I was talking to a doctor's wife who was very sane
and simple. She told me a beautiful story of how her own
prayer had been answered. Her little maid saw that she
was troubled about some family matter and got her to make
the twenty-four days' prayer. She confessed that she had no
faith in it at all so the girl offered to make it for her. Several
times on the twenty-fourth the girl asked her if she had yet
received a rose; the last time, before she left in the evening,
she said rather sadly: 'Well, I suppose you won't be getting
your request.' Before midnight the lady's light was on as
she was expecting her husband back from a sick call and
there was a loud knocking on the back door. When she
went down she found it wasn't her husband but her next-
door neighbours. They had been out to their country house

and had found in their conservatory a great lot of roses. There was quite an armful of them and this lady said, 'We saw your light was on and we brought these in to you rather than let them be wasted'. She put most of them into the sink until morning and it was only when she brought one of them upstairs with her in a glass that she remembered that it was the twenty-fourth day.

And Maritain: Father has several times written about him in his letters. There is something about the mixture of sophistication and childlike belief both in the best French writers and French saints which gives expression to the spirit of Aylesford. Parts of Kent have been described as 'being so English that they are almost French'. Certainly with their squat Norman-towered churches and mansard-roofed houses some of the villages, notably Aylesford itself, speak of the Faith and civilization which first crossed the Channel to Kent.

Though Aylesford itself was never anything but English it was never less than European. In The Friars dates are irrelevant; she is one with Christendom. In her very Catholicity is the communion of the living with the dead, the people whom the Faith has made and will yet make.

Perhaps in this context it is right to conclude with a vignette of one of the greatest living philosophers, Jacques Maritain. It comes from Father's Newsletter of February 1967.

Jacques Maritain is rightly regarded as the great Catholic philosopher of our time. During the War he was in the States and I have met Sisters who knew and regarded him with reverence. He is a philosopher but he is also a very holy man and now venerable in his more than eighty years.

He is now back in his native France and spends much of his time with the Little Brothers of Jesus of Charles de Foucauld at their principal Study Centre. In his lectures, which the Brothers cherish, he regards as *disastrous* the neglect of the Communion of Saints. By this neglect believers have lost an essential dimension; in fact it accounts for the great loneliness which afflicts so many.

The chief reason for this suffering is lack of faith in the Church Triumphant, what is described as the immense 'converse' perpetually going on in heaven: 'The Blessed, the joyous bodies beyond the whole of the Universe and of space, are still present here by their love and by their action, and by the inspiration they give us and by the effects of their prayers. And the love they had on earth for those they cherished, they retain in heaven, transfigured, not abolished in glory. . . . You will remember that famous saying of St Thérèse of Lisieux: "I want to spend my heaven doing good upon earth." The other world is present to our world. It penetrates into it like lightning invisibly.

Maritain goes so far as to say that when we adore the Blessed Sacrament, 'virtually all the saints of heaven are in your chapel around your tabernacle: and actually and in a more especial way there are those who love you and whom you love as your own, adoring Jesus with you. And if we cannot imagine them we can love them. And if there is a terrible curtain between the visible and the invisible world, love makes us pass behind. It is the same love of charity that is in them that is in us. We reach them with our love as they reach us, and with our prayer as well.'

In earlier days there was a great and profound familiarity between the saints and the Christian people. But now as Maritain says: 'Popular devotions have given place to self-styled rational mentality, which in reality is simply an anaemic and aseptic one which admits of practically no living contact with the saints. And this to me is disastrous. For the part which popular piety plays in the life of the Church, both at its own level of course and below that of the Liturgy, is an essential one, because it expresses the direct and

spontaneous movement of souls with regard to their daily
lives and their individual destinies in the world. . . .

'In this sense it may be said that while the Liturgy is
absolutely necessary, it is not enough, first because any live
participation in the Liturgy will always be restricted to a
relatively small number of people, despite all efforts to the
contrary. Then because the popular piety, the piety of the
Christian people, of God's *little* people, has to do with the
demands and initiatives coming straight from their hearts
in particular circumstances and adventures, and with the
whole temporal contact of their existence and the motions
of the Holy Spirit making their way through it all. And
this is an indispensable piece of the life of the Church
Militant, an aspect which is more and more neglected.

'There is Lourdes of course and the other great pilgrimages and a few particularly famous saints and also that para-
liturgical sort of adoration of the Blessed Sacrament. But
as regards that whole huge people making up the Mystical
Body in the state of glory, popular piety has fallen apart
and been reduced to ashes. One would think we are so
stupid as to believe that they are asleep in the Beatific
Vision, want to have nothing more to do with us, and
have in fact forgotten us.'

In his leisurely way Jacques Maritain discusses with the
Brothers the practical aspects of our belief in the Communion of Saints. After much reasoning he comes to the
conclusion that the number of the saved is numerous beyond
all imagining and that many of the good little people go
straight to heaven: 'God is not so sparing of his Grace and it
is we who have not enough practical faith and are not
attentive enough to the glory of those who have gone. I
well remember the Curé of La Corneuve, the famous Père
Lamy, as he was then generally known, telling us the story
of Notre Dame des Bois and of the day he carried the statue

of Our Lady through the wood to the little old house which he was turning into a chapel: he was accompanied by the saints in procession through the trees.

'What he meant by the saints in this instance were not St Peter and St Paul, but the Holy Souls in all their glory, of people he had known, simple country folk who had been members of his family or who had lived in his native village. And could any of us believe that these saints whom we have known, with whom we have special ties, have forgotten us, or that they do not wish to help us or that they do not have a better idea than we do of what is best for us?'

Maritain believes that all our prayers, even with the saints, always have the qualification: 'If it be God's Holy Will.' The saints are still involved with the building of his Kingdom here on earth. It is impossible to think of them as not being joined to the Church Militant, and they are great helpers in the designs of God.

And now this book must finish; it is a pause perhaps, an intermission; for the only ending for real stories is the running out of space. Thinking around and within the Faith is a continuing process. Of the harvest of thought which such thinking brings this is no more than a basket of gleanings; but Aylesford stands – an expression in stone of the unchanging quality in the Church's perpetual deliberation.